# THE SILENT CHILDREN

# THE
# SILENT
# CHILDREN

A Parent's Guide to the
Prevention of Child Sexual Abuse

## Linda Tschirhart Sanford

**McGraw-Hill Book Company**
New York   St. Louis   San Francisco   Bogotá   Guatemala
Hamburg   Lisbon   Madrid   Mexico   Montreal   Panama
Paris   San Juan   São Paulo   Tokyo   Toronto

*Sara Lea . . . this one's for you.*

Reprinted by arrangement with Anchor Press/Doubleday
First McGraw-Hill paperback edition, 1982
1 2 3 4 5 6 7 8 9 0    FGFG    8 7 6 5 4 3 2

ISBN 0-07-054662-2

**Library of Congress Cataloging in Publication Data**
Sanford, Linda Tschirhart.
  The silent children.

  (McGraw-Hill paperbacks)
  Reprint. Originally published: Garden City,
N.Y.: Anchor Press/Doubleday, 1980.
  Includes bibliographical references.
  1. Child molesting.  2. Child molesting—
Prevention.  3. Incest.  4. Parenting.  I. Title.
HQ71.S312  1982        649'.65        81-19392
ISBN 0-07-054662-2                    AACR2

# FOREWORD

Linda Sanford has managed to dispel myths about child abuse while at the same time putting it in a proper perspective. She helps parents (in fact all adults) understand how they can rear a child to be aware of these dangers without being paranoid. She conscientiously avoids an alarmist attitude while pointing out to us concrete things we can do or say to our children to make them aware of abuses.

Not only does her advice about helping our children develop a good self-image so that they develop an "inner voice" (alarm system) address the immediate problem of child abuse but it is very practical advice for other facets of child-rearing. As you read these pages you will be given guidelines on family communication, for example, how to criticize effectively; how to praise a child in a way that *teaches*. In short, the basic thrust of her book tells you how to help a child have a good self-image so that he/she is less likely to be victimized. But, if abuse actually occurs through force, such a child will not fear telling his/her parents. Trust will be established in the home so the child will not feel at fault or guilty for something over which the child had very little control.

Ms. Sanford goes on to describe the various types of abuse and the emotional difficulties with which the child must deal. For example, father/daughter incest has different emotional results than mother/son. A person's sexual behavior can be influenced for years because of such incidents—especially if they are not dealt with adequately.

Perhaps because I am a doctor I have always dealt more with the *physical* well-being of children—they handle stress and strain better if they feel good; once they feel good they behave better. But what happens to the well-adjusted child who experiences a trauma such as sexual abuse? One hopes that parents who read this book will see that some of the most well-intentioned things they do may be creating a potential victim. If Susy has to kiss grandpa and doesn't want to, does our forcing her begin a mental chain of thought that ends with "well, he's a grown up—I have to do what he says"? In short the submissive attitude of a victim.

Why do some children have no compunction about saying "no" while others are easily a victimized? This book will make us all stop and think about our child's point of view and the hidden messages that we send them about themselves. When you see yourself in Ms. Sanford's examples I hope you won't feel guilty, but instead learn a better way of dealing with your children so they will develop an "alarm system" to avoid being abused in any way.

If you or your child were victims of abuse this book will help you understand the emotional side-effects you or your child have suffered.

It is impossible to live in another person's body and perceive their perceptions. Ms. Sanford digs around in the inner world of childhood and helps us remember how we thought and felt when we were children.

Lendon H. Smith, M.D.

# CONTENTS

# ACKNOWLEDGMENTS

Ben Eide, M.S.W., of the Children's Home Society in Seattle, Washington, was part of the initial concept of this book. Although the form and content have gone through many changes, I am grateful to him for his expertise, insights, and especially his friendship.

Three talented women assisted in the preparation of this manuscript. My good friend Kathleen Willard had the thankless job of editing final drafts, and she did so with enthusiasm and skill that I very much appreciate. Lorraine Pozzi of Almost Publishing in Seattle, Washington, contributed not only her professional talents but also her experience as a parent. As the first reader of most of the manuscript her direction was important and always welcome. Julie Albright, in Vermont, prepared the final sections of the manuscript in a professional and efficient way, and I am thankful that Julie was part of this project.

I was fortunate to benefit from the professional training of three excellent librarians at the Norman Williams Public Library in Woodstock, Vermont. Virginia Christy, Debbie Howe, and Marjorie Vail searched out sources and located obscure articles on a regular basis. Because of their skill and willingness to help, I had the resources of a big-city library while working in rural Vermont.

Dianne Douglas Wood, also of Woodstock, offered her vast library on the formation of self-concept in small children as well as her insights as a mother for Part One. Dianne, along with Pat Honabach, Bill Eck, Fred Merrill, and Peggy Merrill, shared family anecdotes with me. As a result, the theory in Part One came alive. And I am thankful to William Boardman for completing the project with insightful consultations on very short notice.

Part Two was perhaps the most challenging part of this book for me to write. I can't imagine writing this section in *quite* the same way without my two-year professional correspondence with Roger Wolfe, M.A., of Northwest Treatment Associates in Seattle.

A. Nicholas Groth, Ph.D., of the Connecticut Correctional Institution at Somers, expanded my West Coast work with Roger. Nick and the men in his child sexual offenders group influenced my view of offenders as troubled men, and I am grateful to them for their openness.

Toni Clark, Ph.D., and Gary Wenet, Ph.D., of the Juvenile Sexual Offenders Project at the University of Washington in Seattle were significant sources for the Adolescent Offenders section. Toni and Gary, among the first therapists to recognize and treat teen-age sex offenders, were always accessible and openly shared their innovative work.

Gene Abel, M.D., Judith Becker, Ph.D., Christine Berguast, and Barry Flanagan of the New York Psychiatric Institute provided me with new material, and their contribution was valuable to me. Also, Miriam Kerster, director of juvenile services, Brooklyn Legal Aid Society; Michael Murphy, special assistant to the executive director of Covenant House in New York City; Detective Gary Trent of the Bellevue (Washington) Police Department; Gerry Holtzinger, therapy supervisor at the Western Washington State Hospital Sex Offenders Program; and Julie Baute of the King County (Washington) prosecutor's office all granted interviews that were informative, and their answers became part of this project. I am grateful to each of them.

Part Three came out of my previous work at the Rape Prevention Forum in Seattle, Washington, and was developed, in part, through the Parent-oriented Prevention of Child Sexual Abuse grant, funded by the King County (Washington) Mental Health Board. The information was delivered in lecture form to hundreds of parents in day-care centers who gave us feedback. My close friend and colleague Claudia Black, M.S.W., helped the advice section reach its final form along with Lieutenant Noreen Skagens of the Seattle Police Department, who offered excellent suggestions both as a police officer and as a parent.

Thank you to Sandra Butler, Sandra Elkin, Bill Price, Florence Rush, and the National Gay Task Force in New York City for sharing material with me during the writing of this book.

The Woodstock Writers Group gave me constructive criticism and encouragement at many Thursday night meetings as I read various drafts of the manuscript. The group is unique in its professional quality and personal caring, and I am glad they were there to make a difference.

Two editors deserve special mention. Lindy Hess was the editor of my first book and was supportive in the beginning of this book. She is a good friend and excellent teacher. Marie Brown, my current editor, has influenced the final product both with her talent as an editor and parent. Her editorial decisions were always on target and made in a constructive manner.

My agent, Frances Goldin, has been with me since the beginning of my writing career, and her political sensibilities, technical expertise, and most of all her friendship have influenced me in more ways than my writing.

No project as long and as consumptive both emotionally and professionally is completed without the encouragement of many people. Old friends in Seattle, new friends in Woodstock, Vermont, and political sisters in New York City helped me to move ahead happily. I would especially like to thank my parents, Dick and Kay Tschirhart and my brother Tom. I could always count on them, and many times I benefited from their support. And, for my "extended family," Lou and Vera Theiss, who have been part of so many of the good times and there through some exceedingly bad times.

Finally, I express great appreciation to Susan Bandler and Bill Peabody, who made valuable contributions to my life during the writing of the book. And my friendship with Mary Ellen Donovan has been the very essence of sisterhood. She became an important part of my life during the last half of the book. Our long talks about the craft and political beliefs we share were major sources of support and stimulation.

# PART ONE

---

## THE FAMILY ATMOSPHERE

# INTRODUCTION

The purpose of this book is to examine and understand the crimes of child sexual abuse. Once we have a working knowledge of the circumstances of child molestation and incest, and insight into the motivations of the offenders, we, as adults, will be able to translate this information into warnings to our children. We can adapt our instruction to the child's age and to the values and lifestyle of our family. In doing so, we will be taking the first step toward the prevention of child sexual abuse.

In America today, there is a *one-in-four* chance that a little girl will be the victim of incest, child molestation, or rape by the time she reaches eighteen years old.[1] Reporting of these crimes is happenstance at best, so we might assume the odds are even more dramatically against reaching adulthood as a nonvictim. We have no idea of exactly how many boys are victims, but we know it is not a rare occurrence. Obviously, our old ways of warning (or simply *not* warning) have not worked.

While we do our best to warn our children about the proverbial stranger in the car or the bothersome man in the movie theater, we tell them little of *why* these situations mean trouble. We warn them about *settings* that are no longer—if they ever were—the bulk of settings of child sexual abuse. Part of the dilemma is that we are attuning their "radar" to a few specific circumstances and ignoring the majority of crimes, which involve friends or relatives and take place in familiar places. The more important difficulty with our old warning systems is that children have no understanding of *why* they should be concerned at all about child sexual abuse. Sometimes the warnings are given without mentioning sex or its abuse. If this is the case, the child is not prepared to prevent the crime. How can she stop something about which she has no knowledge?

This book is an offering of a different way to warn our children about child sexual abuse. Because the teaching is most effective when the child is younger, the text is aimed at parents of children seven years old or younger. Hopefully, the child will be aware of the problem of child sexual abuse before he ventures off on his first solo journey—going to school. However, it is never too late to begin rational, instructive discussions about child sexual abuse, so there will be material relevant to almost every age group. Of course, the readers' focus will be different depending on their needs. The parent of a four-year-old girl will be looking for slightly different answers than the parent of a thirteen-year-old boy, but information is here. The content should be considered, integrated, and eventually taught to our children; not taken automatically as gospel. Also, any adult can make use of this information; parents alone are not responsible for the prevention of child sexual abuse. Child-care workers, teachers, friends of the family, and other adults would do well to familiarize themselves with the problem of child sexual abuse.

Perhaps part of the reason we have had so much difficulty teaching our children about child sexual abuse and its prevention is that no one ever taught us. We have never had any working definition. As children, and sometimes as adults, child sexual abuse had a very vague meaning. "It" was something strangers did to you. We knew they shouldn't do it, but if they did, then it was "curtains" for us. We didn't know the logistics of "it," but we believed "it" was an experience few people (at least in our fantasies) survived in one piece. If we still hold onto that notion, then it is no wonder that we are reluctant to discuss child sexual abuse with our children.

For the purposes of our discussion, child sexual abuse is any inappropriate suggested or actual sexual (involving genitalia) exposing or touching between an adult and a child. The activity is inappropriate because the child does not understand the nature of the request and/or is coerced into the activity through deceit, threats, or because the activity is offered under the guise of normal affection. Simply, if the child understood the request and was aware of the consequences of the activity, he or she would not agree to it.

As it is, too many children do comply with the inappropriate request, but not because children are precocious or stupid. They comply because they are uninformed and unlucky to be in the presence of an adult who will take advantage of the child's innocence or needs or fears. If we teach our children about the circumstances of the crime, we can improve their luck by helping them to recognize and avoid the troublesome circumstances. And if the children are *informed* about child sexual abuse, they will be better able to react to the request as *inappropriate*. The process of informing is complicated. This book will consider many components of this education, and we will begin where the procedure begins—in the family.

The child's isolation from a helpful or protective adult is inherent in the nature of the child sexual abuse. It is the child alone with the offender. Thus, she needs to learn some skills that she can use on her own. Along with the facts about child sexual abuse, we need to teach healthy self-sufficiency. The following vignette brings home the combination of understanding and skill needed to prevent child sexual abuse.

Imagine that your four-year-old daughter is playing alone in your living room when you receive an emergency phone call. You need to go out unexpectedly and there are no regular baby-sitters to be found. As a last resort, you decide to ask your neighbor for this favor. She is not home, but her husband, the father of your daughter's friend, offers to come over and watch your child. This man often plays with the neighborhood children, and your daughter loves the stories he tells. You are grateful for his willingness to help out on such short notice, and as you go out to attend to the unexpected business, you leave your daughter in his care.

Your daughter is glad to see him. They talk as she plays with her trucks. After a while, she asks him if she can hear a story. He pulls her up on his lap, tells her favorite story, and then asks her if she wants to learn a brand-new game.

"What kind of game?"

"A very secret and lots of fun game," your neighbor replies. He tickles her and she laughs.

"What am I supposed to do?"

"It's easy. You just sit here and rock against me, really close. And I'll rock against you right there (pointing to her genitalia) and we'll both feel really good."

At this point, many varied elements will determine if your daughter will agree to play this "secret game" or not. Does she recognize the game for what it is, or does she not understand the sexual nature of the neighbor's request? Does she question why the game needs to be a secret? More importantly, what is her *immediate* reaction to his request?

The immediate reaction is her "voice from within"—that is, what she says to herself before she speaks to him—which will determine her spoken answer to the offender and subsequent behavior.

The "voice from within" is universal. Adults have conversations with themselves that have a bearing on the outcome of events. Pretend you have been cajoled into a tennis game. You don't feel your skill level is adequate but you will play anyway. As you walk out onto the court, you say to yourself:

"I'll just get this over with—I'm such a klutz," and your game is, in fact, not too co-ordinated.

What if instead you said to yourself: "Maybe this will be good practice and I just might surprise myself!"

And, in fact, your chances of playing fairly well are better than if your "voice from within" had cried, "Klutz, klutz!"

The child's "voice from within" works the same way, and it can say any of the following:

I don't like this, but what do I know? I'm never right about anything.

I really want this person to like me—if I hurt his feelings by not playing this game, he won't like me anymore.

My mom and dad told me to do what he says, so I guess it's O.K.

He seems to feel *so* bad—I want to make him feel better.

I don't want to run away and look like a sissy.

This guy is an adult and I better do what he says.

I never know what to say, I always mess things up. There's no point in trying to stop him.

I really don't want to do this but it is rude to say "No" to people.

I know if I tell anyone about this, they'll get mad at me for making trouble.

Nobody else likes me, not in the whole world, except for this person, so I'll do what he says.

I have to be nice to everyone and kiss them and do what they want—so what's the difference with this game?

Of course, children do not think in such adult terms or concepts, but these statements reflect the *feeling* state of the child. She may not be able to articulate her immediate reaction in any of the above statements, but her behavior may be determined by the beliefs inherent in any of these compliant statements. The beliefs and feelings comprise the "voice from within." Hopefully, this little girl will say to herself:

This is wrong—I'm not going to do it. Then I'm going to tell someone what he asked me to do.

And she subsequently tells the neighbor, "No, I don't want to play that game. I'm going to play with my trucks."

There is an obvious world of difference between this statement and the other "voices from within." Before continuing with the molestation, the offender will take his cue from the child's willingness (or lack of it) to co-operate with him. The child's immediate response can make an intended *completed* act of child sexual abuse merely an *attempted* act. Because there are as many responses as there are children, it is important to explore why one child responds with the above healthy statement while another responds compliantly.

It will probably come as no surprise that the child's "voice from within" is learned at home. In the context of the parent-child relationship, how do some of the following questions shape the child's "voice from within" and affect the child's ability to refuse the neighbor's request?

- Is the child taught to put other people's rights and needs before her own?

- Is she taught that adults are more important than children?

- Is she taught that she must obey *any* adult?

- Are rules about what she *should* do in a given situation so rigid that they totally ignore the child's feelings?

- Can the child say "No" to *anything* or is absolute compliance demanded at all times?

- Where could the child go with questions about confusing situations?

- If she tells someone about the neighbor, is she confident they will take her seriously?

- Is the child encouraged to follow her own "intuition" about the rightness of situations or are her feelings discounted?

- Do *other* people always know what's best for the child?

- Does the child have any doubts that she is lovable, therefore vulnerable to the flattery of others?

- Does she feel justified, based on her own worthiness, to remove herself from a situation that might cause her harm?

Parents come up with surprising answers to some of the questions; answers they don't particularly like. In that case, they might want to step back and examine specific areas of their parenting. A few changes here and there might enhance the child's safety.

Wanting to make changes does not mean the parent was inadequate or harmful in the past. Parenting is an overwhelming job, and most people begin with the best of intentions. Virtually no parent could answer all of those questions with absolute certainty that they were not limiting their child in some way. Demands for perfection in parents are damaging both to the parent and the child. So the questions are offered as vehicles for examining *specific* areas of parenting, *not* as an assessment of the parents' innate worthiness.

Most of us have been handicapped by a lack of training for the job of "parent." We rely on "on-the-job training" and learn as we go along. We have our own parents as an example, but beyond that, the mystical endeavor known as parenting is open to individual interpretation. To some extent that is probably as it should be, but the assumption that parenting is a native, inherent ability has been under some attack recently.

The discrepancy between valuing our children on the one hand and our failure to give parents specific training for their job on the other hand seems to be based on the assumption that *if you are a human being you should know how to raise one.* [emphasis added][2]

And if we don't know how to raise another human being, unfortunately we take this as a measure of our worth as people rather than an indication of the lack of training available to us. This section intends to offer some training and resources needed in the realm of preventing child sexual abuse. It is offered with the belief that it is wrong to expect perfection from parents.

Realistically defining parenthood is one of the first steps to freeing ourselves from that "I can't do anything right with this kid so what's the use?" feeling that stops us from learning ourselves and short-circuits our teaching the child how to become a healthy adult. One helpful definition of the parent-child relationship is:

Primarily, it is a bond of mutual involvement and dependence that touches our deepest personal needs and feelings. As such, its richness consists of the satisfactions it provides both parent and child. As a parent, you will derive your satisfactions mainly through your role of caring, protecting, nurturing and teaching your child. This makes you feel needed and respected. Your child will receive the satisfactions of feeling wanted, of being protected by your support, of being encouraged to explore new experiences when bolstered by your companionship and his own developing knowledge and power. Each of you gets something essential from the other.[3]

There is nothing mysterious or confining about this understanding of parenting. With plenty of room for mistakes and subsequent learning, we are more likely to identify a less-than-perfect specific area of parenting and work to change it. It is this very give-and-take, this exchange between parent and child and the resultant skills that are the essence of the child's healthy "voice from within." If the parent understands his or her role as a guide and model, as well as a fellow traveler with the child, debilitating demands for perfection can diminish. And if the child is not limited by or molded to the parent's needs to do everything right, he or she will have the peace and quiet and opportunity to develop *his or her* own voice.

However, the responsibility for the raising of a healthy child is unfairly placed solely on the parent. As we isolate the parent as *the* cause of the successful or troublesome child, we ignore the responsibility of our institutions such as schools, church, and the media. And those of us who are nonparents cannot sit back complacently and think of the well-being of children as "none of our business."

As a nonparent I asked myself, "What do I do to help or hinder parents in their struggle to raise healthy children? Have I ever enhanced a child's self-concept? Do I make unnecessary demands on a child for obedience? Have I discounted a child's questions, feelings, or fears in a way that inhibited the child from acting in his or her best interest? Have I ever trespassed on a child's emotional or physical territory to the point where the child was confused or overwhelmed and interacting with me when he or she really didn't want to?"

The answer to all these questions, from time to time, has been that I was *not* a constructive influence. Many of my mistakes came freely to my mind. But in keeping with the premise that we should not be immobilized by our mistakes and their indications of our imperfections, I will discuss and find solutions for these mistakes throughout Part One. It is equally as important to recognize what it is that we do right. Nonparents have a tremendous potential to be a positive force, and after thinking long and hard, I was able to think of times when I was a helpful part of the ongoing process of child rearing.

Jill, the daughter of one of my friends, is very assertive and precocious for her age of ten. As a result, she has some inevitable and normal conflicts with her mother, and some other adults find her "not enough of a child" to feel comfortable around her. She is also very sensitive and knows when adults don't like her. I have always liked her tremendously, especially for her frankness and mature thought processes. With my friend's blessing, I began to develop a friendship with Jill, taking her places, talking with her, expressing my affection for her. When Jill was ten and I was twenty-eight, she gave me a copy of Judy Blume's *Forever* (a book about a teen-ager's first sexual experience) so that I would "understand about sex." When Jill is not comfortable talking with her parents, she can take her questions to an adult who has gone through her "train-ing program."

Another example concerns two of my closest friends, Mike and Mary Ann. Their eight-year-old daughter, Julie Ann, is also my friend. One night at our usual Sunday-night dinner, I announced my intention to move from Seattle to Vermont. Julie Ann seemed very unimpressed by this; it was as if I were moving to another town. One day she was playing a geography game with her parents, and she noticed *where* Vermont is in relation to Seattle. Julie asked them, with concern, "She's going a long ways away, isn't she?"

She hid on the day I said good-bye to them. Very soon after I had settled in Vermont, I received the following letter:

> *Dear Linda,*
> *I hope you ar having a wondfull time, I am going into third grade. My famly really misses you. And I pray for you.*
> *I love you.*
>
> > *Your friend,*
> > *Julie Ann*
>
> *Have a wondfull time!*

It was the first letter Julie had ever written. Mary Ann told me it was also the first time Julie Ann had ever expressed love to some-one outside her own family. To this day, I still write to her about the "wondfull" times I have in Vermont.

Each of us has the potential to be helpful, and it is important that we think of children's well-being as our responsibility. Two par-ents (and many families no longer have two live-in parents) are usually not enough to deal with the complexities of raising a child. Nonparents have the energy and can develop the sensitivity to re-lieve some of the parents' isolation and offer a child additional guid-ance and nurturance. Although this section focuses on the *family* atmosphere and its impact on the child's "voice from within," we all contribute to that same voice. The advice offered to parents should also be considered by nonparents. The problem of child sexual abuse and its prevention is as relevant to *all* adults as it is to *all* children.

The "voice from within" is formed over many years and is a function of many different areas of the child's life. Returning to the previous scene, we would all hope that the little girl will know the neighbor's request is wrong, refuse it, then tell us about it as soon as possible. However, we may not be too sure of how to instill that sensibility in our child. We may be reacting to or teaching our child in such a way that a more helpless or compliant voice is fortified. As we will find in the "Overview of the Crimes" part of this book, the child's refusal to co-operate will prevent child sexual abuse in the majority of cases. This section will teach us how to teach our children to say "No."

# FEELING GOOD ABOUT YOURSELF IS THE MOST IMPORTANT FEELING IN THE WORLD

Child sexual abusers manipulate the self-concept of the child victim. The offender will choose a child who seems insecure and will hold out the promise of eternal love and friendship *if* the child will only co-operate with him. How solidly the child likes herself will determine her vulnerability to the offender's promises.

Self-concept is a term we hear a lot lately, but what exactly does it mean? In the realm of child sexual abuse, it means that the child feels good about herself. The molester's enticement of *really* liking her if she lets him put his hands down her pants is not effective with her. She likes herself, so it's nice if he likes her, but O.K. if he doesn't. And certainly she doesn't need to *perform* in any way to get people to like her.

The formation of the child's self-concept is an ongoing process. The child does not decide suddenly at age seven that she is a wonderful person and everyone who has a different opinion can go jump in the lake. However, the child does have a basic trust in herself— she thinks of herself as a friend—someone who is nice to be around. With that core feeling, she is confident to explore, to grow, to succeed, and thereby to enhance further her self-concept. She does not believe new experiences are doomed to failure because she is basically no good.

The process of building self-image goes this way: a new reflection, a new experience, or a new bit of growth leads to a new success or failure, which in turn leads to a *new or revised statement about the self*. In this fashion, each person's self-concept usually evolves thoughout his lifetime.[4]

Common sense tells us that any child derives a large portion of her self-concept from her family experience. But what if the parents have ambivalent feelings about themselves; they are consumed with self-doubt, never satisfied with their performance, and constantly confused by their emotions? In the section on incest, we will see a direct connection between the parents' self-concept and the commission of the crime. Even in nonabusing parents, the adult's self-concept paves the way for the child's sense of self. We now realize how problems such as battering and alcoholism (all of which are reflections of poor self-concept) are passed on from generation to generation. How can a parent teach a child to like herself if the parent is a stranger to that feeling?

Under the best of circumstances, being an integral part of teaching a child to like herself is an intimidating proposition. If our own parenting was not particularly helpful, we are more overwhelmed. We have no point of reference, no positive action to imitate. Too often we rerun our own childhood experiences with our children and we don't realize it, as this mother found herself doing:

> I remember as a kid I was always so frustrated—no matter what happened to me, my mother would always be aloof and offer only platitudes like "That's nice, dear," or "That's too bad." That's all she ever said and I really wanted some emotion. I wanted her to be angry at the people I was angry at and happy for the things I was happy for. Now, with my own daughter, I catch myself doing the same thing. I'm so worried about saying the right thing. I don't want to smother her with my joy or overwhelm her with my anger. I'm afraid most of the time so I don't take any kind of stand that I can be accountable for. It probably seems like the same kind of aloofness that I resented in my own mother.

Or, at other times we don't rerun, but we try very hard to counteract our own experiences, to correct our parents' mistakes through our own child-rearing practices. One nonparent observes:

> I'm one of those Korean War babies who was taught that education and purpose were everything. I remember my parents saying time and time again that all you can do for a child is give him a good education and from there on, it's up to him. We were good people if our grades were good and we accomplished something. Now I hear my friends with small children

say, "All you can do for the child is teach them to really like himself and to have good relationships with other people. If they have that, then everything else will be O.K." We found that our accomplishments were rather empty and we are strangers to intimacy. I wonder if twenty years from now we will have a generation of adult derelicts who like themselves, or will some contributing, healthy people come out of all of this?

Parents certainly do have varied perceptions of their role. Some parents see their role as "proctor" or as the child's "inner conscience." They believe it is their duty to point out the child's mistakes and tell him how to correct them. When the child does something right, they take it for granted, after all, the child *should* do things right. Like this father, they speak only when criticism is warranted:

How's my kid going to know when he screws up if I don't tell him? I'd much rather have him hear it from me. It would be embarrassing to him to have someone else tell him, so I keep a close eye out, and I always tell him that it's wrong and how to fix it.

In their own way, these parents love their children and believe they are doing what's best. But for the child, constant criticism can culminate in the "voice from within" saying, "I don't like this. But what do I know? I'm never right about anything," or, "I never know what to do, I always mess things up. There's no point in trying to stop him."

A balance between praise and criticism is crucial to the child's positive self-concept. However, some parents believe *any* praise at all will "swell the child's head," make him difficult to deal with, and give him a false sense of himself. Inappropriate or dishonest praise can do this, but no praise at all is perhaps worse. If the child does not receive adequate praise at home, she will be hungry for it and will possibly seek it from an offender in return for her cooperation.

Praise or positive reinforcement is *not* permissiveness. We don't have to like everything our child does or profess our love every hour on the hour. Praise is an exchange of good feelings. When both the parent and the child feel good about something that has just happened, praise should follow. Insincere, dishonest, or inappropriate praise comes when the parent does not feel good about the child's behavior and offers praise to manipulate him to stop, as we find in this situation:

> A good friend of mine has a son who whenever he doesn't get what he wants, he tells her, "You are the *worst* mother in the world" and starts a screaming fit. Instead of telling him to do that somewhere else or to stop it, she runs over to say, "I love you. Do you want a hug?" Of course he stops crying and says "Yes," even though she's the worst mother in the world. Then he asks again for the same thing and if he doesn't get it, which is about half the time, he does the whole fit over again. You can set your watch by this kid pulling this act to get affection. She really resents his behavior and can't see how she's feeding into it.

This child will grow up very confused about what acceptable behavior is because he has been praised for inappropriate actions. What a rude surprise when, after telling someone that he or she is the worst person in the world, the person either walks away or counters with a list of *his* faults. He can expect few hugs in the real world.

Praise has the most meaning to the child when it is *specific*. General statements like "I love you" or "You are a wonderful person" are valuable, but nothing will enhance a child's self-concept as well as a specific statement following good behavior. The child makes the connection between what he did and your approval. This increases the likelihood of his repeating the behavior.

| SITUATION | GENERAL PRAISE | SPECIFIC PRAISE |
|---|---|---|
| After much coaxing on your part, your child voluntarily cleans his room before visitors come. | "You are a good boy (or girl)." | "I really like it when you see what needs to be done, then you go ahead and do it. It makes me trust you more. You're really growing up." |

| | | |
|---|---|---|
| You feel sick and stay in bed late one morning. Your child fixes you breakfast in bed. | "Oh thanks, dear." | "You are so special because you are sensitive to other people and are willing to give something of yourself. I feel better already." |
| Your child brings home a good report card. | "Very good, honey." | "Some kids don't like school very much or don't try very hard, but you like to learn and that is a very good thing about you." |
| Your older child keeps her younger brother from playing with a strange animal in the park. | "Thank goodness you were there." | "Wasn't I lucky you were there watching your brother so carefully *and* you could think so quickly." |

Again, general praise is *not* bad and it certainly is better than no praise at all. However, specific praise bolsters the child's self-concept. The child acts, the parent gives the child specific feedback, and the child learns a little more about himself from the parent's perceptions. The parent is not manipulating or defining the child. Specific praise is in response to the *child's* behavior. As an adult, the parent is offering the child a positive way to look at his behavior.

By the same token, *criticism* needs to be specific. Criticism of our children usually comes both from our genuine concern for them and the disappointment of our expectations. When we criticize our child, he does not question our expectations. He questions himself and internalizes the labels we put on him in *our* disappointment.

| SITUATION | LABELING | SPECIFIC CRITICISM |
|---|---|---|
| Your child's room is always messy and she refuses to clean it. | "You are the biggest pig I've ever seen." | "I am really tired of walking in here and seeing this mess. You have a choice: Clean it up, or stay in here for the rest of the day." |

| You asked your child not to run through the new garden, but he forgets and leads the neighborhood through the new beds. | "What! Are you deaf or stupid?" | "I thought I made it clear. Try harder to remember in the future." |
| You catch your child in a lie about spending allowance money on candy. | "You are a liar." | "It makes me very uncomfortable when you lie like this. I want to trust you, but right now it is difficult." |
| Your child accepts a ride home from a stranger because it was raining. | "You get what you deserve when you do that. . . ." | "That upsets me. I want very much for you to be safe, and that was dangerous. Let's talk about it." |

A parent might say, "Well, those are only words. What's the big difference?" But they are powerful words. A child receiving the above "labeling" messages will conclude that he is a stupid, deaf, lying pig destined to be murdered in a stranger's car. Just as the child builds his self-concept from the praise he receives, he also takes on criticism as part of the same building process. As a matter of fact, some children dwell more on their failures than they do on their successes, so there is a potential for the labeling to outdistance whatever praise there might be. Something like that happened to this parent's child:

My daughter was just getting into riding horses and seemed to like it a lot. We were teasing her, and I thoughtlessly called her a "scaredy cat" because she doesn't like to ski. She's afraid of the heights and I thought big horses would scare her as much as ski lifts. Obviously she didn't see the connection, and she's always been hypersensitive. All of a sudden she didn't want to go to riding lessons. I knew something was going on—it wasn't like she wasn't interested. It was more like she was pouting.

Finally she told her father she didn't want to go because she might get thrown and be a "scaredy cat" like I said. I'd really hurt her and she was willing to give up all the good things about riding because of it.

The parents' *words* might go in one ear and out the other, but the judgments that accompany the words stay inside the child. The judgments gather until there are enough to create a "voice from within." The quality of that voice will be a function of praise, labeling, and specific criticism, or a combination of all three.

Notice the striking difference between the words used in the Labeling column and those in the Specific Criticism column. In labeling, the parent *is* defining the child: *"You are . . ."* In specific criticism, the parent is expressing disappointment but is not making any conclusions about the child's entire being. The child's behavior is at issue, not his worth as a human being.

Which form of criticism we choose will be a reflection of our expectations. Children also have expectations for themselves, partially as a mirror of our expectations. If we want to enhance the child's self-concept, we must be careful not to pile our own *unrealistic* expectations onto the child's. *The Parent Book* outlines the child's self-deprecating expectations, which, when combined with our own, can mean trouble:

If you look closely, you will notice your child tends to have unrealistic expectations in four major areas. First, about time. He often expects things to happen right now, even sooner. Second, he is unrealistic about his performance. He expects to give a superior performance with little training, effort or experience. Third, he compares himself unrealistically with others. And, finally, he believes that fallibility and failure are unique to him, that only he makes mistakes. He doesn't realize that it's always easier to imagine and wish for success than to achieve it.[5]

Although we need to work to help the child gain perspective in these four areas, the last expectation mentioned is a particularly important one in the realm of child sexual abuse. The child not only feels he is the only person who makes mistakes, but also he can exaggerate his mistakes to be the *worst* thing he could have possibly done. He does not realize that there are levels of mistakes, and it is difficult to maintain a good self-concept if you believe you are the world's leading reject.

Akin to making mistakes is feeling "different," as in "not fitting in" or feeling like "a fish out of water." Although all children feel "different" at some time in their lives, some children are more vulnerable to the label. It is important that the parent recognize the child's feeling and work with him to lessen his isolation, and this is discussed fully in the section on the child's mastering his environment. "Different" children are often victims of child sexual abusers who offer the "special friendship," the "you and me against the world" bond. Isolation commands the "voice from within" that says, "Nobody else likes me, not in the whole world, except for this person, so I'll do what he says."

Self-respect also lessens the child's vulnerability to sexual abuse. In fact, self-respect is just another way of saying, "I feel good about who I am." Dorothy Corkille Briggs, author of *Your Child's Self-esteem,* believes there are two main convictions on which self-respect is based:

I am lovable (I matter and have value because I exist).

I am worthwhile (I can handle myself and my environment with competence; I know I have something to offer others).[6]

Translated into a response to a molester's approach, these convictions would sing out, "I don't have to trade access to my body to gain affection or friendship."

Instilling these convictions is not easy; there is no exact formula. A balance of praise and specific criticism over the years will enhance the child's self-concept. One without the other, or the absence of both, leaves the child generally vulnerable:

If your child receives only support (praise), he will inevitably remain weak and spoiled, self-centered and incompetent.

If your child receives only challenge (labeling), and possesses an active temperament, then he will inevitably become rebellious and act out his resentment.

If your child receives only challenge (labeling), and possesses a passive temperament, then he will inevitably become crushed. [parentheses added][7]

Many times we assume our children know we love them, therefore we don't have to tell them. Children don't intuitively know any such thing, and they need to be reminded, just as this father tells us adults do:

One day I was complaining to my wife about how I never hear her say, "I love you." That's always my biggest gripe with her— I never know how she feels and once in a while I'd like to hear it. I don't think that's asking a lot, especially if she really feels that way. Then I stopped and tried to remember when I last told my son that I love him. I honestly couldn't remember—it had been so long. I guess I should take some of my own advice.

Children often interpret this silence as "I am not lovable" or "Nobody likes me." This belief has perhaps the largest impact on the "voice from within." If the child knows he is both loved at home and lovable to other people, then he is less vulnerable to the promise of love from an offender.

Feeling good about ourselves *is* the most important feeling in the world. Our "voice from within" is a reflection of this feeling and it provides the basis of our other successes. We will not deteriorate into chronic selfishness just because we like who we are and refuse to become victims to compensate for our lackings. As *How to Be Your Own Best Friend* states:

The Bible says, "Love thy neighbor *as* thyself," not "better than" or "instead of" thyself.[8]

# CHILDREN SHOULD NOT BE LIMITED
# OR MADE MORE VULNERABLE
# BY SEX-ROLE STEREOTYPING

Expectations of behavior based on the sex of the child are prevalent not only in our general society but in the dynamic of the child sexual abuser as well.

Little girls are supposed to be ladylike, polite, accommodating, nurturing, entertaining, and helpful. It is an unfortunate coincidence that these are the very traits the offender seeks in a girl victim. He takes advantage of her willingness to be a *good* girl. When he approaches her, her "voice from within" may tell her, "He seems to feel *so* bad. I want to make him feel better."

Little boys are supposed to be brave, adventurous, curious, able to handle *any* situation. When confronted with a potential abuser, his first reflex may be to run away, but his "voice from within" may rule, "I don't want to run away and look like a sissy."

Even though we might strive for well-mannered daughters and self-sufficient sons, we never intend for them to be caught in the pitfalls of the labels. How are such radically different and potentially harmful messages transmitted to our children? Our goal may be well-intentioned; we want our children to be happy, to find a place in life, and to fit into the scheme of the world. But too often they are limited by the role we impose on them based on our stereotypes. *Growing Up Equal*,[9] a source book for parents, cites four influences in the detrimental sex-role stereotyping of children:

First, parental perceptions of an infant begin the process. Babies are totally ignorant of which sex they are; it will be some time before they notice the differences between them and the opposite sex. Nonetheless, the people around the baby will perceive them differently according to sex. One study asked thirty pairs of new parents (fifteen couples with baby daughters and fifteen couples with baby sons) to describe their baby twenty-four hours after its birth. Although there were no differences in the size and weight of the new-borns, after only twenty-four hours of life, the parents' perceptions were, "Daughters, in contrast to sons, were rated as significantly softer, finer featured, littler, and more inattentive." And so the life-long message to the girl begins.

Parents have no corner on the market for value-ladened percep-tions based on a child's sex. Nonparents and even children follow the same party line. One teacher tells of her experience:

In my sex-education class, I asked how you tell a boy baby from girl babies. These fourth graders seriously told me, "The girls wear pink and the boys wear blue." I asked them, "But what if the baby wears yellow or green or white?" Then they knew to look at the genitalia, and of course they knew the dif-ferences, but that wasn't the first thing that came to mind.

Second, children imitate the behavior they see in the adults they admire and spend time around. If a little girl sees her mother, female teachers, and other women in society acting in a self-deprecating other-oriented manner, she will conclude this is how she should be. To be an adult woman usually means to be like Mommy, so if Mommy always compromises her own needs to ac-commodate a man, the little girl is more likely to do this. A psy-chologist offers an excellent case in point:

I was working with this little girl who had two brothers. They played house for hours on end. The five-year-old brother was the father and the three-year-old brother was the baby. As soon as the game started, the "father" would climb in his play car, wave good-bye, say, "See you at dinner," and leave for hours on end. The little girl made mud pies and sat in a chair watch-ing the "baby." That's all she did—cook and sit in a chair. And she was only four years old.

On the other hand, if girls have contact with assertive, self-sufficient, nonvictim women, then being able to take care of herself will become part of her idea of "what she should be when she grows up." The less accommodating she is to men, and the more she is encouraged to act in *her* own best interest without expecting other people to protect her, the less vulnerable she will be to a potential child molester.

Little boys who never see adult men express fear or sadness will come to believe these are emotions they should avoid. To be tough and brave, no matter how you *feel* inside, means being like an adult man. A child molester can have an uncanny ability for sensing when a boy won't cry or run away. He will choose this boy and challenge him to stay and "be a man." Adult males who show the boy it is all right to run away, *not* to meet every challenge (especially if it is something that will hurt him), provide the boy with some of the best prevention sensibilities he could have. The lesson for this family was difficult:

One time the whole family was out together. We were trying to go to a big event in the park, and trying to park the car was difficult. Jim tried to pull into one place just as another guy was pulling into the same place from the other direction. Well, we really didn't see him, but he thought we did it on purpose. The other guy got out of his car, and was walking toward us, obviously really angry. Jim told us to lock our doors, and he just pulled out as this guy was pounding on our hood. Our eleven-year-old boy questioned Jim—he thought his father should have gotten out of the car and fought with the man because we were there first. We spent the rest of the day explaining physical violence wasn't warranted over a parking place, and I think our son finally respected his father again, but I could tell he had strong ideas about the "shame" in leaving the scene in a locked, speeding car.

Third, differential *treatment* of the child according to sex cements sex-role stereotyping and its injurious effects. Consider the following situations and examine how you (this is applicable to nonparents too) would handle the situation if a boy or girl is involved:

• Your child comes in crying because the neighbor man "teases" him or her and he or she doesn't like it.

• Bullies frighten and bother your child on the way home from school.

• While out playing, your son or daughter encounters a transient in the park and gives his or her allowance because he or
she feels sorry for him.

• A man you hardly know tells you, in a suggestive manner,
your child is the "most beautiful kid he's ever seen." You have
an uneasy feeling; how do you react?

• Without your knowledge or permission, your child and a
friend accept a ride home from an adult acquaintance.

Not only is the child likely to encounter a different reaction, based
on his or her sex, to each situation, but also each example is a possible prelude to a sexual-abuse situation. The child's behavior and
the adult's reaction could be a "rehearsal" for a future outcome.
Also, the child checks out the validity of his or her feelings against
the reaction of the parents. In any of the given situations, if it is
permissible for the girl to be afraid but not the boy, changes in
the child's feelings and resultant behavior may result. A father
shares with us:

I remember reading about this study that sure said a lot about
how I treat my kids. They showed a picture of a little kid falling down and they asked the girls to complete the story—what
happens next sort of thing. The girls said they'd go home and
their parents would wash off the hurt, put something on it so
it wouldn't get infected, and then bandage it up and tell her
it will be O.K. The boys said the kid goes home and the parents
tell him "life is rough," it's no big deal, you shouldn't get so
upset over a little bruise. I know I treat my son's hurt very
differently than my daughter's.

Yet, it's the same bruised knee and the same soreness. The sex of
the child dictates both the child's feelings about the bruise and the
parent's treatment of the mishap.

Last, sex-role stereotyping is learned through the culture. Books,
television, language, and advertising amplify the differential messages we give to our children. Our culture is much more male-
oriented than female-oriented; girl children do not receive equal

time. The conclusion: Girl children are not as important as boy children.

For example, a 1974 study of sexist language in the Random House Dictionary found that 68 per cent of the words were masculine-gendered, 23 per cent were feminine-gendered, and the remaining 9 per cent of the words were androgynous.[10] Girls speak a language that is relevant to them only 23 per cent of the time. Volume alone is not the problem; the values inherent in the words are telling. The masculine-gendered words connotated achievement, ambition, aggression, competitiveness, competence, dominance, and intelligence. All of those qualities are necessary to avoid victimization. Contrast those qualities with the values of feminine-gendered words: weakness, incompetence, submissiveness, dependency, and timidity. This is the quintessential description of a victim.

Television is a strong cultural influence, and while much has been done to combat television violence, sex-role stereotyping is alive and well in children's programming. America's population is approximately 48 per cent male and 52 per cent female, but not so in children's television. If what we view is any indication, females represent a significantly smaller, less powerful portion of the population. Consider these findings:

• On "Sesame Street" 78 per cent of the characters (including muppets) were male; 87 per cent of the announcers/narrators were male; males were found to initiate action more often than females, and females were found in nonactive roles three times more than the male characters.

• On "Electric Company," 69 per cent of the characters were male; there were twice as many male announcers/narrators as females; action and talking roles were divided evenly between males and females.

• Percentage of males for four other children's shows were: "Villa Alegre," 69 per cent; "Zoom," 53 per cent; "Carrascolendas," 49 per cent; and "Mr. Rogers' Neighborhood," 74 per cent.

• On Saturday-morning cartoons—some of the most violent programming on television—males were shown in forty-two roles while females were in only nine roles; and males were shown as being adventurous, knowledgeable, independent, aggressive, sturdy, and bold, as compared to females' portrayal as romantic, submissive, fragile, timid, and patient.[11, 12]

Not only are girls/women not portrayed enough to be deemed important, but also, when they are on the screen, it is in the role of victim.

All four influences combine to impact on how little boys or girls perceive themselves (self-concept) and what they consider their options to be; from what they will be when they grow up to how they will react to a potentially dangerous situation.

Expectations of *protection* seem to be at the crux of differential attitudes found in sex-role stereotyping. Simply, girls look to other people to protect them, while boys, cast in the role of the *protector*, are prepared to cope independently of other people's help. The girl is in sorry need of that protection when the offender (a man) banks on her inability to protect herself from his sexual abuse. When she primarily relies on men to help her out of difficult situations and develops no resourcefulness of her own, a confrontation with a child molester will be like a hen asking a fox to help her to the other side of the road.

Attention and affection are also important issues. Just as most women do not fit into the sexist image of the *Playboy* bunny or sex kitten, many little girls are not cute, adorable, and "sugar and spice." A girl may be athletic, intelligent, or talented but not particularly pretty or "cuddly." She may be acutely aware of not "fitting in," and her isolation and lack of self-esteem, despite all of her assets, make her vulnerable to the flattery of an offender who thinks she is "special" or "beautiful." Again, from a teacher:

> I have a classroom of sixth-grade girls who already hate their bodies. They endlessly discuss how they don't look like Cheryl Tiegs and how they can maybe look more like her. No matter how many times I tell them they are only twelve years old and have plenty of time, and it really isn't that important, and Cheryl Tiegs in real life probably doesn't look like Cheryl Tiegs, it does no good. They are already defeated, and define themselves by what they haven't got rather than by all the good, individual things in them.

On the other hand, a miniature "Cheryl Tiegs," defined by her beauty and coyness, may seek affection as a form of validation. Entertain is what she does best, and she is vulnerable to the exploitation of those she perpetually entertains.

Little boys really never grow out of their need for affection, but after a certain age, they may receive it only from their mothers, if at all. Boys do not learn about appropriate affection in a vacuum; without experiencing affection from a nonexploitive male, the boy may be vulnerable to the attentions of the offender. How else will they know the difference between normal affection and child sexual abuse? This mother tells of her family's affection:

> Sometimes my husband comes home really tired and feeling awful. He'll just sit at the table, really wiped out. He'll ask me to come sit on his lap and just hold him. My nine-year-old son usually sits and just watches for a while, but then he'll crawl in his father's lap and give him a hug—he'll say, "I love you, Dad." It's a very important part of our family life. They also still kiss each other good night, and my husband's father thinks this is terrible. He is very critical of it every time he visits.

This boy could probably tell the difference between genuine affection and a "special game" a molester would ask him to play. But other boys with unsatisfied needs for affection may not know the difference. If they don't fit into the mold of stoic, athletic, rowdy boys, they are especially vulnerable to the affirmation a buddy/child molester will offer.

Few parents deliberately set out to stereotype and shape their children according to sex roles. We do it unconsciously because the influence is everywhere, and after all, it was done to us and perhaps we haven't made sense out of it yet. To assess the extent to which sex-role stereotyping is part of family life, *Growing Up Equal* suggests the following questions as a measure:[13]

> Is there a difference between female and male behavior, emotional responses, preferences, abilities, and/or attributes?
>
> Does age make a difference?
>
> Do girls act differently when they are with boys, and vice versa or when they are in mixed-sex groups?

Do children adhere to traditional expectations for their sex?

Do they live up to the stereotypes?

Do they stereotype other children by sex?

How do other people (friends, parents, relatives, other children) channel your child into conventional roles—by word or by action?

How does your child respond?

Many of us are aware of the confinement and damage of sex-role stereotyping, and the situation is beginning to change some. Girls are becoming more assertive; their options seem to be more varied than ever before, but to what extent have little boys been able to behave in previously unsanctioned ways? According to this teacher:

Hardly any girls in my classes say they want to be mommies anymore. They *do* say they want to be teachers, doctors, actresses, and the like. At least they are thinking about supporting themselves and maybe having kids later. But the boys haven't changed. They sure aren't saying they want to be parents, but more interesting, they still aren't saying they want to be nurses, beauticians, or ballet dancers either.

Perhaps some of the most serious work left to be done concerns opening up some humane options for little boys as well as girls.

Differences among children, in and of themselves, are not so bad. This would be a very boring world if we were all the same. But why should the differences be based on *sex* and be as sweeping and confining as they are? Why not have natural differences, emanating from the varied personalities and interests of each *individual* child? Why not let the children have some say in what those differences will be?

As it is now, members of one sex, females, are inadequately prepared to prevent their own victimization. Boys are prepared to defend themselves but are sometimes hesitant, afraid of looking like a "sissy." If we are to have differences, why does it need to be between strong and weak, competent and incompetent, giving and taking? The dichotomy reaps some heavy personal consequences for the child, not only as victim, but in many other ways as well. *Growing Up Equal* has inventoried the important studies on the effects of sex-role stereotyping, and it is wise to review the results:

• Starting at age six months, girls receive more physical contact and are talked to more than are boys.

• Fathers display affection more with girls.

• Girls learn to rely more on the opinion of others.

• Parents are more likely to accept clinging, dependent behavior from girls.

• Parents respond more to boys' large muscle movements.

• Boys are encouraged not to cry while girls usually receive support for doing so.

• Boys and girls are given different kinds of toys: girls' focusing on nurturing and domestic skills and boys' on career skills and muscle development.

• Girls learn to be more concerned with their appearance—they are usually not allowed to get dirty but are supported in being perfect in grooming, thus inhibiting active playing.

• Boys learn to be more concerned with their physical prowess—fathers roughhouse with them and teach them sport skills.

• Parents encourage boys to solve their own problems, while they more often help girls solve theirs.

• Parents are more protective of their girls.

• Parents encourage their boys to be more independent than they do their girls.

• Parents are more tolerant of assertiveness and physical aggression in their boys than in their girls.

• Mothers sanction boys negatively for imitating their ways (such as in domestic activities) while encouraging girls.[14]

Sex-role stereotyping is one of those bad habits; we can't remember *not* having it but we know it is harmful and we can't seem to stop. It is a basic matter of treating a child differently according to sex rather than the child's needs or interests. It is a simplistic, not very well-thought-out scheme. It markedly contributes to our children's victimization and it is worth our time and energy to assess and change our individual contributions to this habit.

# THE CHILD NEEDS TO KNOW
## THAT THE PARENT WILL LISTEN TO HIM
### AND TAKE HIS FEARS SERIOUSLY

Almost every adult can remember a time in childhood when he or she wasn't believed. Who hasn't been impacted by an unscrupulous or unbalanced adult in authority who told a lie about us? No matter how many times we tried to explain the truth to other adults—parents, school principal, etc.—we were not believed. The bottom line was that we were only children, and the adult telling the lie was believed because he was an adult. Years later, the very thought of that incident can bring back strong feelings of helplessness and betrayal, as this woman remembers:

> I'll never forget this nun who seemed to like me in the second grade. She was always asking me to do her favors, like stay after and help with the blackboards or something. Well, I was very assertive and had better things to do. So, after I refused her a few times, she called up my mother and told her I had been skipping out on classes and would *have to* stay after. It totally flipped me out. I hadn't skipped anything except not staying after with her. I tried to explain it—as best I understood it—to my mother, but she kept on saying, "She's a nun, why would she want to lie? She wouldn't do that, it's a sin." I think that was the worst year of elementary school for me.

Child molesters are well aware of who will win if a battle of veracity ensues. As an adult, especially if he is close to the family, a child molester can insist the child is confused, vengeful, or fantasizing. He may go so far as to warn the child that no one will believe her if she tells. The child is more vulnerable if her personal experience confirms his admonition. If the word of adults has more value than the word of children, she may never tell. If her everyday fears and questions are not resolved, but instead regarded as nuisances, her "voice from within" will tell her, "I know if I tell anyone about this, they'll get mad at me for making trouble."

Our children come to important conclusions based on how we do or do not listen to them. If we are attentive and take them seriously, we are more likely to hear about a potential or actual incident of abuse. We would all agree that we want to know about these things. If they feel discounted or limited in the types or amounts of questions they can ask, then they will keep the offender's secret because they have no place to go with it.

We are often not aware of our patterns of listening to our children. *Your Child's Self-esteem* asks four questions to assess such patterns:

1. Who does most of the talking?

2. How do you respond to your child's messages (questions)? Do you use the traditional "feeling stoppers"? (Judgment, Reasoning, Cheering, Denial)

3. Are you merely quietly attentive or do you actively reflect back his total message empathically?

4. How would you feel if your messages (questions) were handled as you treat your child's? [parentheses added][15]

The last question is perhaps the easiest way to determine how much of a resource we are to our children. If you were in his or her shoes, would you tell your parent about the "strange" man who hangs around the swimming pool? Would you ask your parent questions about what it means if someone puts his hands down your pants? Would you tell your parent about the baby-sitter asking you to play that "game" last night? Or would anticipated reactions of hostility, hysterics, or just plain ignoring you prevent you from speaking up?

The probability of child sexual abuse flourishing will significantly diminish if the offender's secret is *not* kept. The child's confidence in his parents' willingness to listen is developed a long time before his first experience with potential child molestation. When he was afraid of ghosts in his bedroom, did someone explain to him about ghosts and reassure him, or did they answer, "Don't be silly, there are no ghosts." If no one will talk openly about ghosts, then he certainly isn't going to risk admonishment by talking about child molesters. As this mother discovered, the parents' willingness to listen can be very reassuring and constructive for the child:

Our son was having a bad time with dreams when he was around seven years old. He'd wake up screaming in the middle of the night. My husband and I handled it really differently. He insisted we shouldn't ask Noah about the dream because then he would be more into it, it would scare him more, and he'd start to use it for attention. I didn't think that was right, I thought we should talk about it, but I deferred to my husband. Noah's dreams kept on getting worse and worse, so finally, *I* talked about it with him. It turned out he and his friend had been playing with matches, and they were scolded, but weeks later, Noah was having dreams about burning alive. It really alarmed me, but we talked about all kinds of things like how he shouldn't still feel guilty, and we only scolded him because we loved him, and what to do if there ever is a fire, how to get out of the house. I'm not sure which thing really helped, but the dreams *did* go away once I listened to him.

Listening is the best policy, and asking direct questions is the most helpful way to go about developing this all-important skill. Let the child know you *recognize* his state of mind and you want to know more about it. *Direct,* action-oriented questions get at the heart of the matter:

- "How are you *feeling?*"
- "What are you *thinking* about?"
- "I really want to *listen* to you."
- "What can I *do* to help?"
- "Won't you *tell* me what's on your mind?"

Children need a direct cue to be sure that the parent is interested. Many victims report they wanted to be the offender's "special friend" because "he always listened to me . . . he cared about me." Children are less likely to enter into a secret bond with a child molester if they believe their concerns are taken seriously at home.

Every time we *don't* listen to our child or we disregard questions, we not only diminish their curiosity, we also teach them that we don't want to be bothered with them. The following responses can discourage the child from communicating with his parents or any other important adult:

- "Don't bother me now, I'm busy."

- "Can't you see I have someone with me? Go out and play."

- "I've answered that question a thousand times."

- "Go ask your mother (father)."

- "What a silly thing to think of. Where did you ever get an idea like that?"

Of course we can't always drop everything to attend to every question; however, the *quality* of time spent on the child's concerns might diminish the number of questions asked. Before children become totally discouraged with asking for help or information, they will make one last valiant effort with a barrage of questions. On the other hand, if they *know* you are accessible to them, the need to test and prove your interest can decrease. Accessibility can be enhanced by statements like:

I don't know the answer to that, but let's look it up, and I'll show *you* how to look this up too so you can find the answer for yourself.

I don't really know, but maybe your mother (father) will know when she (he) gets home from work. Let's ask.

I'm in the middle of something now, but I will talk with you about this when I'm finished, so please don't forget your question.

I remember being afraid of ghosts too. Let's check the rooms, make sure nothing is there, then we'll talk about ghosts.

It's been a *really* rough day—I need fifteen minutes of quiet for myself, then I'll be glad to talk. O.K.?

You seem to be asking that question a lot lately. Is there something *else* bothering you? Or maybe we should write the answer down, do a drawing of it, or make up a story about it to help you remember. What do you think?

None of these responses are pampering the child or interfering unreasonably with the parents' life. They are instilling a sense of legitimacy about the child's concerns. And remember, it isn't the parents' responsibility *alone* to answer all questions. The genuinely curious child might need some supplementary program where he or she can learn about a specific subject of burning interest.

It is that sense of legitimacy about concerns that encourages the child to share experiences and questions with the parent. Without it, the child becomes silent and loses an important resource. Virginia Satir, author of *Peoplemaking* and *Conjoint Family Therapy,* agrees that we can't always be there to listen to our child, but through her savings bank analogy, she stresses the importance of listening as often as possible.

Applied to issues of trust and being believed, the savings bank works like this: At birth, parent and child open a savings bank together. Trust and caring are the currency. Every time we seriously consider our child's fears or concerns, and answer the best we can, we are making a *deposit*. Every time we tell our child to go away or when we discount fears or questions, we make a *withdrawal*. In the natural course of family life, withdrawals are inevitable, but if we are not cautious, the withdrawals can easily pile up and *overdraw* our account. When there is an overdraft, the child concludes he is not important; thus the "voice from within" tells her, "I know if I tell anyone about this, they'll get mad at me for making trouble."

Four basic requests can also be adapted from *The Parent Book* to comprise the transaction of the savings bank:

- *Companionship* because he is lonely;

- *Reassurance* because he is afraid;

- *Activity* because he is bored; or

- *Answers and information* because there are things he does not know.[16]

Although these may seem like insurmountable needs to the child, incidents involving each type of need can be dealt with in perhaps only ten minutes of the parents' time. Reassurance or giving an answer does not need to be a major production. Directing the child to some activity or form of companionship can also be a simple matter. Of course, it is not *always* a simple matter, but in individual incidents, ten minutes of the parents' time can make the difference between a deposit and a withdrawal.

Faced with a potential child sexual abuse situation, a child should not have to debate who to tell about the incident and worry about whether she will be believed or not. She needs a *reflex* that says, loud and clear, "I'm going to tell my parents about this, right away." That reflex is instilled through previous experience, which has taught her that feelings of fear and questions are acceptable and will be taken seriously. With this knowledge she is less impressed with both the child molester's willingness to listen to her and his contention that no one will believe her anyway. The health and strength of the "voice from within" are partly determined by how well that voice is listened to, both by the child and the parent.

# CHILDREN NEED TO LEARN
# HOW MUCH OTHER PEOPLE
# CAN PHYSICALLY AND EMOTIONALLY
# ASK FROM THEM

By the intrinsic nature of child sexual abuse, the offender will be many years older than the victim. In a world where there is a quantum gap between children and adults, what are the implications of this fact?

For all too many children, the difference in ages will add up to the "voice from within" that commands, "He's an adult and I'd better do what he says," or "Mom and Dad said to mind him—if he says to do this, it must be O.K." But if a child develops a sense of *territoriality*, then he will not mindlessly obey the adult.

Territoriality means the child recognizes that his own best interest is a separate entity from other people's needs and cannot always be defined by them. Because he is a separate person, he has boundaries—both physically and emotionally—that no one is allowed to cross. The child will examine each request, agree if it does not invade his territory, and refuse if he feels the adult is trying to meet his or her own best interest at his expense. Simply put, a child with a sense of territoriality will not follow every command from an adult just because it emanates from someone older.

This does not apply to commands to clean up the bedroom or to stay out of the street. In this context, territoriality applies to *hurtful* requests made by adults. In the opening vignette, a child without a sense of the emotional and physical limits would agree to the molester's request to play the "new game." A child *with* a sense of territoriality would question the molester's request, consider whether that amount of touching was comfortable, and if she already had been warned about "games" by her parents, her "voice from within" would, almost by reflex, tell her: "This isn't right. I'm not going to do it, and I'm telling someone about it right away."

When our children were infants the boundaries were fuzzy. To some extent they needed to be; the child depended on the adult for daily survival and didn't have the resources to defend his own territory. However, as the child grows older, she naturally gains these resources. First comes the *feeling* that she has a mind of her own, that she sometimes knows what is best for herself. Of course, a large dose of guidance and experience must accompany this budding sense of separate personhood. Problems begin when we insist that *we* know what is best for our children and that if the children will only obey our every command, without question, life will be good to them. Perhaps it will be—until they become adults and find they have no sense of themselves outside of our direction. The child ruled by the parents' voice, at the expense of her own "voice from within," is likely to heed, without question, the commands or requests of any adult. A graphic situation is offered by a mother of three boys:

> We were out in the desert on a long trip, and we had pulled over to the side of the road. The boys were playing on the other side of the road when these two men in an old beat-up truck drove up next to them. They were really gross-looking—very filthy and it seemed they had been drinking. They called toward our oldest son and Billy, who was nine then, immediately went over and talked to him. I couldn't believe it, and I was really worried. Billy was at the passenger side of the truck, so I couldn't see what was going on, but I could just imagine. So I went over there and told the boys we needed to be going. I could smell the liquor on the men's breath. I asked Billy why he had gone over to the truck. He said, "Because he asked me to." I really had gone out of my way to raise my children to be polite, but enough was enough—I sure never meant for them to be *that* polite.

Billy's parents happen to be very good parents. Although they have instilled some excellent values in their son, one important virtue was missing, at least in this situation. That is a sense of territoriality. At nine years old, it would have been right on target for Billy to say to himself, "Why should I talk to those gross guys? Just because they say, 'Come here, kid,' doesn't mean I have to *do* it."

So, in the context of child sexual abuse, the essense of territoriality is: When a child is faced with an unwanted approach, what is his first priority? Is it his own safety or being respectful to his elders?

Assertiveness and self-protection are the tools of territoriality in general and the necessary skills for the prevention of child sexual abuse in particular. The child will not suddenly pull these skills out of a hat when approached by a child molester. He will have developed—or not developed—them over time as an outgrowth of his family atmosphere. The likelihood of trusting his judgment and acting in his own best interest will be reflections of how often he is allowed to exercise that judgment and the degree of acceptance of his self-protective actions. Without knowing it or meaning to, we short-circuit a child's sense of territoriality.

Again, consider how important adults are in the child's life. Do adults reign absolutely supreme? Or is there some room for the child's wishes and needs? In our desire to raise "nice, polite children" we sometimes forego the development of "self-sufficient, assertive children." For instance, if a child has been sitting comfortably in the same chair for an hour, does she have to get up and give it to an adult who just entered the room? If so, why? Is it because the adult's comfort is more important than the child's? Is it because that's "good manners"? The child may come to some different conclusions, such as, "Adults are more important than kids," or "What I want isn't at all important," or "Good manners means giving up myself for the sake of an adult." If the message comes up repeatedly, it will not enhance a healthy "voice from within." Instead, the "voice from within" will say, "This guy is an adult and I'd better do what he says."

Mandatory forfeiting of the child's rights *is* different from consideration of other people's needs, as this mother of two pubescent boys tells us:

> We have this real old lumpy couch and one part of it is definitely more comfortable than the rest. Whenever my mother comes to visit, I have to ask the boys, if they are sitting on the comfortable part, to move and let her sit there. I get so frus-

trated, I wish they would just think of her and offer her the comfortable part.

In this case, there is a sound reason for the children giving up their seat to their grandmother. They are not asked to do it merely because she is an adult and they are children.

Conversation sometimes falls into the same category of "not as important" if children are involved. How many of us have interrupted a conversation we are having with our child when an adult comes on the scene? Suddenly, what the child has to say is no longer interesting and we turn our attention to the adult, telling the child to "go off and play now." Certainly adult conversation can be *more* interesting than talking with a child, but that really isn't the issue here. When we cut the child off, what is that teaching her? How does that message interface with the considerations of the previous section on listening? The child can conclude that what she has to say isn't very important, thus fortifying a silent quality in her "voice from within." If adult conversation has supreme priority, then the offender's voice can drown out her own insignificant mumblings.

There are ways to accommodate the child's need to talk along with our own needs for adult companionship. A mother of a three-year-old child offers her own experience:

There are always a lot of people around the house, people that I like to talk with. At the same time, my son Paul is also very talkative—it must run in the family. If we are involved in something like telling a story (*he* makes them up) then the adult who comes in is invited to sit down and listen to the rest of the story. If it seems to be going on, we pick an ending point we like and tell him how much we liked the story. That makes him happy—that's what he was waiting for. If it's the other way around—the adult was there first and Paul wants to talk—we've taught him to say, "Excuse me, Mom, I have a question—" or whatever. He realizes he's important and can interrupt us, but he also knows there's a right way to do it so that his question gets answered and I'm not totally undone by it. After all, his father or I have to say, "Excuse me . . ." to each other if we interrupt, so it only seems right.

That is a fine balance; other people's privacy and the child's needs. However, it would seem Paul was well on his way to speaking up when he needs to without running roughshod over those around him. More importantly, he is developing a sense of legitimacy about what he has to say, which *is* as legitimate as any adult's utterings.

The bathroom is another arena of child vs. adult prerogatives. In that it involves the child's sexual territory as well, it is one to consider carefully. Many of us have probably encountered the situation described by this father of a seven-year-old boy:

> After the kids were out of the toddler stage, my wife and I started to insist on our private time, like in our bedroom and unless there was an emergency, they couldn't come into the bathroom if either one was in there with the door closed. But if we needed to go in to gather up the dirty clothes or we needed something out of the bathroom, we would knock and go in if our kids were in there. Well, one day I knocked and as usual without waiting went on in. My son, who was six then, pulled me up short. He told me, "We can't come in here when you are in here, so why can you come in anytime you want, even if I'm in here?" He was obviously disturbed, and I started with one of my "because I'm the daddy" lines, but then I figured he really had a point. He wasn't ever going to learn to *give* the privacy his mother and I were asking for if he couldn't enjoy its privileges as well. I mean, why should he respect our privacy if we were going to do as we please?

This is the essence of territoriality. The child must believe, "As a member of the human family, I am entitled to the same rights as anyone else. What is *expected from* me must also be *available to* me." Without this belief, the child will be trapped in a double standard, which when applied to child sexual abuse, amounts to the belief that the offender's need to touch her sexually is important and her need for control over her own body is insignificant.

Prolonged or enforced nudity is a variation on the issue of the child's sexual territory. Nude children do not provoke child molesters, but flagrant public nudity can give a child a false and injurious sense of how much access adults should have to his body. The following incident, offered by a nonparent, demonstrates the dilemma:

I was living in a commune on a very busy street near a university. The two children in our house were two and five, and the parents in the house would *un*dress their children to go out and play in the summer. Soon the other neighborhood kids were mimicking them and their parents came over to our house very upset. They asked us to please confine the kids' nudity to our own house or backyard, and they didn't feel it was safe for the kids to be playing nude next to the street in plain sight of everyone. The parents in my house told these other parents that they were sick and deranged, that the body was beautiful and shouldn't be hidden behind clothes. Everyone on both sides got real upset. Our kids still played next to the street in the nude and the other kids weren't allowed to play with them. In response to the parents in our house, I suggested that if they thought the human body was so beautiful, maybe the next time it was their turn to mow the commune lawn, they would like to do it in the nude. I meant it seriously, but they didn't really get the point.

Nudity within families, depending on the family's style and the age of the children, can be a liberating experience. However, nakedness on public thoroughfares liberates no one. The children involved in this case were too young to protect themselves from adults' reactions to their nudity. With no sense of sexual limits, the "games" the child molester wants to play may not seem out of the ordinary to the perennially nude child.

Akin to sexual territory are the relationships that envelop that territory. Friendships, affection, choosing to be with some people and not with others are all exercises in the child's development of assertiveness and self-protection skills. But here again, we often scramble the normal development without meaning to.

Kissing is an excellent example. All children have needs for personal distance, but we barely notice, let alone respect this. It begins when they are babies. Often when we pick up a baby or toddler, the child will squirm or cry. Instead of putting him down, we hold on tighter, because we want to express our affection. If this happens repeatedly, the mindset the child will develop is obvious—if an adult wants to touch him, he will be touched, and that's all there is to it. What the child wants done to his body is irrelevant. The implications for this mindset in child sexual abuse are also obvious. Probably each of us knows how it feels to be slobbered on by someone we want to get away from; yet, as adults, we allow this to happen to our children in the name of affection.

As the child grows older, he is subjected to verbal as well as physical affection. While we stress not talking to strangers, we can allow family, friends, and acquaintances to unleash their affection on our hesitant children. The message can be confusing to the child, as a four-year-old girl recently told her mother:

> You tell me to *never* say "hello" to strangers, but when you have me in the shopping cart in the store, all those goofy old ladies come up and tickle me and try to kiss me and you *make* me be nice to them.

To tell the child, "Well, I'm with you," or "I say it's O.K.," is more confusing. So many times the offender *is* a friend of the family. The parent has allowed the offender (unknowingly, of course) to express "normal" affection within the family. And, just to confuse the issue unwittingly a little more, the child may have been told, "Now, you do what he tells you to do while I'm gone." Thus the very good reasons for the child's "voice from within" answering the offender's approach with, "Mom and Dad told me to do what he says so I guess I'd better do it," or "I have to kiss everyone else and be nice to them—so what's the difference with this game?"

Magically, the child is supposed to know the difference between a child molester and someone—such as the ladies in the grocery store—whom the parents allow or encourage to touch the child. True, chances are slim that the elderly woman in the store is really a male child molester in disguise, but the point is that *forced* affection is forced affection. After repeated instances of being "loved" against her will, the child will think there is nothing out of the ordinary about someone touching her when she does not want to be touched. There will be nothing alerting her self-protection skills if the scene is commonplace.

Combined with the social pressure to accept unwanted affection graciously (which people of *all* ages must contend with), children have the combined problem of being outweighed and outsized by those giving the affection. The world is peculiar enough with a viewpoint that is at eye level with most people's hips and groins. Complicate that with big people pushing their faces into the child's, and the child finds himself in a genuinely exasperating situation. One of the first skills taught in effective communication with children is to sit or position yourself so that adult and child are at *eye* level. By not towering over the child but instead meeting him at his own outlook point, the overbearingness inherent in the size difference is diminished. With this kind of experience in talking with adults, children might be better able to push away unwanted affection without feeling something comparable to Skylab falling on them if they don't co-operate. To gain an understanding of the impact of the size difference on a child, imagine if you were suddenly transported to a world of twelve-foot-tall adults!

Children can have opinions about both a person's affectionate behavior *and* the person himself. Often a child will not like a specific adult, and when we ask her why, she really can't explain. The adult may not be behaving inappropriately, but for whatever reasons, the child intuitively doesn't like him. And sometimes we scold the child, telling them it's "not nice" to dislike their uncle or neighbor. Children are not that inherently opinionated—there is probably some good reason for not liking the adult, even if the child can't verbalize it directly. Unless *we* respect the child's feelings, discuss them, and decide what to do about them, it will be asking a lot of the child to cope with a child sexual abuser in a straightforward manner based on her feelings of dislike or uncomfortableness. One mother of a young son gives us a good solution:

One night Doug and I wanted to go out to dinner—on the spur of the moment. We called all the baby-sitters, and as luck would have it, the only one available was one our son didn't particularly like. He was about eight then, so we sat down and explained that we really needed to go out, and would he mind staying with her. He said he really didn't like her; he couldn't say why, he just thought she was "weird." I really trusted him— I knew he wasn't trying to ruin a good time for us. I just couldn't see us going out at his expense after he'd made it clear he would be uncomfortable, so my husband came up with a good solution: The three of us went out to dinner together. My husband and I didn't have the privacy we wanted, but we *did*—all three of us—have a good time.

After a few experiences like the above—being listened to, being taken seriously, and finding a solution—it will seem in the natural course of events for the child's "voice from within" to say, "This is wrong. I'm not going to do it, and I'm going to tell someone right away," if ever approached by an offender.

Perhaps the child just needs time to get to know someone, or the circumstances around their interaction are strained. In these cases, it is still inappropriate to tell the child, "Be nice," or "Don't hurt his feelings by not liking him." Compulsory friendship curtails the child trusting his sense of other people—a prerequisite to recognizing a dangerous situation for what it is. Statements like, "Give it a little time, honey," or "Do you think you'd like him any better if he didn't baby-sit but just came over as a relative?" respect the child's "alarm system" and instill a healthy sense of territoriality. A male nonparent friend of mine gave me an excellent example of a child's feelings being respected, and through the outlet of her expression and the passing of time, it all worked out for the best.

When I moved into Emily's house, she was four and a half. She had seen many of her friends' parents divorce, and I think she was afraid that my moving in meant her father would move out. We explained to her that that wasn't going to happen. But still, she didn't like me. One day, she came up to me, tapped me on the shoulder, and said, "You know, Steven, you could get a real nice apartment in New York City, with lots of room for yourself. Real cheap." Obviously she hadn't adjusted to my moving in, but no one yelled at her, told her she was bad for saying that. I respected her need for distance. In a couple of weeks, she began to like me. Now that we share games we both like to play—like Monopoly—we are good friends.

Emily had some valid concerns that were resolved as time went on and as she saw that her father intended to remain in the house. Steven is an adult, and if he is crushed by real-estate advice from a four-year-old girl, then that is more his problem than the child's.

Emily seems to have some gifts of perception that were enhanced, not discounted, by the adult's treatment of her needing distance from Steven. Instead of thinking to herself, "This guy is an adult and I better do whatever he says, even though I don't trust him as far as I could throw him," Emily looked to the New York *Times* classified ads. Such resourcefulness will not be easily undone by a potential offender.

As usual, the family is the place where the child most often practices defining territory. An important consideration to remember is that children's needs change. As the child grows older, her territorial boundaries change. Sometimes these changes are not respected in the growing child, and much confusion results.

An excellent case in point is "Daddy's little girl." As she approaches puberty, she casts off cute nicknames and no longer wants to be kissed every night. She still cares very much for her parents, but growing up demands more autonomy and their physical affection is seen as confining. If left to her own devices, chances are she will find *new* ways to express her affection—special activities they will share or deep discussion about important issues. Sometimes we don't recognize the new behavior as a more mature form of trust and affection and we long for the old childlike ways. This is natural, but we could be unintentionally undermining the child. For instance, if the father persists in his old expressions of affection, the child may give up her needs for distance against her better judgment, in order to please her father. Resentment is sure to follow along with a basic mistrust in her own ability to define her territory. More often, open hostility can develop over where the boundaries will be. However, if the parents can respect her needs—as confusing and fast-changing as they can be—then the most basic and essential lesson of maintaining personal integrity is learned. And it isn't *all* pain and confusion, as the father of a teen-age girl shares with us:

When Janine went to junior high, she didn't like to wrestle or let me call her "Peanut" anymore. I knew in my mind that she was just growing up, but inside of me I felt like I was losing her. I was real confused and didn't know what to do—I basically did nothing, which I think *she* took as rejection. Then one night we were watching "the Mary Tyler Moore Show" to-

gether. Ted, the anchorman, was about to meet his new stepfather, and he didn't know what to call him. He asked Lou
Grant what his daughters call him, and Lou said something
like, "When they were little, they called me Pop, then when
they got older and went to college they called me Father. Now
that they are married with their own families, they call me Pop
again. I like Pop best. Father cost too much money." Not only
was it funny, but it said something about what we were going
through and also reassured us that somehow she would always
be my Peanut even if I couldn't call her that now. We talked
a little that night, and from there on, through a long, arduous
process of elimination, we decided on playing tennis together
each week, as our time. I miss the wrestling, but I know this
is best for her.

Here the adult's need for contact was no more important than the
child's need for distance. There are no easy solutions, but an episode
at home where the child's territory can be redefined and respected
has a long-lasting, healthy effect on the child. Unfortunately, in
cases of incest, the natural redefining or pulling away is not expressed or not respected.

Boys have their own issues with distance. A specific case that
worries most mothers concerns little boys' use of public rest rooms.
Around four years old—or sometimes earlier—little boys refuse to
go into the ladies' room with their mother. They also refuse to go
to the bathroom before the shopping or theater trip, and choose
only those times when their father is absent from the outing. Most
mothers want to respect this budding independence, but they are
not willing to let the little boy enter the world of large, confusing
men's rooms on his own. Part of this is fear of the unknown: Most
women have never been in a men's room, and can't imagine what
*really* goes on in there. Whatever it is, they are sure it is beyond
the coping capabilities of a four-year-old boy.

Compromises can be made. Suggest to the boy that he go into
the ladies' room with you, but he can go into the toilet stall *all
by himself*. This will satisfy your son's need for privacy for some
time. Eventually he will want to venture forth to the men's rooms
by himself. When he does, you might want to stand outside the

door and talk to him while he is inside. True, this does provoke strange looks from adult men, but it is a definite form of protection. After a few successful experiences, your confidence and his skill will increase, and the issue will fade away.

Although the concept of sexual limits is by far the most crucial in relation to child sexual abuse, it is also the most intangible form of territoriality. As an introduction to the concept that there are limits to what people can emotionally or physically ask of you, use a tangible object as the focus of boundaries. Children who are required to share *everything* (bedrooms, baths, clothes, toys, and books) are going to have a harder time grasping what it means for access to their bodies to be off-limits. It's hard enough sharing parents with siblings without complicating matters by not having anything that is all their own. One mother tried this concept with her four-year-old son with great success:

> It was Timmy's fourth birthday and while he was excited, he also seemed a little down, a little nervous. I had to ask him what was wrong quite a few times and he finally told me that he liked having a birthday, but at the party he had to share all his toys, so other kids got to play with them before he did and sometimes they got broken in the process. I think he also felt a little guilty about feeling selfish although he couldn't really explain it that way. I know I lean on the generosity thing a lot. So we talked and I told him it wasn't selfish to want to share some toys and to keep the rest to himself. We decided together that a fifty-fifty split was good. He would be generous with half and put the other half away for his own private time.

Through that experience, Timmy is learning the skills of assertiveness and self-protection. At four he knows what off-limits means in terms of his toys. He can be generous without being controlled by the needs of other people. The next step—to understand that his body is off-limits to adults and that it does not exist for other people's pleasure—is fairly close at hand now.

Of all the concepts discussed so far, territoriality is the most nebulous. A common fear is that selfishness will be cultivated in the child. Let a young child define parts of his own world and deem them "no trespassing" to other people and you will have a maniacal toddler on your hands. We have all known such little tyrants, but I contend that did not happen because the child had a healthy sense of territoriality. This vignette observed by a non-parent captures the real point:

> I was visiting my friends' house one day. They have this totally undisciplined five-year-old, Theo, who I feel sorry for because he is so obnoxious and overbearing at this age, I can't imagine what he'll be like later. Anyway, we were playing an Elton John record, and all of a sudden he throws a temper tantrum saying he can't stand Elton John. First his parents ignored him, so he got more and more hysterical. Then they finally turned to him and said, "Theo, you're being unreasonable." They kept playing the record and kept on telling him how unreasonable he was until finally he hyperventilated himself during this tantrum. The most unreasonable thing about it was these adults expecting a five-year-old to understand and change his behavior because they said he was unreasonable.

The problem here was not that Theo had too strong a sense of territoriality; he didn't. He had no sense of other people's territoriality or rights. More important is the fact that the parents lacked any sense of territoriality themselves. The simple act of removing this screaming child to another room, explaining it was their private time, seemed out of their grasp or belief system. So without a healthy model of territoriality, Theo is bound to be confused about where his rights begin and where other people's rights also lie.

In our respect for other people's boundaries, we model for our children both self-respect and a recognition of other people's emotional and physical limits. The clincher in American child rearing has been that territory was to be acquired on the child's eighteenth birthday. But what is she supposed to do with it? Until this mystical day, no one cared about *her* emotional and physical limits. Subsequently, she doesn't care about other people's dignity. And even if she did care, with no instruction and certainly no practice, she cannot suddenly define what she wants and act on it.

Not all of us are so extreme in our lacking of territoriality, but it is a new concept when applied to children. Adults fumble their way through the wants and needs of important adults in their lives, but children are another matter. As an example, if a child does not like a friend of the family, he is told to be "nice" or scolded and told that he doesn't know what he's talking about. If, on the other hand, our spouse does not like that same friend of the family, chances are much better that other arrangements will be made and the adult will not be subjected to that person's company. We cannot and should not live our lives by our children's whims, but unless we respect the same sense of prerogative in them that we value in ourselves, they will never develop their own sense of self. Dorothy Corkille Briggs examines the larger issue, but what she asks has a definite bearing on the double standard regarding territoriality:

> Ask yourself this question: "If I were to treat my friends as I treat my children, how many friends would I have left?" Few of us would think of shaming or analyzing friends in front of others, jerking them up short with sarcasm, humiliating, embarrassing, hitting, or ordering them about like soldiers under our command. Of course not . . . Repeatedly we treat children as second-class creatures devoid of feeling; and yet, we prize them! At times we blatantly disregard their sensitivities.[17]

Perhaps as children we were treated exactly as Dorothy Corkille Briggs describes. If we are one of many mothers entering into assertiveness training or one of many fathers learning communication or sensitivity techniques, the concept of a healthy sense of territoriality may be too new to instill it in anyone else. Still, our child will learn the most by watching us and through the ways we respect and help him define his emotional limits. This is the chance to correct the imbalance in the double standard and to create those all-important skills of assertiveness and self-protection. This is at the core of our ability to take care of ourselves on all levels; and as the world changes, it is no easy proposition.

I guarantee the little girl now learning a lack of regard for her own feelings and without the skills to draw boundaries around her will be the woman thirty years from now who, even though she has strong feelings that there is something "not quite right" about the man asking to come into her home, will say to herself, "Oh I'm just being silly and I don't want to be rude," and lets him in. We know today all too often the man is a rapist, literally preying on the woman's lack of territoriality. It doesn't need to be this way, but the learning must begin early. Possibly there is no more valuable or life-affirming lesson than that of territoriality.

# CHILDREN NEED TO LEARN
# TO MASTER THEIR ENVIRONMENT:
# TO TRUST THEIR INSTINCTS
# AND ACT IN THEIR OWN BEST INTEREST

Previously we have been discussing feeling states: self-concept, trust, and dignity. In this section, we will discuss the action component of these feelings—mastery over the environment.

In the context of child sexual abuse, mastery over the environment means the child listens to his feelings of uncomfortableness with the offender's request, then follows his instincts to refuse by saying "No" or leaving. This *action* comes from the "voice from within," which says, "This is wrong. I'm not going to do it, and I'm going to tell someone about this."

Children are not *born* with the skills to take charge of a situation, and certainly they do not instinctively know how to cope with a situation as confusing as potential child sexual abuse. Mastery is a learned skill, and it is developed in very small steps over a long period of time.

As with territoriality, there is a necessary imbalance between our parents and ourselves in infancy that must be realigned throughout childhood. When we were infants, we depended on adults to master our environment. Adults decided when and what we should eat, what we should wear, which places were safe for us. As we grew older and gained more skills, we began to make those decisions for ourselves. The process of mastering the intangible parts of our environment—how we will react to a situation, who will be our friends, what personality traits will be developed—was basically guided by our parents. Now that we are adults, perhaps with infants of our own, the cycle begins again.

Parent and child together cope with the little challenges along the way. As the child makes decisions and acts more from her own sense of self and less from the parents' directive, she is mastering her environment. With each challenge she successfully meets, she begins to believe in herself and her ability to assess and control some of the events around her. This confidence quiets the "voice from within" that says, "I never know what to do, I always mess things up. There's no point in stopping him."

The concept of mastering the environment sounds ominous unless we consider the process an accumulation of conquered situations. Some of the smaller steps that lead to action-oriented confidence could be:

• The first time your child tells someone else that he doesn't like what he is doing and he isn't going to stand there and watch it continue.

• Your child comes and tells you something wrong has happened even though she realizes you might be angry.

• Your child expresses she wants to leave a place because she doesn't like it; she doesn't want a particular child-care person because she doesn't like him or her; or expresses other personal preferences in a straightforward manner.

• Your child hesitates before attempting a new task, assesses her previous skills, and decides to wait a while or learn some new skills before trying it.

• Or the child, after careful assessment, decides to take the risk and expand her skills.

• Your child picks another child to befriend and initiates the friendship.

None of these tasks are intrinsically life-endangering. Each is necessary for the child's development to a healthy adulthood in the long term, and mastery of his environment in the short term. A child who consistently forfeits decision-making in these small, everyday areas to someone else is not learning to master his environment. Having never followed through on his judgment before, he will be totally unprepared if confronted with a potential child sexual abuse proposition. The little challenges would have put him in better stead for the "big" one.

It is easy to understand why we sometimes overprotect our children rather than become active participants in their process of learning to master their environment. Perhaps we do not feel we have that much impact on our surroundings. Or maybe we fantasize that they will be protected just because we *really* want them to be safe from harm or disappointment. We can put enormous energy into protecting our children from failure without realizing, at the same time, that we are also sheltering them from success. *Your Child's Self-esteem* states:

> Imagine that your blueprints are such that your child can fit them, but only with strenuous effort. You churn out the designs for his feelings, attitudes, values and goals. You know best, and you teach your child *not* to listen to his inner promptings. He becomes a highly dependent puppet, moving as you pull the strings. His reward? Your approval. The youngster then places his psychological center of gravity outside himself. Others have his answers and his own *self*-confidence never has a chance to flourish.[18]

What if an offender is one of the people who offers the child the answers he looks for in others? When confronted with possible child molestation, what if the parent is nowhere to be found? In incest, we will see that the parent in the situation described above *is* the offender.

This is not to say that only children who cannot master their environment are molested. The point is that the child's trust of his own judgment and willingness to take action based on that judgment are prerequisites to prevention of child sexual abuse. And the benefits of mastery skills go far beyond the prevention of these crimes.

Under the guise of well-intended protection, we will, rather than discuss or guide, autonomously make the decision that our child is *not* ready for some step that is not life-endangering, and discourage her from trying in order to shield her from the possibility of failure. The message to the child is: "Don't do that—you'll fail and

you can't stand to fail. It hurts too much and isn't worth the risk."
An adult woman shares with us:

> When I was in junior high, I was really shy, but I belonged to
> a hospital guild like all the other girls. I remember our spon-
> sor—she was an older woman with no children and I adored
> her. She was very sensitive to my acute shyness. About midway
> through my first year there—we had just moved—the secretary
> of the guild moved away. One time I wasn't there, and the
> sponsor suggested that I be the new secretary. I think she
> thought it would help me. The other girls elected me, and I was
> so excited. I felt so important—like I never had before—almost
> like a normal person. Well, my mother forbade me to go back
> to the group. She told me I didn't have the time, and she was
> afraid I wouldn't do a good job, then my feelings would get
> hurt. So what if I did make a mistake? It wasn't going to hurt
> anything—there wasn't any money involved or anything like
> that. I think the other kids would have tolerated a mistake, and
> who knows, I could have learned something from it. I never
> went back to the group. I never saw the sponsor again.

It would not be at all surprising if this girl had developed the "voice
from within" that would tell her, if confronted with an offender,
"I never know what to do, I always mess things up. There's no point
in stopping him." Indeed, she had experienced neither success nor
failure and subsequently had not learned anything about herself.
She was denied the opportunity to make the connection between
what she *feels* (what she wants or what is best for her) and how
she *acts* (doing something in her own best interest). Her mother
was not deliberately evil. She probably just couldn't stand to see
her daughter hurt. She forgot that the child might not be afraid
of failure, and after all, it was her daughter's life.

At the base of this woman's predicament was a lack of friends.
Either through circumstances such as moving, discrimination, long
absences, or lack of social skills, some children are basically friend-
less. Actually reaching out to be friends with someone is one of
the most necessary mastery skills for both life *and* preventing child
sexual abuse.

Child molesters use a process of "making friends" with the victim that is surprisingly similar to the way in which two children become friends. A child with few friends of her own, and unfamiliar with the "let's be friends" transaction, will be very impressed by the offender's desire to befriend her. As a result, she may not question his request for sexual favors in return for his friendship. She will be ruled by the "voice from within" that says, "Nobody else likes me, not in the whole world, except for this person, so I'll do what he says."

Just like all other mastery skills, making friends is a learned skill. *The Parent Book* offers excellent suggestions on how parents can help to teach this important skill:

There are a number of ways to help your child make new friends, but they require effort on your part. The rule is: Don't let him give up.

*Encourage your child to risk possible rejection.* Tell him, "I'd really be proud of you if you would take the initiative. After all, everyone feels the same way. Everyone is afraid of being turned down. It's a chance we all have to take. Besides, people especially like the person who takes the first step—he makes it safer for them."

*Be available to comfort him when he is rejected.* Not every attempt he makes will be successful. Some efforts at friendship simply don't work out. Say, "Not everybody you want for a friend is going to like you, any more than you're going to like everybody who wants you for a friend." Ask him about the children he knows, the ones he likes and the ones he doesn't. Ask how things are going in these relations.

*You can serve as a bridge.* Offer to bring your child together with a possible friend in some kind of activity. A visit to the zoo, a ball game, or an ice-cream parlor will often start off a friendship much more quickly than the hesitant, hit-or-miss, trial-and-error methods most children usually employ.

*Prepare* your child for mixed feelings in his friendships. Tell him it is inevitable that there will be times when he will feel upset with his friends. Emphasize that only relationships which have survived the test of bad feelings and disagreements are truly solid. This knowledge will prepare him for occasions when he and his friends disagree. It will enable him to understand that he doesn't have to lose a friend every time they don't see eye to eye.

If your child never asks for help in making friendships, you may assume that your offer of assistance would constitute an intrusion into his private territory. This is not the case. It isn't that your child doesn't want your help—he may not know how to ask for it. He'll be very gratified to find out that you know something about—and care enough to show him how to manage —such private feelings as his loneliness and fear.[19]

Child molesters, fearful and lonely themselves, especially seek out children who have not learned how to manage the same feelings. "Popular" children, or those with an adequate number of friends, are also molested, but they are less vulnerable to the long, consuming relationships some offenders demand. Having mastered the skill to seek out friendships, "popular" children do not need that single "special friend." Children who can reach out to each other are not as prone to the "voice from within" that rules, "I really want this person to like me—if I hurt his feelings by not playing the game, he won't like me anymore."

Teaching our children the ropes of making friendships is one of the more directed and straightforward tasks of mastery over their environment. For the most part, children will choose when and what they want to learn to master, with little regard for our timetable or how confident we feel about teaching them. The child's own senses of curiosity and direction are healthy for her, but usually frustrating and bewildering for us. There are other times in raising our children when we wonder where the childhood went; they seem to be so adult in some of their behavior. As they master more of their environment—exercise control over it, make choices, and act in their own best interest—they do appear to be more adult than child. However, sometimes in the chaos of redefining of roles, in our *own* self-defense, we squelch some of these "adult" characteristics that are reflections of the child's mastery skills.

It might be helpful to try to think of our child with these *same* attributes twenty years from now—even as we feel flattened or confused by this self-confident "monster" we think we have created. The same behavior in children and adults is labeled *very* differently:

| BEHAVIOR | IN A CHILD IT IS CALLED | IN AN ADULT IT IS CALLED |
|---|---|---|
| Telling Steven about apartments in New York | rudeness | being helpful |
| Asking someone to blow their cigarette smoke in another direction | insolent | assertive |
| Not doing a job until the financial arrangements are clear | greediness | good business sense |
| Refusing to give up the chair he has been sitting in for an hour | selfishness | standing up for rights (who would think of asking an adult to do that?) |
| Not eating everything on the dinner plate | picky eater | not hungry |
| Cutting in front of a line (with "good" reason) | pushy | in a hurry |
| Asking someone how much their new car cost | nosy | direct |
| Knocking something over and breaking it | clumsy | had an accident |
| Strikes a bargain: "I'll be glad to do this if you help me with . . ." | calculating | negotiating |

If we can think of some of the "obnoxious" behavior in terms of the self-protection it will later provide the child, perhaps we will be more able to tolerate it.

As painful as it is to watch our children fail, or as exasperating as it is to be the brunt of their assertions, guiding them to master their environment is integral to their growth to healthy adulthood. Through the *action* of mastery, the *feelings* of good self-concept come to fruition. If a child does not feel good about herself, she will want to retreat, she will master little, and she will remain more vulnerable.

The coming together of these complicated concepts can be found in the following quote by Erik Erikson in *Childhood and Society*:

> From a sense of self-control without loss of self-esteem comes a lasting sense of goodwill and pride; from a sense of loss of self-control and of foreign overcontrol comes a lasting propensity for doubt and shame.

It is that doubt and shame that lie at the very heart of child sexual abuse.

# FAMILY ATMOSPHERE AND THE PREVENTION OF CHILD SEXUAL ABUSE

Now we have a sense of how to teach our child to be a *non*victim: Enhance self-concept; eradicate sex-role stereotyping; be there to listen; instill personal integrity; and teach the child to master his environment. What's a mother or father to do in face of such a tall order? Beyond the development of the "voice from within," how closely connected are these fine goals to the prevention of child sexual abuse?

Sherry Angel, a mother in Anaheim, California, provides us with some connection in a thought-provoking article in *Redbook*, "Don't Be Afraid to Say 'No'!" The article is a letter she wrote to her young son about her own victimization as a child and offers her prevention advice to him.

She describes her own victimization involving a longtime, trusted neighbor, Bill, who molested Sherry when she was six years old. Bill had molested both of Sherry's sisters, and the article was prompted when the three sisters, now grown with families of their own, finally broke their secret bond with Bill. It was not a bond made out of loyalty to Bill; Sherry and one sister were unsure of how to tell anyone else about the abuse. Not wanting her son to have the same experience, she tells of her own experience.

It was a typical case of child molestation. On her way home from school, she stopped to show Bill the stars on her perfect assignment. He asked her to come into his radio shack, where he pulled her onto his lap and fondled her. Out of confusion and innocence, this scene was repeated for two years.

I was compelled by the misconception that I had to obey Bill because he was an adult. I had been taught to respect my elders, and I feared that if I challenged his authority, I would be the one who was punished—either by him or by my parents.[20]

The neighbor implored young Sherry to keep their "game" a secret. Sherry had a happy family life, but still she was unsure of where to go with her confusion, and feared a situation worse than the abuse she was enduring.

I was torn daily between a growing knowledge that what Bill demanded of me was terribly wrong and the fear that if I told anyone—even my own parents—we all would somehow be destroyed in the fallout.[21]

So confident after the successful molestation of two sisters, he attempted to molest the third in her very own front yard! The girl ran and got her parents. Due to the young girl's trauma, they decided not to press charges against Bill. He did stop molesting Sherry, so she saw no reason to tell her parents what had happened to her. Many years later the neighbor moved away.

Sherry Angel does not blame her parents; she understands Bill is totally responsible for the crimes. However, she brings together the basic principles we have been discussing (this book and her article were written totally independently of each other) with her own experience. She writes to her son:

Once I began to understand what had happened to me, I was able to see what my parents could have done to protect me. And now I feel confident that I can teach you how to deal with the threat of sexual abuse.

First you must know that your opinions and feelings are important and you have a right to express them—even if that means disagreeing with an adult. Your home will never be a place where children are seen and not heard. If you ever feel you have been punished wrongly, I want you to tell your father and me. We're not afraid to change our minds if we think you're right.

We want you to respect adults—but only up to a point. If an adult—any adult—ever asks you to do something you sense is wrong, don't think you have to obey. Use your best judgment, and then tell your father and me about it right away so that we can help you with any worry you may have.

Please, please feel free to talk to us about anything. I think I would have told my parents about Bill without hesitation if we had already talked openly about sex. But I was eleven years old when my mother explained the "facts of life" to me. We had many open talks about sex after that. She taught me that sex is beautiful when it involves adults who love each other, and I'm sure her attitude is what helped me overcome any fears I might still have had when I married your father. But your grandmother now realizes that she should have started that dialogue with me when I was much younger—as I plan to do with you. With that knowledge, I hope, you will be able to recognize the difference between the right and the wrong kind of authority.

So please remember:

Don't be afraid to stand up for yourself if you feel an adult is trying to take advantage of you.

Your body is very special, and you don't have to let anyone touch it unless you want to. Don't be afraid to say "no."

If you are disturbed by something, tell me about it, no matter what it is. I will never punish you for being honest. And although I may sometimes disagree with you or disapprove of your behavior, I will never judge *you*. I love you and nothing can change that.

Love. That's the most important thing. Your grandparents gave me enough affection to convince me that I could never do anything to cause them to stop loving me. They taught me to like myself. And that helped me realize that I was not a bad little girl and that I was not to blame for what happened to me.

Thanks to your grandparents' support and their open attitude about sex, what could have been an emotionally crippling experience for your Aunt Jill and me is over. And I'm confident that it's over for good because I now believe that I can protect you from ever becoming a victim.[22]

The chances are that Sherry Angel probably will be able to protect her son from becoming a victim by teaching him how to protect *himself*. If he is victimized, it will *not* be because his mother and father failed him, nor will it be a result of any inadequacy on his part. The crime will be the *offender's* responsibility.

The nonvictim personality is important for a child in more ways than preventing child sexual abuse. However, it is more difficult to raise a nonvictim; most of us were raised to be victims of one sort or another, so the five principles we've discussed can seem truly overwhelming. The principles are not a recipe for the perfect child, nor are they the keys to the meaning of parenthood. Given what we know about the circumstances of child sexual abuse and what the offender looks for in a victim, the principles will enhance a child's safety.

An inventory or summary might be helpful at this point. The long list of what we should strive for is impressive in that it demonstrates what a difficult job we have as parents. There is no passing grade; no tabulating system to see how many you get right. The list is a point of reference, something to check back with in the interest of raising a nonvictim child:

- Be as consistent as we can in the enforcement of agreed-upon rules.

- Adopt the Golden Rule; treat my child in the same way I would like to be treated.

- Address the child by name, not with degrading nicknames ("you brat") or without respect ("hey you").

- Avoid exploiting the inevitable size difference by physically abusing the child.

- Point out the child's mistakes with ways to correct them rather than by humiliating, punishing, hitting, or shaming the child because he failed.

- Point out the successes and positive aspects of the child just as quickly and forcefully as we point out the mistakes.

- Teach the child the value of privacy by respecting your

child's needs for privacy and sharing your own consistent private time together.

• Acknowledge the presence of fear, uncertainty, failure, and frustration in life rather than denying their existence or punishing the child for having these feelings.

• Avoid domination by parental authority and help guide the child to her own sense of *self*-authority.

• Exercise fair and constructive limits so that the child can imitate with healthy *self*-imposed limits.

• Allow each child to move at his individual pace.

• Encourage the child to make decisions or expand territory but be available for nurturance and redirection if the child fails.

• Be open and constructive in feelings of loneliness, fear, and sadness so the child will recognize the feelings as normal and learn to manage them.

• Connect feelings to behavior; crying when we are sad and explaining why we are sad.

• Do not question the child's right to say "no" to matters of personal preference that do not endanger the child's safety or unduly disrupt other family members.

• Stress the importance of friendships outside the family and realize that good family relationships are the beginnings of good relationships *outside* the family.

• Understand that there are many levels of "wrong" or misbehavior and try not to react to every misdeed as if it was the *worst* of all possible fates.

• Assume the child is telling the truth until the parent knows for a fact that she is lying.

• Allow the child to have time and things all to himself free from sharing.

• Intercede with unconditional love (not recrimination) to set limits when the child is overtired or overextended and unable to cope on her own.

Again, if we don't perform to optimal potential on each point at all times, our children will not vanish into perpetual victimization, nor will they grow up to be no-good derelicts. Expectations of perfection imposed on parents are equally as damaging as expectations of perfection on children. We all basically do our best. Perhaps the inventory can remind us what our best is or it might introduce us to a new way of looking at "best."

The bottom line on most advice to parents is to treat the child as the parent would like to be treated if he were in the child's shoes. What would we need to help us grow? It primarily comes down to safety, love, and becoming competent. Oftentimes we react in an authoritarian manner to ensure safety or are overly permissive under the guise of love. Achieving competence is the school's responsibility. Yet we have the potential *and* the responsibility to contribute to all three needs. Hopefully at the end of this section, we will have learned that the raising of a healthy child is not an either-or proposition. The development of a nonvictim requires a fine balance of all of the above.

The answers are not always easy, or even apparent. Sometimes when in the thick of raising our children, we can't remember what the question was. The best we can do is give it our most sincere effort, congratulate ourselves and each other on our successes, recognize and learn from our mistakes, and hope that our child remains safe and loved and competent. After all, it is our job to teach them the "hows" of life. Eventually the child reaches an age when she takes responsibility for her own life and decides "what" to do and "where" to go with our "hows."

When she takes responsibility for her future, she will be in good stead if she is basically a nonvictim, if her "voice from within" is strong and clear and tuned into her own best interests. Although the principles and lists and all the things we want to do for our children require enormous effort and, at times, excruciating self-examination, we would all agree they're worth our most conscientious effort.

# EXERCISES

## EXERCISE ONE ADDITIONAL READING

The following books are highly recommended for more information about the formation of a healthy "voice from within" and related matters:

Ames, Louise Bates, and Ilg, Frances L. *Your Two-year-old,* 1977; *Your Three-year-old,* 1977; *Your Four-year-old,* 1977; *Your Five-year-old,* 1979; and *Your Six-year-old,* 1979; New York: Delacorte Press.

Bakker, Cornelis B., and Bakker-Rabdau, Marianne K. *No Trespassing: Explorations in Human Territoriality.* San Francisco: Chandler & Sharp, Inc., 1973.

Bessell, Harold, Ph.D., and Kelly, Thomas Jr. *The Parent Book: The Holistic Program for Raising the Emotionally Mature Child.* Sacramento, Calif.: Jalmar Press, 1977.

Boston Women's Health Book Collective. *Ourselves and Our Children.* New York: Random House, 1978.

Briggs, Dorothy Corkille. *Your Child's Self-esteem.* Garden City, N.Y.: Doubleday & Company, 1975.

Carlson, Dale. *Girls Are Equal Too.* New York: Atheneum Publishers, 1973.

Jenkins, Jeanne Kohl, and McDonald, Pam. *Growing Up Equal: Activities and Resources for Parents and Teachers of Young Children.* Englewood Cliffs, Prentice-Hall, 1979.

Phillips, Paul, Ed.D., and Cordell, Franklin. *Am I O.K.?* Niles, Ill.: Argus Communications, 1975.

## EXERCISE TWO     FEELING GOOD ABOUT YOURSELF

As a family ritual (at dinner, before bedtime, during breakfast, or whenever it feels best to you), make a *specific* positive statement about each family member. "I like (or love) you because . . ." Each family member takes a turn making a positive statement about all other members. This should be done *at least* once a week. The statements do not need to be profound; just say one thing that you like. Chances are, it will be a surprise to the recipient.

After you've had some practice, make a positive statement about *yourself*—"I like myself because . . ." You will most likely be self-conscious at first, but try it anyway. This is the beginning of a good self-concept. Everyone has his or her turn saying what they like about themselves. Trust me, it seems more natural as you go along. A variation on this exercise is to write the statements down. Have a family blackboard or large sheet of butcher paper on the refrigerator where people can write down both what they like about each other and what they like about themselves.

Invite guests and honorary members of your family to join in on this exercise. There can *never* be *too* much of this sort of thing around the house!

## EXERCISE THREE     BEING SPECIFIC

Make two charts for yourself like the ones found on pages 16 and 17. First, think of your most common phrases of general praise and the situations that evoke them. Try translating them into *specific* praise. Next, practice the specific criticism. Identify the source situation and most common labels that you might use. Use the chart to translate the labels into *specific* criticism. If you practice ahead of time, your chances of naturally using the specific criticism or praise will increase.

EXERCISE FOUR    MY SON IS . . . MY DAUGHTER IS . . .

Fill in five adjectives for each of the following statements. Fill in only one at a time, approximately three weeks apart from each other, and *no* peeking at what you wrote three weeks before!

A good little girl is:    A good little boy is:    A good child is:

1.                        1.                        1.

2.                        2.                        2.

3.                        3.                        3.

4.                        4.                        4.

5.                        5.                        5.

After filling in all three columns, what differences are there between good boys and good girls? Who comes closer to being a good child—the boy, the girl, or are they all fairly close in quality? This exercise gives you a chance to assess your own propensity for sex-role stereotyping. If you are uncomfortable with your lists, the books listed in Exercise One offer excellent strategies for change.

As an interesting aside, go back to your lists after you have finished reading all of this book. If you were a child sexual abuser, how would you react to the qualities you list as being a good boy, a good girl, or a good child? Would they be encouraging in your choice of victim or would they be discouraging?

If your children are of school age, make a game of filling out the lists *with* them. This is an excellent technique to discover and discuss whatever ideas the children have about sex roles. It gives you a chance to correct misinformation or to strengthen healthy attitudes. It also gives the children a chance to talk about sex roles that might seem arbitrary and confusing to them.

## EXERCISE FIVE     I'M HERE TO LISTEN

Set aside thirty minutes each week at a consistent, predetermined time to spend alone with *each* child. Let them know they can count on you for undivided attention during that time. The time is yours to share—playing cards, answering questions, reading stories, or whatever you decide to do.

To accentuate the time as a sharing and listening period, I suggest you begin by together reading the book *There's No Such Thing as a Dragon,* story and pictures by Jack Kent (Racine, Wis.: Golden Press, 1975). This is an excellent story about a mother who won't listen to her son. It is a humorous, sensitive short story with a happy ending, perfect to open discussions about "scary" things and to reassure your child that you *want* to listen. The story will set an honest, giving tone to your weekly private time.

Establish your own one-to-one time with your spouse, significant other friend (or, better yet, time *all* to yourself), and help the children to understand that is *your* time to talk to someone else without them. Make other arrangements for child care during that time, and as much as possible stick to your weekly allotment. As long as your children also get their one-to-one time, you will be setting an excellent example of the fine balance between accessibility and privacy. And they will always know they have that one time out of a hectic week to share their private joys and fears, and they can count on being listened to.

## EXERCISE SIX     ALL MINE AND NOBODY ELSE'S

Ask your child to pick out one toy, book, or possession that he doesn't have to share with anyone else. Talk about it and carefully choose which item will be off-limits to other people. Once a reasonable choice is made, help him develop ways to straightforwardly and nonviolently keep his possession to himself. Think up possible situations and help him learn to say "No" assertively. Be creative about ways in which he can protect himself from possible intrusion.

## EXERCISE SEVEN    I *CAN* DO SOMETHING RIGHT

If your child seems to be having some trouble mastering parts of his environment, sit down and decide together what it is that the child would like to learn to do. Arrange it in a hierarchy, beginning with the easiest task and working up to the most difficult. For each task, agree on a reward once the child has accomplished it. The list should be no more than five tasks long. A sample list for a seven-year-old is:

| *TASK* | *REWARD* |
|---|---|
| 1. Take the dog for a walk without getting tripped. | Stay up late one night. |
| 2. Eat my dinner without spilling food on myself. | Extra quarter for a Good Humor. |
| 3. Play with my little brother for one hour without fighting. | Spend the night at a friend's. |
| 4. Ride my bike without training wheels. | *Star Wars* T-shirt. |

The purpose of the chart is to encourage the child to try and to reward successful efforts, thus increasing his confidence. If he gets stuck on a specific task, then retreat, define some other tasks with reward (choose tasks that he has a greater chance of achieving), and return at a later date to the uncompleted task. Reassure him that in *trying*, he hasn't failed. In fact, not trying at all is the only failure. The rewards should be well defined and do not need to be elaborate. However, your affection and verbal praise upon completing the task will be the greatest rewards.

## EXERCISE EIGHT    GIVE YOURSELF A BREAK TODAY

Adapt Exercise Two to boost your confidence as a parent. If you
have a two-adult/parent family, tell each other, "I think you are
a good parent because . . ." and be specific. Once you are comfortable, make the statement, "I think I'm a good parent because . . ."
This is a good habit to get into.

This exercise is greatly enhanced by *writing* the positive statements
(both your own and those coming from other people) down and
keeping a list that is easily accessible when you feel and believe
you can't do anything right. Note cards are handiest. Encourage
informed nonparents to contribute one or two positive statements
to your list. Also, set an example; when you see a parent/friend
do something with his or her child that you especially like, instead
of thinking to yourself, "That was pretty terrific," *say it out loud.*
It's a long journey for everyone involved, and we need all the explicit support we can get.

Eventually, as you gain confidence and integrate the list, perhaps
you might work up to take the risk and ask your child what he
or she likes about your parenting skill! Children are very observant,
and as they grow older and gain judgment, it is likely they will
make comparisons between you and other parents they know.
Chances are some of those comparisons are favorable to you and
their thoughts would be surprising to you. And who would know
better how you are doing as a parent?

# PART TWO

---

## OVERVIEW OF THE CRIMES OF CHILD MOLESTATION AND INCEST

# INTRODUCTION

Now we are ready to examine two specific crimes of child sexual abuse—child molestation and incest. These two crimes comprise most of the offenses considered as child sexual abuse.

We will find that offenders in both groups have much in common. We consider the crimes separately, however, for specific reasons. First, child sexual abuse is many different crimes along a continuum. At one end of the continuum is the child cornered once in a public place by a stranger—lewd suggestions are made and the child escapes. On the other end of the continuum is the child who is sexually victimized many times, over an extended period of time, by a close relative or guardian. Each has its own undesirable effects. The motivation, dynamic, and aftermath of these two crimes can be radically different. It is important to recognize that there are various frequencies and circumstances in child sexual abuse.

Second, the *relationship* between offender and child can be very different. Although many child molesters are acquaintances or friends of the victim, they can also be strangers. In contrast, incest is almost never perpetrated by a stranger. Instead, the offender has an ongoing relationship with the victim that reflects great differences in power, resources, and knowledge. It is basically this relationship (and most likely a blood relationship) that defines the crime of incest.

The sexual activities themselves are very much the same in both incest and child molestation, so it is the relationship of offender and victim that determines how the crime will be defined. The section on child molestation deals with sexual activity by adults who are *not* relatives or guardians of the child-victim. The section on incest concerns sexual activity between a child and an adult who is directly related to and/or lives with the child.

We must keep in mind that the child needs the *same* defenses if confronted with either crime. Part Three explains what those defenses could be and how to teach them. However, this section should not be skipped over. Before we can instill a healthy sense of awareness in our children, we must understand the realities of child sexual abuse. We would not take a medicine before knowing what was making us ill. By the same token, the necessary defenses are meaningless unless we have a thorough understanding of what we are protecting ourselves against. The goal of this book is to guide parents in teaching their children how to protect themselves against sexual abuse. As a prerequisite, the parent must understand the nature of these crimes.

When learning about a topic such as child sexual abuse, there is a great danger of overidentification by the reader. Parents may read sections on incest and recognize some of the characteristics of their own family or a friend's family. This does not automatically mean the family in question is incestuous. It would take a combination of *many* of the characteristics for a family to be considered potentially incestuous.

The situation is similar to that of a beginning medical student who finds in himself symptoms of a variety of terrible diseases. We've all heard stories about celebrities doing public-service announcements, describing the symptoms of a specific disease, and in the name of the organization asking listeners to see their doctor for a preventive checkup. In the middle of the first taping, the celebrity is speechless—he can't go on. He suddenly is sure that *he* has the disease. And almost every family has been "blessed" with a new student of psychology who now can explain all of your idiosyncrasies in terms of Freudian traumas in their various stages. Better yet, the student can summarize the pathology of the family's interactions in twenty-five words or less. As another example, I was reading *Helter Skelter* the other day, in which the author gives a very detailed background of Charles Manson's early life. He mentions that both Manson and Adolph Hitler liked dogs. I immediately thought, "Oh my God, I'd better go turn myself in before it's too late." Of course, I realized that my caring for animals would not necessarily lead to my becoming a mass murderer. But this is a common and human response to descriptions of "causes" or background of any abhorrent crime.

Another danger that the parent should be aware of is that,

out of wanting to do everything possible to protect her children, she may find it too easy to seize any "answer" and run with it. In this spirit, parents sometimes overreact to well-intended advice. Millions of teen-age boy baby-sitters are put out of business because of the statistics on adolescent pedophilia. Many boy baby-sitters are competent as well as trustworthy. The job of baby-sitting can enrich their experience and prepare them to be better fathers, while giving them a way to earn money. For the child, the care of a younger man breaks down those stereotypes (formed very early) about child care being "women's work." Mothers no longer let their husbands change their daughters' diapers. In such a case, the mother not only misses the point about incestuous fathers, but she also denies herself a very important sharing of child-care responsibilities. The community, in attempting to protect its children, may use an animated device on TV to teach the child about "dangerous strangers"—which may teach a child not to accept rides with people who wear black capes and have light bulbs for eyes. Children take this warning very literally—they will never accept a ride from someone wearing a black cape with eyes that light up. Yet they never recognize a potential child-molestation situation involving a "normal"-looking person.

It is up to the parents to examine the material presented and to interpret it through their own lifestyle, values, and circumstances. The parents need to explain the information to the child in a style that is consistent with the rest of the child's life. We caution parents to consider *all* of the material, not just the parts that hit close to home. React to it as a body of knowledge, not as an omen or prediction of doom.

Many of the statistics are presented in ranges, rather than as one specific percentage. This is because many studies do not agree, and it is important to note the different findings. Also, the sources of many of the studies are prisoners or in-patients convicted of child sexual abuse. We must realize that this is not the total picture; many child molesters and incestuous fathers never enter the judicial system. Fewer still are found guilty, so there is much research in non-prison populations to be done.

Self-reporting by any sex offenders is a controversial area. Often when the offender's version of his crime is checked against police

records, we find much embellishment. It is dubious, at best, to look
to a sex offender for prevention advice. He has a large investment
in maintaining his position of omnipotence. Keeping this in mind,
most of the statistics used are less influenced by the self-report than
others that might have been used.

As we examine the crimes of incest and child molestation, three
phrases will be repeated many times: power, knowledge, and resources. Crimes of child sexual abuse are considered in the context
of the great discrepancies between the victim's and the offender's
*power, knowledge,* and *resources.* The exploitation of these differences does the most serious harm to the child.

*Power* is one of those words that probably means something different to every person who uses it. The perception of physical
power cannot be overlooked. In the vast majority of the cases, the
implied use of physical strength can be found. Although few physical injuries occur in child sexual abuse, this is not due to the
benevolent disposition of the offenders. The child need only look
skyward to estimate that the offender is twice her size. As a child,
she is always relying on "bigger" people to lift and carry or do other
physical tasks beyond her strength. Little boys or girls might aspire
to superhuman, or at least adult levels of physical prowess, but they
are clearly aware that they are *not* that strong yet. The child, understanding very clearly those differences in power, most often acqui-
esces, thereby avoiding the need for any physical showdown.

Emotional power is a very important factor. Many children derive
their "sense of self" from adults. If adults like them, they consider
themselves "good kids." The child might especially value the opinion of the offender; a compliment from him puts her on the top
of the world. The withdrawal of affection or love is a considerable
influence over children. Probably all of us have used expressions
of our dissatisfaction with the child as a means of discipline. This
is a widely accepted practice. We have all found it to be an effective means of making children do something they don't particularly
want to do. While its utilization may be useful to teach a child
to stop pounding on his brother, it is also one of the tools of the
child sexual abuser. Often he tells the child, point-blank, that he
won't like her or his feelings will be hurt if she doesn't play that
"special game" with him.

The disparity of *knowledge* between adult and child is obvious. It is clear and unavoidable that the adult has the advantage. In matters of child sexual abuse, one of the basics of this imbalance is the adult's knowledge of *what is* sexual activity. To the younger child, the "tickling" of his genitals may not seem to be sexual activity at all. To the child, it is a "game." The adult surely knows this is no game. Fondling of the child while she is being towel dried after a bath may seem to be pampering to the child. That "physical examination" the little boy must submit to from the coach of the team might seem different from the doctor's examination, but he really wants to be on the team. The offender uses his superior knowledge to exploit the child. The child is participating in something she would probably not do if she had knowledge of the true significance of the activity.

Knowledge of the *meaning* of the sexual activity is also a key. If an older child is concerned about the sexual advances of a father or a stepfather, but he assures her, "This is what people who love each other do," she will probably take his word for it. By having the advantage of knowing the implication of the activity, he can exploit the child. Later, when she learns the *meaning* of the activity (very often people do love each other without engaging in sexual activity), she feels betrayed by the offender.

Knowledge of the *consequence* of sexual activity cannot be overlooked. Adults, to some degree, have knowledge of legal, medical, and psychological ramifications of sexual activity with children. Often, children do *not* have this knowledge. They think they are entering into a "special relationship" with an adult or learning a new game. The adult knows this is not the case. He understands that there are very real legal consequences for his behavior. He understands, at some level, that harm could come to the child because of his actions. He enlists this child in a conspiracy of silence to avoid legal consequences and chooses to ignore any harm he may cause. Any psychological confusion or damage from the molestation, he rationalizes, is offset by the "specialness" of the relationship. Knowing that the child will not come out of the relationship without some turmoil, the offender places his own impulses and needs above the health of the child.

The last consideration, *resources*, is also very apparent. If the child depends on the offender for her continued existence, then resources take on a special meaning. The child may be coerced into the relationship by the threat of removal of resources she presently has (food, shelter, education), which she knows she is still too young to obtain for herself. While the relationship often begins with the inequality of resources and the victim in a powerless position, this inequality takes a special toll when the victim tries to end the relationship.

In cases of incest, it is virtually always the daughter who severs the relationship. Her lack of resources often is felt vividly at this time. Usually, she wants the relationship to end long before she is ready to go out into the world and support herself. The fourteen-year-old girl who can no longer bear the confusion and shame of an incestuous situation is in no position to venture forth to find a new life. All resources for her continued existence revolve around her father. He is breadwinner, rulemaker, and executor of resources. Severing the relationship seems like severing access to everything she needs to grow up.

Resources in the access to material goods is a given discrepancy between adults and children. This imbalance is used in *both* expressed and implied ways. The child may be bribed into sexual activities by the stranger with gifts. In family settings, there may be a threat to withdraw an allowance or a promised present if the child does not comply with the adult's sexual demands. For some children in a certain phase of their growth, material goods may be their main source of good feelings. They are happiest when they have a new baseball mitt or money to spend with their friends. The child may derive his sense of self by having the newest playthings to share with his friends, the most money for treating the neighborhood to jawbreakers, or the best sports equipment to get him on the team. It is extremely sad that we teach some of our children to depend on external "things," rather than their wealth of inner resources, to make friends, yet this is not an uncommon attitude in children.

For any victim of sexual abuse, but particularly in cases of incest, resources are an issue. When they decide to tell of the incident or relationship, whom should they tell? They may feel they can tell no one. If the offender is a relative, they may feel that no other relative will listen to them. Even if the offender is a stranger, the child needs to know that someone will listen before she will speak up. It is not uncommon for children to think that no one will believe them or take them seriously. If their other fears or concerns were not respected, then they are not anxious to bare their souls about sexual abuse.

If they *are* believed, what will happen next? Should she tell the police? Will they believe her? After all, it is her word against his. Who believes a child over an adult? If the offender has threatened the child with injury or death, what resources does she have to protect herself? These are all very real questions for the child who wants to end her victimization.

As we can see, the child's best defense against sexual abuse is a sense of her own power; knowledge of what constitutes child sexual abuse; and resources available for support and protection. The offender plans on an imbalance in each of these areas. Without this imbalance, he cannot abuse.

The parent is extremely important in giving information and guidance to offset any imbalance. Returning to an original point, before the parent can teach the child, the parent must understand the nature of these crimes.

# CHILD MOLESTATION

## Facts and Patterns

Few other crimes in our society conjure up such universal repulsion as child molestation. Upon hearing the words, disturbing visual images crowd our minds. We feel a little physically unsettled, and a gnawing fear creeps in. We hope "it" never happens to someone close to us, because, after all, what would it mean and how would we deal with "it"?

Stereotypes about child sexual abuse serve to calm those fears. Our most prevalent stereotype is that child molestation is something that happens to other people's children. "It" could never happen to our children; they are well taken care of and loved. "It" happens to children of neglectful families, in less fortunate neighborhoods. Look at the statistics, we say. "There hasn't been a reported incident of child molestation in my neighborhood in years."

We like to think that "those kinds of people"—both offenders and victims—aren't any part of our lives. Child molesters are dirty old men in black wrinkled raincoats who sit on park benches, only on cloudy days, offering candy to little girls. We watch out for the cloudy days and carefully eye the old men in black raincoats. And "those" victims, precocious beyond their years, tempting and teasing with their curls and fluttering eyelashes. As long as our children are neat, well behaved, and respectful of elders, they will be safe.

In reality, the elderly flasher rarely molests Lolita. Yet we do find some comfort in these persistent stereotypes. They offer us considerable personal distance from the crime. Unfortunately, it is not the type of distance that cultivates objectivity or preventative analysis. It is the type of distance that instills a false sense of security and immunity.

Stereotypes that are the antithesis of who we think we are create a conspicuous offender and victim. Consequently, there will be no surprises and we believe we are protected from the randomness of the crime. All we have to do is be aware of people noticeably different from ourselves and we can prevent the crime. We reduce a complicated dynamic to a simple formula: Listen to our stereotypes and we will be safe.

It is natural to want to remove ourselves from dramatically unpleasant situations. No one wants to see herself or those close to her involved in *any* crime, let alone child sexual abuse. Yet the facts tell us that wishing it just doesn't make it so. An estimated two hundred thousand to five hundred thousand sexual assaults on female children four to thirteen years old occur each year.[1] The above figure does not include assaults on boys, or on girls under four years old or over thirteen years old. There is no reliable reporting system at this writing. The FBI gathers statistics on sexual violence but does not break the figures down according to the age of the victim. The molestation of a six-year-old and the rape of an elderly woman are considered one and the same. Estimates are based on reported cases and we have enough information to know that no one is absolutely immune from a crime that happens to *at least* two hundred thousand girls each year.

Studies differ as to the average age of the victim, but the majority of child victims are not worldly, sexually curious postpubescent children. The averages range from eight to eleven years old, with the stronger bias toward the average age being on the younger side.[2] From 60 to 90 per cent of the victims are girls, and *one* aspect of our stereotypes is true: *Men* are child molesters in at least 97 per cent of reported cases.[3] They may not be old, but they certainly are men. Approximately two hundred to three hundred men are prosecuted for child sexual abuse for every one woman prosecuted.[4] One large sex-offender treatment program on the West Coast has had only four women residents in recent years. All four women, in tandem with their husbands, were involved in incest.[5]

Contrary to our elderly bench-sitter vision, offenders tend to be young. One investigation revealed that virtually all of the studied child molesters had committed their first offense by age forty, and 80 per cent had committed their first offense by age thirty.[6] Elderly men sometimes commit these crimes, but they certainly do not have a corner on the market. Nor is the offender necessarily the occasional slobbering, sex-driven teen-ager. Another study found that half of the offenders were at least ten years older than the victim.[7]

Approximately three fourths of the offenders are known to the victim—possibly as family friends, neighbors, baby-sitters, or school or church personnel.[8]

> I took a lot of pride in Scouting and worked really hard to build up my troop. I even got a community award and got my name in the paper a lot before all this happened to me. [twenty-eight-year-old offender]

> I really liked all three boys I was sent up for, so I'd spend a lot of time with them after classes. [thirty-year-old offender]

Warning our children about taking rides from strangers is only 25 per cent effective; they are three times as likely to be molested by someone they know.

Familiarity is not a coincidental feature of these crimes. The offender *depends* on it, as Vincent DeFrancis of the American Humane Association explains:

> The offender relies on the child's wish to *not* displease him, even though to the child the request may have seemed unpleasant or distasteful or even bizarre. In other words, the child's *need* and *wish* to please was exploited by the offender. In some instances, the child was assured that what was requested was perfectly normal and proper between them *because* of the relationship.[9]

Given the essential ingredient of familiarity, it is no surprise that the child will be molested in his home or in the home of the offender in over 50 per cent of the cases.

> I'd volunteer to baby-sit a lot, then I'd put the younger kids to bed so I could be alone with the oldest kid. [thirty-four-year-old offender]

> George was always around the house, helping my mom with odd jobs, so he'd watch me while she was out and that was when he wanted to play those funny games with me. He never wanted to do it when she was around. [seven-year-old victim][10]

Automobiles or outdoor spaces are the next most frequent places of molestation. We do find a minority of the incidents in public places such as movie theaters, swimming pools, or public rest rooms. We seem to spend an inordinate amount of time warning our children about the man who might sit next to them in the movies or try to follow them into the bathroom stall. Prevention will be much more of a reality if we spend more time teaching our children about the potential offenses happening in the home.

Along with strangers and parks, we caution our children about the dark. Child molestation, for the most part, does not happen in dark places, deserted alleyways, or in the glare of bright city lights. Approximately two thirds of the crimes are committed between noon and 8 P.M., before dark sets in.[11]

The vast majority (79 per cent) of offenses involve only one child molester.[12] This is an interesting criminological phenomenon. Sex offenders do not share the camaraderie found among other criminal groups. Movies like *The Hot Rock* and *Butch Cassidy and the Sundance Kid* portray burglars and armed robbers who work closely together. Jewel thieves, although they usually work alone, have knowledge of each other's "heists" and organize into a hierarchy of accomplishment. Even "hit men" get together once in a while or at least know each other's style. Child molesters work alone and do not share the details of their crimes.

Working solo does not impede the offender's accumulation of victims. The most extensive study to date reports that the average molester of girl children will molest 62.4 victims in his "career," while the average boy molester studied offended 30.6 victims.[13] A few child molesters might offend *just once* and never do it again, although this is the exception rather than the rule.

Chances are good that many of the individual offender's victims will have age, physical appearance, or personality traits in common. Child molestation is not a happenstance crime; the offender has preferences for the sex and type of victim as well as for the desired circumstances of the crime. It is not a "catch as catch can" situation; his approach varies little and he seeks the same gratification repeatedly.

Considerable thought and planning go into the offense. After choosing a specific victim, the offender may ingratiate himself with the child's parents to gain their trust and diminish any suspicions.

It took me a long time, but I finally became part of the family. I just helped out when I could, dropped in unannounced, became friends with the father—I did anything I could so they'd think there was nothing unusual about me spending time with their son. [twenty-four-year-old offender]

So the decision to molest a child is not any more spontaneous than the choice of victim is random. This crime is not the unhappy result of the offender momentarily taking leave of his senses when, coincidentally, a "provocative" child appears before him. Generally there is a period of time between the decision to molest and the actual commission of the crime, as this report explains:

Neither rape nor child molestation is commonly an act of the moment, performed as a whim when all is going well. Rather, the typical offender knows in advance when the "urge" is creeping up on him. He may wake up in the morning feeling restless. As the day progresses, he may find his thoughts turning more and more often toward his "outlet"—his preferred offense. The offense itself may occur that night or next week or next month; only rarely does it occur without such a warning or "prodrome."[14]

A minority of offenders have no specific victim type or pattern of offense, and they are considered less treatable and more dangerous. For them, *any* child will do.

I saw this client on referral last week. Over the course of six months, he had not only molested the little boy he was arrested for, but he had also exposed himself to adult women and engaged in various acts of bestiality. Then, at the end of the intake, he tells me he is primarily interested in little girls. [psychiatric social worker]

If the offender has a pattern, treatment will attempt to identify, understand, and replace that pattern with a more appropriate, adult situation. However, if the offender has no specific preference, it will be difficult to counteract his free-floating urges for children.

Regardless of the offender's choice of victim, the sexual activity he engages the child in is relatively immature. His choice of sexual expression correlates more to the age of the child rather than to *his* age. Exposing genitals, stroking, and touching are common interactions between victim and offender. As the victim grows older or the relationship progresses, mutual masturbation or oral-genital contact might be introduced. Intercourse or some form of penetration may be attempted with older victims or in violent cases, but for the most part, the immature sexual activity is easily disguised as a "game" or "playing."

It took me forever to figure out what was going on. He called it "roughhousing" and wanted to do it every time he was alone with me. In summer camp, that happened to be a lot of times. When I got older, I realized he was having erections when he rolled all over me. [sixteen-year-old past victim]

We never thought too much about it. Our daughter had a lot of tomboy friends and one of her friends' father wrestled with them. It wasn't until many years later that we found out he undressed them in the process of wrestling. [forty-two-year-old mother of a victim]

One study reported that 85 per cent of the sexual activity between offender and victim was nonorgasmic, and another found that sexual activity ceased before any type of genital stimulation took place in one fourth of the cases.[15] In short, the offender is "playing doctor" with the child, mocking the normal sexual exploration that possibly happens between the child and her peers.

When confronted with his crime, the child molester calls on a very strong denial system. Almost half of the offenders in one large study categorically denied the offense.

It never happened. That kid is lying. I wasn't even around her when she says I did it. [thirty-two-year-old offender]

It's her mother—she's giving me this bum rap because I walked out on her. She's trying to get even. [thirty-six-year-old offender]<sup></sup>[16]

Of the remaining half, many admit the offense, but minimize its importance.

It only happened once. I said I'd never do it again, so I don't know what the big deal with the police is. [twenty-four-year-old offender]

It was an accident, the kid came in while I was going to the bathroom, and now she says I exposed myself and tried to do things to her. So she saw me in the bathroom. I forgot to close the door. So what? [thirty-year-old offender]

Others have external excuses for what happened.

Well, I had been drinking really heavily and I guess I forgot what I was doing. [twenty-eight-year-old offender]

See, I get these really bad headaches, and when I do, I become another person. I don't remember what happens. [forty-two-year-old offender]

Projection of responsibility onto someone else—victims or family or society—is another popular rationalization.

I just had too much pressure on me—the wife was always nagging me, I hated my job, the kids weren't behaving. This was the only thing I could do to make myself feel better. [thirty-five-year-old offender]

This kid has been hanging all over me. She comes on with a lot of the guys in the neighborhood—what could I do? For a ten-year-old, she really knew it all. [twenty-six-year-old offender]

There are some definite trends in who denies most often.[17] Molesters of children under nine years old deny 55 per cent of the time, as compared to the 40 per cent denial rate of molesters of older children. Interestingly, aggressive offenders deny 68 per cent of the time, whereas nonviolent offenders deny only 40 per cent of the time, and twice as many boy molesters deny as girl molesters.

As self-righteous as the individual offender might be, his generosity in ignoring the impact of the crime does not extend to other offenders. In one study, only 36 per cent of the offenders considered their own justifications as valid justification for other child molesters.[18] Rather, the majority described *other* child molesters as "off their rockers," "weak," "had no excuse," and, in general, "very different from myself."

The facts, from choice of victim to strong denial systems, add up to a profile of the child molester being an immature and rather self-centered person who lacks a sense of the consequences of his behavior. A. Nicholas Groth, an experienced prison psychologist, sums up the personality characteristics of the child molester:

> If they share any common psychological traits or characteristics, these tend to be a sense of isolation or alienation from others, an ineptitude in negotiating interpersonal relationships, deep-seated feelings of inadequacy, and a tendency to experience themselves as helpless victims of an overpowering environment.

> The child offender appears handicapped by poor impulse control, especially in regard to sexuality; poor ability to tolerate frustration or to delay immediate gratification of his needs; and low self-esteem. He is relatively helpless in meeting psychological life-demands and appears to be concerned only with his own needs and feelings. There is a relative insensitivity or unawareness of the needs and feelings of others and little insight into or understanding of his own behavior. In essense, he is a psychological child in the physical guise of an adult.[19]

People become child molesters for various reasons. In the next three segments, we will explore the backgrounds that lead to these offenses. First we will consider the adolescent offender. He is too young to be *permanently* classified as a child molester, yet he does molest young children. Adults become child molesters either because they have had a lifetime *fixation* on children as sex objects, or because as a "normal" adult, they felt it necessary to *regress* from a demanding adult to the emotional safety of children as sexual partners.

## Adolescent Offenders

As stated before, perhaps more than any other category of child molesters, we must be careful when defining the adolescent offender. He or she *is* a person in teen years who molests children. However, the adolescent offender usually has not had enough varied sexual experience to *choose* child molesting as the preferred sexual expression. Rather, the offenses are reflections of a disturbed state of his life at that time.

We assume that any teen-ager needs time and a variety of experiences such as different jobs, college, and travel before he can make an intelligent decision about long-range career plans or getting married. The same holds true for developing our sexuality. Child molestation may be the adolescent offender's *first* sexual expression, and while the offender should be accountable and treated for the offense, it is clearly inaccurate and not at all productive to label him a "child molester" forever.

Two thirteen-year-old boys masturbating each other are *not* child molesters. Assuming they both are at the same level of power, knowledge, and resources, they are simply exploring with each other. Experts in this field agree that a five-year age difference between the offender and the victim is a safe guideline for defining exploitation. Of course, there are exceptions where the imbalances of power, knowledge, and resources between the offender and the victim are great, although the age difference might not span five years. However, there are fewer gray areas than we might expect; in two important studies, the average age of the victim of the adolescent offender is six years old.[20]

For those of us who have thought about the existence of teen-age child molesters, a certain stereotype comes to mind: a fat boy with thick glasses, slovenly in appearance, baseball cap on backward, food smeared all over his sweatshirt, and saliva drooling out of the corner of his mouth. As with most stereotypes, the picture fits only a few offenders. There is no one type of adolescent offender, but they do have some characteristics in common.

The majority of adolescent child molesters are boys. Dr. Toni

Clark and Dr. Gary Wenet of the Juvenile Sexual Offender Project*
at the University of Washington have seen only eight female clients
out of two hundred referrals. Clark and Wenet believe that there
are probably more female adolescent child molesters, but their offenses are not being identified or reported. Also, our society does
not value and cultivate aggressive females in the same way we raise
aggressive males. Although the existence of female offenders cannot
be questioned, it is safe to assume that the vast majority are boys.

Adolescent offenders are involved with children victims in very
acceptable settings: baby-sitting, Sunday-school help, coaching a
sports team, or volunteering to take neighborhood children places
the parents don't have time to take them.

> Tom had always been such a friendly and polite boy. My kids
> were crazy about him and *asked* if he could be their baby-
> sitter. I never would have guessed he would have done any-
> thing like this. [mother of a four-year-old victim]

The danger inherent in identifying teen-age offenders in child-care
roles is that all teen-age boys will be purged from our churches
and neighborhoods for fear *they* are child sexual abusers. Many
boys genuinely enjoy contact with children and should be encouraged to participate in the guidance of younger children. Child-care
experience for teen-age boys breaks down sex-role stereotyping and
prepares them for many nontraditional jobs. A telling sign of a teen-
age boy who might be tempted to exploit children sexually is a lack
of contact with his peers. If the boy's willingness to help us with
small children isn't *balanced* with an interest in peer activities and
relationships, there might be reason to be concerned.

The adolescent offender is basically nonviolent in the commission
of his crimes, and his victims are strangers in only 20 per cent of
the cases.[21] Because the offender and the child know each other,
the sexual abuse is often carried out during the course of a "game."

> I was playing strip poker with this little girl and of course she
> kept on losing, so when she was finally undressed, the rest was
> real easy. [seventeen-year-old offender]

* At this writing, the Seattle project is the only out-patient treatment facility
in the nation for teen-age sex offenders.

Two thirds of the victims are little girls, and the sexual activity is basically nonorgasmic, including exhibition, mutual masturbation, and sometimes oral-genital contact.

The majority of these offenders will stop the approach or sexual activity if the child begins to cry or protest. Approximately 20 per cent of the offenders will continue the molesting, and they are considered more violent.

> I had to hit the kid because he was making so much noise. I thought it was real strange—an eight-year-old boy crying. But when it was all over, I really think he liked it, you know, once he got used to it. [fifteen-year-old offender][22]

Those who use force or coercion are acting alone and are usually not part of a gang. They are merely more intent on getting what they want.

Clark and Wenet found that molesting sometimes followed a bout of frustration or anger. If the offender had been rejected by his peers, had difficulty at home, or had problems in schoolwork or on a job, he would seek out children shortly after the troublesome event. He is not angry with the child, but sex is one of many ways to release tension, and for the adolescent offender who is overwhelmed with stress, the molestation of children is a pleasurable outlet.

> Everything seemed to be going wrong in my life. My parents and teachers were on my back about my grades and I'd been doing lousy on the track team. I had all these feelings building up, and nothing to do with them, so I figured maybe I'd feel better if I fooled around with this Mike kid. [fifteen-year-old offender]

Most offenders, in Clark and Wenet's experience, are not aware of their pattern of hostility followed by molestation.

The teen-age child molester is like any other teen-ager in many ways, except that he may have more difficulty in initiating and maintaining friendships in his own age range. He may have an interest or aptitude in sports, music, or cars, just like any other teenager, but somehow he can't easily share those activities with his peers. Perhaps he has missed out on some very valuable childhood training, beginning in elementary school.

As children, most of us had a same-sex friend as our "best friend." Although we had some interest in the opposite sex, our "best friend" was the most important. Through that friendship, we learned *how to* be friends; we invited someone to play at our house, asked them to keep our secrets, planned some future activity and, in general, reached out and shared a part of our life with them.

Around twelve years old, a transition begins; our same-sex "best friend" fades in importance as we venture out into the world of dating, "making out," and "falling in love." The transition seems awkward at first—neither boys nor girls are sure how they feel about these changes, and at times they seem out of their control. Yet, they know how to connect with another person, they have years of same-sex friendships to fall back on. Eventually it all works out, and many boys and girls together continue in their development of peer relationships.

For a variety of reasons, the adolescent offender did not have meaningful same-sex relationships as a small child.

We moved around so much, I never got to know anybody. After a while, I was having so much trouble in school, I really didn't care if I knew anybody. [sixteen-year-old offender]

I was huge for my age—they all called me "Jolly Green Giant" and stuff like that. All they did was make fun of me. [fourteen-year-old offender]

I was real shy and I didn't exactly live in the kind of house where you wanted to take kids home to it. [fourteen-year-old offender]

Therefore, as a teen-ager, he does not know the ground rules of making friends and he has not experienced success at reaching out to other teen-agers, as the Seattle project's 1976 study states:

The majority of child molesters were described by the project staff as either marginally adjusted socially or as social isolates. Typically, they had no friends, or if they did, these were friends with whom they felt no closeness. This was in contrast to the "adjusted" youngster, who had at least one close friend as well as a group of acquaintances with whom she or he interacted regularly.[23]

The teen-age offender's social isolation does not go unnoticed by other teen-agers. At best he is excluded from their activities, and at worst he is ridiculed as "weird."

> Nothing would have surprised me about that guy—he was so goofy and always by himself. We used to make fun of him in the locker room, but he never said anything back to us. [classmate of an adolescent offender]

The offender has the same desires, needs, or fantasies as any other teen-ager; but he lacks the wherewithal to make things happen for himself. The experience of dating is an excellent example.

When a dance is coming up, teen-age boys usually pick out the girl they would *most* like to go with. The boy checks around with his friends to determine her availability. If she is unattached, he administers many tests to gauge her interest in him, such as asking her to study with him, teasing her mercilessly, or tripping her in the hall. If she responds to his machinations in a favorable way, he proceeds to the next step. Not wanting to appear foolish if his assessment is off-base, he asks his friends to pass a message along to her friends that he is possibly considering taking her to the dance. If she sends an affirmative message back through the chain, then he takes the big step and actually asks her. The teen-agers who go to the dance are survivors of this "trial by ordeal."

The adolescent offender has visions of going to the same dance. However, he tends to pick the type of girl many other peers would consider taking, so the competition is tough. He does not have the confidence to approach her for a preliminary reading, nor does he have access to an intricate grapevine to determine her availability. He definitely does not have the resources of three or four friends to carry a message to her. Wanting desperately to belong but not having the skills to conform to the usual way of asking for the date, he might work up the courage to take the plunge. He calls her to ask her to the dance. She may not even know he exists, and if she does know him, she thinks someone must be playing a practical joke on her because she would never go out with "that creep." Even if she does politely turn down his request, chances are good everyone in school will learn of his rejection.

> Just one time I asked a girl out for a date. It turned out that she was going steady with one of the "jocks," except I didn't know it. She was nice enough about it, but the next day her boyfriend and his friends gave me a hard time, really bugged me about how I wouldn't know what to do with her anyway. [sixteen-year-old offender]

He will not consider asking a girl who will more likely accept his request. He must go to the dance with someone who will ensure his acceptance. Anyone less than a "popular" girl will confirm the label that he is "different."

Needless to say, this chaos in peer relationships limits the offender's normal sexual exploration. How can he kiss girls if they won't be seen talking with him? Not all adolescent offenders stand out as the "class dolt," and some have had sexual experiences with teen-age girls, but generally their shyness and lack of skills or of confidence do affect their sexual development. On the other hand, children will not only talk with the offender and be his friend, they will also express affection. Often the sexual abuse begins under the guise of the affection the offender so intensely needs. Again, from the Seattle project study:

> We sometimes observed in our target population that the sexual behavior may have originally been motivated by ignorance or curiosity. Unfortunately, it seems that the actual *performance* of the act may so impress the youngster offender that the sexual behavior may become a pattern of its own, independent of the *original* motivation. [emphasis added][24]

The elements of ignorance and curiosity are significant. The adolescent offender probably cannot express his sexual curiosity with other teen-agers, and he may be ignorant of what sexual exploration *really* consists of. Once the child has met those needs, and the offender for the first time feels powerful and satisfied, he is likely to repeat the behavior again, even though he had every intention of "just trying it once to see what it was like."

Dr. Clark states that many of her clients deny they know what masturbation is:

> Some of these kids are the brunt of teasing by other boys, such as being put down by being told to go "beat off." They connect masturbation to something very negative and therefore won't do it. Or, if they do it, they won't admit it.

Ridicule around sexual issues heightens the offender's confusion. In the case of masturbation, a normal form of sexual exploration is abandoned or at least skewed by the shame attached to the act. More importantly, the offender becomes aware that little children do not tell him to go "beat off." They look up to the offender, and he feels more comfortable with them because they are more equal in the realm of sexual knowledge and experience.

> I liked the little kids in my neighborhood because they didn't bug me. They were nice to me, and we listened to each other and every day asked each other how things are going. [thirteen-year-old offender]

As another reflection of the offender's poor peer relationships, we find little experience with drugs or alcohol. An alienated adult can easily obtain drugs or alcohol on his own, but the teen-ager needs either the street sense or a trusted relationship with a pusher to obtain the substances. Both seem out of the question for the adolescent offender.

The family situation provides us with some clues as to why the teen-ager becomes an offender. The absent father is prominent in the family dynamic. The offender's father may be dead, separated, or divorced from the boy's mother. If he does live in the home, he may be emotionally aloof from the offender. On the one hand, this complicates the boy's problems with other teen-agers. He has no one to turn to with questions. He has lost an important confidant.

> I used to try to ask my dad about things like dating, you know, starting out by asking if I could use the car, but I wanted to know if he had any good ideas about *how* to ask a girl out. He always said to ask my mother. He said it in a real mean

way. I'd rather die than ask my mother that. [sixteen-year-old offender]

On the other hand, the absent father exacerbates the offender's sexual confusion. Boys look to their fathers or other significant male adults as models of adult male sexuality. If he has no father to imitate, or if his father will not discuss his future as an adult male sexual being, the boy's alienation and floundering sexuality are magnified.

The reason I did this thing with the kid was to get my father, or somebody, to talk to me about sex. I figured they'd notice then. [thirteen-year-old offender]

When teen-agers in the general population are asked which parent they favor or identify with, the breakdown is fairly equitable between mother and father. In marked contrast, perhaps due to the absent father, 80 per cent of adolescent offenders identify their mother as the preferred parent.[25]

Dad explodes a lot—I like Mom much better. She's better about discipline and problems. [fourteen-year-old offender]

The sense of self that could be derived from a close relationship with an adult male is sadly missing. The teen-age offender either identifies with his mother, or perhaps with *no* person close to him.

Another fact of contemporary family life is a high incidence of physical and sexual abuse of children. It is no coincidence that almost half of the teen-age offenders in the Seattle study were victims of abuse.[26] Not only does this weaken an already poor self-concept, it also isolates them from the normal development of sexuality. The adolescent offender/past victim is vulnerable to all the damage resulting from abuse.

When confronted with his crime, the offender often perceives the punishment as resulting from the fact that he, a minor, had sex.

The reason I'm in trouble is that I wasn't married when I did that to the little girl. If she and I had been married, it would have been O.K. [fourteen-year-old offender]

He believes an adult doing the same thing would be free of consequences. His concern is not so much for the victim as for what the authorities are "doing" to him.

Some offenders maintain that the child, no matter how young she was, gave consent to the sexual activity, even if she didn't understand the sexual nature of the offender's actions.

> I don't know why everyone's making such a big deal. I didn't hurt her. I asked her if she would play a game with me and she said "yes." If she didn't want to do it, she should have said "no." [sixteen-year-old offender]

There is a double standard operating around the offender's lack of understanding or outright denial of issues of consent. The adolescent offender may have worked with small children in a capacity where he was a leader or a teacher. In these situations, it is clear that the children do not have the skills and judgment of a teenager or an adult. If they did, the children wouldn't need the offender to be a lifeguard while they swim, teach them to play a game, or look after them while the parents are gone. While the offender related to the children *because* of the differences in skills and judgment between them and himself, around issues of consent to sexual activity, suddenly small children are the offender's peers.

Finally, we must consider the adolescent offender's future. Will he grow out of the need to offend, or continue to molest children when he reaches adulthood, or will he graduate to more violent crimes? Because there has been little research on or treatment with adolescent offenders—far less than with adult child molesters—we really don't know the answers. The adolescent offender's problems seem to be clear and amenable to treatment. Social-skill development is a specific treatment strategy, and preventive work should be done with teen-age boys in the area of sex education and learning the meanings of "consent" and "exploitation."

Early detection and treatment of the adolescent offender is critical to the overall prevention of child sexual abuse. The teen-age boy's confusion is not yet a pattern, and with intervention, society may be free of one less adult child molester.

## Fixated Offenders

Any adolescent offender has the potential to become an adult fixated offender. His teen-age offenses mark the beginning of his prevailing interest in children as sex partners. A. Nicholas Groth describes the fixated offender as:

A person who has, from adolescence, been sexually attracted primarily or exclusively to significantly younger people, and this attraction persisted throughout his life, regardless of what other sexual experiences he has had.[27]

As a ten-year-old, the potential fixated offender may be sexually active with children close to his own age. At age fifteen, his predominant sexual interest is still with ten-year-olds. This may or may not be disconcerting to him or to those around him. However, when he is a man in his twenties, he is *still* most interested in ten-year-olds as sexual partners. Then it is apparent that he has a problem. The offender grows older but the objects of his sexual arousal do not.

Even though I didn't have sex with a kid until I was in my twenties, I always was interested in them. Most of my friends have always been around ten or eleven. When they got older, I'd find new friends or coach a new team, but I'd lose interest in the older kids. [twenty-seven-year-old offender]

Much of this implies an easily spotted social reject or bachelor as the fixated offender. It isn't that simple. Twelve per cent of fixated offenders are married at the time of their offenses.[28] However, the marriage itself is symptomatic of the offender's problems. One therapist summarizes the fixated offender's marriage this way:

The emotionally underdeveloped man who is unconsciously looking for a mother will often find someone who is seeking a permanent child—one who will not grow up and leave her. "More than the ordinary man, they (sex offenders) are dependent emotionally," continues (Robinson) Williams. "Not having matured in that area, they are still children looking for a mother. Often their wives are maneuvered into being mothers—handling the finances and making all the household decisions. Their wives are many times manipulated into what I call a "bitch-mother," one who is forced into a position of saying "no" to them frequently. The sex-offender husband, through her, finds a justification for being even more irresponsible. He then complains that his wife is unsympathetic and unloving—and thus the vicious cycle continues."[29]

In general, the wife initiates the relationship and continues to dominate it, according to the offender's forfeit or indirect request. One study demonstrated that the offender does not take a long time to choose his wife, with an average "courting period" of five months.[30]

> I married Snookie because she was a terrific cook and she had a good job and was still raising her three kids. We didn't know each other that well, but I saw how she ran things and that's all I needed to know. [twenty-four-year-old offender]

Marriage does not deter his offending. In fact, the offender may find accessible victims in his stepchildren. While giving the appearance of a well-adjusted married man, the offender is but another child to his wife and a peer to his stepchildren. Along with her many other responsibilities, the wife of the fixated offender initiates sexual activity with her husband. He may respond to her, but he is far more likely to initiate sexual activity with children.

> I don't see how men can do that bar scene—jumping from stool to stool, hoping they hit the jackpot. [twenty-seven-year-old offender]

The availability of an adult sexual partner does not alter his desire for children.

The fixated offender is generally overwhelmed by the logistics and demands of everyday life.

> This last time I was arrested, well, it all started with trying to buy a shower curtain. I was trying to choose which color and I have this problem with decisions. Every time I try to make one,

my mind starts to wander. So there I was, I started fantasizing about those eight-year-old blondes. Before I knew it, I wasn't in the store anymore. I was out looking for one like in my fantasy. [twenty-six-year-old offender]

The 88 per cent of fixated offenders who are not married at the time of their offenses will find someone else to fill the role of caretaker. To help him get through life, the offender may still rely emotionally or financially on his parents or perhaps receive state aid. Institutional life soothes the offender's anxieties about making it through each day.

Being in the service was the best time of my life. I just sat there stamping papers and did what they told me. The food wasn't bad, considering, and I had my own bunk. It was really a great life—I was more relaxed then. [thirty-four-year-old offender]

In some extreme cases, prison life is less stressful and more preferable to the offender than the bewildering demands of being on his own.

Many fixated offenders have difficulty with leisure time and are more prone to offend when they are bored. Without the self-sufficiency to cope with a lack of structure, they may seek out the company of children as both a form of entertainment and as an antidote for their feelings of emptiness.

The fixated child molester's self-perceived helplessness has been with him throughout his life and perhaps started in his childhood. Almost half of fixated offenders were victims of child sexual abuse, usually victimized by a nonfamily member in a violent manner.[31] And from this the message begins: The world is a cruel and demanding place, void of love from adults.

The incident or incidents of sexual abuse may account, in part, for his fixation on a specific age, sex, or physical appearance of his victim choice. He seeks to resolve his own victimization by reliving the experience as an adult. He may not be aware of the connection between his own experience as a victim and his career as an offender.

Nothing happens when I'm around older boys. Sometimes I start to think I'm cured but then I get around seven- or eight-

> year-olds and it all starts again. It wasn't until I went to prison
> that I really remembered or talked about being molested by a
> neighbor when I was eight. [thirty-three-year-old offender]

However, child sexual abuse in the offender's childhood is merely
a tangible, although significant, indication of his generally troubled
life. His upbringing was basically insecure, marked by numerous
moves, early physical illness, marital differences between parents,
and the like.[32]

As the offender projects his own feelings of sadness and loneliness
onto his victim, the offender is trying to capture some of the missing
joy of his childhood. He believes that by being a "buddy" to the
child, he is enhancing the victim's life in a way in which his was
never enhanced.

> I choose six-year-olds because that's when it happened to me.
> But I was gentle and took him lots of places, so it was really,
> really different. We really loved each other. [twenty-two-year-
> old offender]

> This guy kept telling me how much I looked like him. He called
> me by the same nickname he had and we played the same
> games he used to like. I didn't see where I looked at all like
> him, but he insisted. [twenty-three-year-old past victim]

Sex with the child is just one aspect of the emotional involvement
the offender wants with the victim. He wants the most warmth and
comfort with the least demands upon himself; therefore adult relationships are too threatening. With a child, the sexual involvement
is the offender's testing ground for the depth of the victim's com-
mitment to him.

> If the child *really* loves me, she will want to do this for me.
> [twenty-three-year-old offender]

In the fixated offender's mind, if the emotional involvement is there,
the sex will follow naturally. Sex is his way of *experiencing* the
child's love.

When involved with a fourteen-year-old, the fixated offender also
becomes a fourteen-year-old. He allows the victim to influence him
to become more of a child.

> If I was with an adult and we had to go on the subway, I'd pay my subway token just like everyone else. But if I'm with a kid I'm involved with, I'd sneak through without paying, even if my pockets are full of subway tokens, I'd do what he did. [thirty-seven-year-old offender]

The offender can show incredible patience in his premeditation of the crime as he waits to be accepted as "one of the guys."

> I got busted for molesting these boys on my baseball team. But it wasn't like I was exploiting them. I'd worked with those kids for a full year on nothing but their batting and fielding before I ever molested them. It took me that long before they trusted me and stopped treating me like a tough adult coach. [twenty-eight-year-old offender]

In areas such as decision-making, sports participation, or conversation, the offender and the victim are equals. In fact, the child may have a little more power in the relationship than the offender. The camaraderie between offender and victim is a double-edged sword. It also serves to place the blame on the victim, at least in the offender's mind. Because the offender is no more mature or responsible than the child, he insists that the victim is powerful and that he, the offender, had little control over his own behavior.

> I really loved this kid—not just for his body—but really just for him. He told me to get the money for the minibike, or he'd leave me. So I stole to get it. What else could I do? [thirty-one-year-old offender]

And, of course, the offender maintains that the child initiated the sexual relationship.

> These kids were really streetwise—smarter than I am. Even the nine-year-old had made it with a lot of guys. They told me if I let them ride in my car, they'd let me "do it." [twenty-five-year-old offender]

In the offender's fantasy life, not only does the child initiate the sexual relationship, but she also encourages it to continue. He may go so far as to believe that the victim's friends seek him out upon her recommendation.

I didn't have any peace or quiet. First she keeps coming back for more, then she broke her promise and told other kids and they started pestering me because they said she liked it so much. It was one of those other kids who blew the whistle on me. I'm still in love with her. [twenty-four-year-old offender]

The fixated offender shows little remorse for his crimes. He may be genuinely sorry he was caught and has to stop his molesting, but he thinks little of the potential damage he has done to the victim and may not recognize the relationship as harmful. He describes his need for sex with children as an addiction or a compulsion. Consequently, the fixated offender's recidivism rate is high; he will follow his drive again and again with little thought of the consequences to the victim.[33]

Perhaps due to his own victimization, which becomes so much of his reality, or his intense need to be loved by the child, he sees nothing particularly out of the ordinary with what he has done.

I'm just a victim of an uptight, Victorian society. If people were more hang loose about sex, if they knew how beautiful sex with kids can be, I wouldn't have been busted for loving Jimmy. [thirty-one-year-old offender]

In many ways, including his sense of right and wrong, the fixated offender is a child. Still, he must be accountable for his offenses.

## Regressed Offenders

Contrasted to the fixated offender, the regressed offender probably has not demonstrated much interest in children until the time of his offense. Again, A. Nicholas Groth describes him as:

. . . a person who originally preferred peers or adults for sexual gratification. However, when these adult relationships became conflictual in some important respect, the adult became replaced by the child as the focus of this person's sexual interest and desires.[34]

Three fourths of these offenders are married, and their average

age ranges from thirty-two to thirty-six years old, whereas the fixated offender's average age range is from twenty-seven to twenty-nine years old.[35] The regressed offender has a strong adult sexual preference and often initiates sexual activity with *both* children and adults. One study reported that among a large group of regressed offenders, adult sexual preference was 83 per cent exclusively heterosexual and 17 per cent bisexual, with the bisexuals stating a preference for women. Interestingly, 71 per cent of the regressed offenders' victims were girls, 16 per cent chose boy victims, and the remaining 13 per cent victimized both boys and girls.[36]

Throughout his life, the regressed offender has been somewhat successful in his peer relationships. For him, life is going along as it should when a crisis, stress, or challenge is introduced. Coping seems beyond his capabilities, frustration and self-doubt result, and he becomes a child molester as a release for these feelings.

My wife was in the hospital having a baby we couldn't afford. All I could think about was how I was alone all by myself. It wasn't long before I went looking for a kid. [twenty-six-year-old offender]

During this difficult time in his life, there is more psychological safety to be found in sexual relationships with children because they are less demanding than adults.

I was having problems with my wife—she couldn't climax during sex. I felt beat into the ground like I wasn't a man at all. So I thought about having an affair, but if I did and *that* woman didn't climax, I'd feel even worse. I turned to kids, where climaxing isn't an issue. [forty-year-old offender]

The stress can be anything: financial crisis, loss of loved one, marital problems, sexual dysfunction, career dissatisfaction, or the onset of physical illness. Whatever the problem, its resolution seems out of the offender's grasp. The molestation is a response to a totally unrelated situation; the sexual and emotional contact soothes the offender's frustration and anger.

I never noticed it, but I guess I always went to visit this neighbor kid after I'd have a fight with the boss. The kid just made me feel so good—it seemed like the thing to do. At the time, it was the only thing I could do. [thirty-two-year-old offender]

One possible type of stress is *aging*. Most of the minority of offenders who are over fifty-five years old are regressed.[37] The fixated offender would have a difficult time offending, throughout his life on a regular basis, and making it into old age undetected.

Many elderly offenders are reacting to loss: retirement, death of wife and friends, decreased sexual functioning, or poor health. They want to recapture the warmth and validation they found in work and relationships.

I was living with my daughter—I hadn't lived with anyone in ages—it was humiliating. I felt like a fifth wheel so I watched her kids and some of the neighborhood kids to make myself useful. I missed my wife, my own home, especially I missed engineering. I say I could have worked a few more years. Anyway, the kids were so affectionate—one in particular was starved for affection. It was just too easy. I really looked forward to seeing that kid every day. [sixty-seven-year-old offender]

Because we have taught our children to be especially nice to, perhaps even pity elderly people, accessibility to children seems to be no problem for the elderly offender. Under the guise of grandfatherly attention, he can develop a relationship with a victim and ensure the secrecy of his offense through the child's loyalty. If he is discovered, chances are he will be treated with leniency, prompted by the belief that he is "harmless."

When I told my parents about my friend's grandfather, they just told me to stay away from him. I overheard them talking later—they said he was too old and sick to know what he was doing to me. [twenty-nine-year-old past victim]

When someone believes "there is no place to go but up," child molestation might not seem like an inappropriate activity. However, somewhere in his consciousness, the regressed offender knows he is wrong. Unlike the fixated offender, he has an *adult* sense of right and wrong. Yet relief from the stress is his priority, so he knowingly suspends his normal values (or is so momentarily distracted by his problems that he momentarily doesn't care) when he molests the child. He may not premeditate the initiation of the relationship; that may be left to opportunity, but once involved with the child, he will plan to hold onto the relationship.

> I took these kids on a field trip—having sex with any of them wasn't at all on my mind. Then one of the little girl students came in—real upset and she needed some affection. Well, I needed affection too—it was a horrible time in my life. Before I knew it, there we were. But after that, it was *me* who kept on getting her to go places with me. I really couldn't help it. [twenty-nine-year-old offender]

Sometimes feelings of guilt and remorse do follow, but the subsequent further loss of self-esteem diminishes the offender's ability to cope. The original problems now seem more insurmountable, and once again, the offender seeks relief in the safety of children. It is the quintessential vicious circle.

> I knew if anyone ever found out about this, it would destroy my teaching career. But I couldn't help it—every day I swore I'd never go near that nine-year-old again and every day I found myself wanting, thinking I *needed* to see her. [twenty-six-year-old offender]

It is important to note that most men go through severe personal and professional crises without molesting children. As overpowered and unhappy as they might feel, they find other solutions to their problems. The regressed offender, on the other hand, uses his life circumstances as an excuse or justification for his offense with the often-heard refrain, "If it weren't for . . . I would never have molested that child." Still, the offender is totally responsible regardless of his life circumstances.

Inasmuch as the regressed offender is probably married and feels he needs an accessible child as an outlet for his chronic dissatisfaction and self-doubt, his own children might be prime candidates. Certainly they are around him more than any other children, he has power over them, and their proximity may coincide with his high points of stress if his home life is a source of problems. Yet we find a curious double standard. Many child molesters believe *incest* is the lowliest of crimes and that it is more "correct" to molest a nonrelated child than one's own son or daughter.

When I was checked into prison, this shrink talks to me. He says on my record it says I molested my two stepchildren and I also got four other kids of my own at home. He says he was wondering if I ever molested the other kids—my own flesh and blood—so I got mad. What does he think I am? I'd never do anything like *that*—molest my own kids. He's crazy. [forty-four-year-old offender]

The regressed offender is as likely to molest a familiar child as he is an unknown child. He maintains his status of adult and elevates the child to a psychological age closer to his own to romanticize the relationship. Whereas the fixated offender takes on the values and interests of the child in order to be "one of the kids," the regressed offender attributes very adult characteristics to the child to gain equality.

Our relationship was what the child wanted. She was the aggressor. [thirty-one-year-old offender]

Cindy and I had a really good relationship. She was very mature at ten years old. We would plan things to do together like camping trips and movies to go see. It was the best relationship I ever had. [twenty-seven-year-old offender]

This one little girl I saw for a while liked me so much she used to have orgasms during our sex. [twenty-four-year-old offender]

The regressed offender deludes himself into thinking the child is his "date," girlfriend, or steady lover. He will not become an authoritarian adult *unless* the victim resists or wants to terminate the relationship. Then the "courting" stops and the exploitation becomes blatant. For all intents and purposes, the adult offender and the child victim are counterparts in an old-fashioned romantic fantasy where the adult remains basically an adult.

It is believed that approximately half of child molesters are regressed and the other half are fixated.[38] The prognosis for the two is radically different. As one prison psychologist tells us:

The treatment issues are very different. With the regressed offender, you are trying to get him *back* to a place he used to be where he had successful adult relationships without a sexual interest in children. On the other hand, with fixated offenders, you are trying to get them *beyond* the place where they are now, where their only sexual interest is in children. Without that prior successful experience with adults to return to, it is much more difficult.[39]

## The All-important Fantasy

We know of some specific characteristics common to offenders of a given age, or pattern. Is there not some overriding dynamic that we can identify as a prelude to child molestation?

To some extent, the answer is yes. Masturbatory conditioning is a key factor in the motivation of the child molester. The process of masturbatory conditioning begins as the offender fantasizes about sexual activity with a child. He does this repeatedly, achieving orgasm many times through the fantasy. The orgasm is a powerful reinforcer and he is inclined to use the same fantasy again. As time goes on, the fantasy becomes unsatisfying—the novelty of the fantasy wears off and the offender needs actual sexual contact with the child.

How does the molester come to choose children as the subjects of his fantasy? Why not the latest pinup or star of a television jiggle show? To understand the differences between the masturbatory fantasies of the non-offender adult male and the child molester, we must go back to their original sex-play experiences. Consider the differences in these two men:

Sam and Tony lived in the same neighborhood and met when they both entered kindergarten. Although the two boys were friends, they were very different. One thing they did have in common was the partner of their first attempt at "playing doctor." Joanna was seven years old when Sam and Tony were six. They played many games together: war games, cowboys and Indians, hide-and-seek, and, of course, doctor and patient. They were at the age where they were curious about their own bodies. This interest

was surpassed only by their interest in the opposite sex's body. Sam
had a sister, but his family stressed privacy to an almost fanatical
extent. Tony had no brothers or sisters yet. The three children had
a "secret" hiding place in the woods near their neighborhood. When
alone with each other, they would quickly pull down their pants
and remain exposed for a few seconds. Sometimes they would touch
each other, and at other times they would just look. All three were
very curious about the differences between boys' and girls' urina-
tion. So they showed each other how to urinate in the woods. After
a few weeks, their curiosity was satisfied, and the weather became
colder, curtailing their outdoor games. For a while, Joanna played
with other girls in the neighborhood. Sam and Tony continued to
spend time together. When the summer came again, Joanna, Tony,
and Sam played kickball and roller-skated, but they had outgrown
"playing doctor."

Tony and Sam had very different childhoods. When Tony was
ten, his mother had another baby. This was quite an adjustment
for Tony to make. His father was in the Merchant Marines and
was away from home a good part of the year. Tony and his mother
came to depend on each other, especially after the birth of the new
baby. Tony was basically shy as a child. With all of his responsibilities at home, he was not very involved in high-school activities.
He rarely went to movies, nor did he read much. He was not noticeably interested in girls. Tony was never asked to a Sadie Hawkins
dance, so it seemed the feeling was mutual. The one outside interest
Tony did have was Sunday school at the church. He was an
assistant to the preschool teacher. He did well at this, and always
looked forward to Sundays. After graduating from high school,
Tony entered the Army.

Sam, on the other hand, revolved his existence around sports.
Playing kickball with Tony was only the beginning. From there,
he went on to Little League, then high-school football. His sports
prowess won him a scholarship to college. It also won him the undivided attention of half of the cheerleading squad. Sam dated
many girls in high school. He became noncommittally involved with
the majority of them. Just before Sam was to enter college, his
parents decided to divorce. This did not have much noticeable impact on him; he was unhappy about it, and concerned for his

younger sister, but he was determined to play professional football, and going to college on an athletic scholarship was the first step to that end.

As the reader may have already guessed, one of the Sam-Tony-Joanna triangle becomes a child molester. Because at least 97 per cent of offenders are men, we can safely eliminate Joanna from consideration. Is it quiet Tony, with his dependence on his mother and interest in helping children? Or is it Sam, with his *macho* boyhood and "wanton" sex life? To find the answer, we must back up to the boys' puberty.

During puberty, or in many cases somewhat earlier, boys begin to masturbate. They may discover the process from older boys or happen onto it by themselves. Before long, they find the activity is enhanced by fantasizing. Everyone starts out at the same place; we fantasize about what we know. All of our initial fantasies relate to something we have actually experienced. So, when Sam and Tony began to masturbate, they both thought of their sexual exploration with Joanna.

For Sam, the novelty of this wore off soon. He looked around at the bodies of the other boys on his sports teams and when he fantasized, he would think of the varied physiques in the shower room. But he became uncomfortable with this. It did not seem congruent with the tenets of team sports. For a while, Sam began to be concerned about his interest in the genitals of the other boys.

But then, one day, an older boy on the team brought a magazine that he had his older brother buy at a pornographic shop. The team passed the magazine around until the corners on the pages were torn and smudged. In this magazine Sam found a wealth of new fantasies. This satisfied his needs for fantasies for quite a while. Eventually he noticed that some of the women in the TV shows he watched reminded him of the models in the magazine and he incorporated television actresses into his fantasies. Before long, Sam was noticing a few similarities between the actresses and the developing girls in his school. He fantasized, sometimes during class, about the more "attractive" girls. It wasn't long before he had the opportunity to live out some of those fantasies. And he had come full circle, back to fantasizing about what he knew.

Tony had a very different adolescence. He also started fantasizing about the times in the woods with Joanna. Those were such special times for him, compared to the routine and responsibilities of his adolescent life, so he did not grow tired of the fantasies. The scene reminded him of a time when he had close friends to have fun with. He didn't feel he had any friends now. Too shy to meet girls, not interested enough (although capable) in athletics to join team sports, Tony remained a loner throughout high school. He made good grades and kept up his part of household duties. Because he was no trouble at all, few teachers or other adults really noticed Tony.

He was comfortable with masturbation. In fact, he enjoyed the release it gave him. Masturbation also connected him with a happier time in his life. Unlike Sam, he was never exposed to pornographic magazines or sex play with girls his own age. For a while, he did fantasize about the young preschool teacher he worked with in Sunday school, but this made him feel guilty. After all, it seemed almost unholy, and she was the person most interested in and kind to him. Tony watched television, but he never thought of the actresses as anything more than people on the screen. He had enough difficulty relating to real people that he could not get excited about someone on television.

Both men married in their early twenties, had families, and settled in semiskilled jobs. The need for masturbation decreased because they were now married. Both men were involved in church or Scouting; the guidance of youngsters was an important value to them.

Tony married a woman who worked on one of the Army bases where he was stationed, and who was as shy as he was. Beyond their shyness, they shared a strong sense of loneliness and a readiness to find one person to give them "meaning" to their life. Tony's wife took the initiative in the relationship. Although it was difficult for her, she asked Tony out on their first date. They also shared a love of children and plans to have a family. After a short courtship, they were married.

The next ten years of Tony's life were uneventful. He stayed at the same job in an automobile plant, and had three children. In his midthirties, Tony began to wonder what it was he wanted from life. He was bored with the job and was having trouble concentrating on his work, which was causing him problems with his supervisors. At home, Tony was beginning to realize that three children were too many. He would lose patience with the children, and was bothered by the fussiness of the youngest child, who was still an infant. His impatience and dissatisfaction were confusing to Tony, as the one bright ray of hope in his weekly routine was the youth group from the church. He led them on nature outings every weekend.

To his wife Tony seemed very preoccupied. She did not understand why family life had not turned out to be totally satisfying to her. She began to look for other interests—a part-time job or perhaps school. While Tony didn't approve, he didn't argue with her. They just grew farther apart. Tony began to drink more often to fill up the empty hours, which helped him forget the feelings of inadequacy that gnawed away at him. He remembered the pleasant sensations of masturbation when he drank. It had been a long time since he had masturbated on any regular basis.

The alcohol diminished his ability to have an orgasm. Tony needed to fantasize to achieve an orgasm. This was a problem. His adult sex life did not offer much material for fulfilling fantasies. A major part of his problem was his dissatisfaction with the marriage; he could not think of any interesting fantasies that featured his wife. His sexual relationships with other adult women had been limited by his shyness. Tony watched television, but the beautiful young actresses were no help at all. As a matter of fact, thinking of them made the situation worse. Tony was reminded of his inadequacy as a man; how could he ever meet and seduce a woman like that? Pornography was not an outlet to Tony. His religion had strict sanctions against the material.

So the predictable happened. Tony reverted to his earlier fantasy life. He thought of the days in the woods with Sam and Joanna. This fantasy worked very well for him. It conjured up youthful curiosity, being part of a group, as well as feelings of warmth and friendship. Time and time again, Tony achieved orgasm with these fantasies.

Eventually, Tony began to need more than the fantasy. His feelings of loneliness and worthlessness heightened. The stresses of his marriage and job became more than he could bear. The element of alcohol impaired his judgment and lessened the amount of control he had over his desires. To obtain the same level of satisfaction, Tony made the fantasy a reality. He molested a seven-year-old girl (the same age as Joanna in his fantasy) in the neighborhood.

The moral of Tony's story is *not* to eradicate child sex play. "Playing doctor" with other very young children is a healthy, normal part of growing up. It did not adversely affect Sam, and therefore cannot be blamed for Tony's sexual interest in children. Many circumstances in Tony's life contributed to his regression.

Masturbation is also not the villain here. We now understand that masturbation is not as evil or catastrophic as we were once led to believe, and some of us know from experience that masturbation does not lead to blindness, excessive amounts of body hair, mental dullness, or sexual perversion. Again, Sam masturbated, perhaps to a nonexploitive fantasy, and remained a solid citizen.

Fantasy per se isn't the problem, although certain styles or content of fantasies are troublesome. Sam probably fantasized about the stars of the jiggle television programs and soft-core pornography. NEVER SHOULD THIS BE RECOMMENDED AS HEALTHY FANTASY MATERIAL. Although it does not deal with the sexual exploitation of children, this material does demean women in no small way. Exploitation is exploitation; it does not matter at whom it is aimed. It encourages the men who ejaculate to these fantasies to look at women as stupid, helpless objects who exist merely for men's pleasure. In that contemporary female sex objects on television and in advertising and pornography are blatantly *child*like, such fantasy material is dangerously close to igniting a sexual interest in children themselves. We need a new, widespread "school" of fantasy about warm, responsive, responsible sexual encounters between two people where one person is no more powerful or subservient than the other.

Tony differed from Sam both because Tony's fantasies were about children and because he did not have the controls to refrain from putting his fantasies into action. Child molesters sometimes read child pornography to find new fantasies or to enhance old fantasies, but many find what they are looking for in the mainstream of daily life.

I especially liked those billboards with the really tan little blond girl and the puppy is pulling her pants down and you can see her white buttocks. I can't remember what it was selling, but I sure liked the billboard. [thirty-year-old offender]

I used to make collages out of the little-boy underwear pages in the Sears, Roebuck catalogue. I'd cut out all the different ages and sizes and arrange them real artistically. [nineteen-year-old offender]

Whatever the source of the fantasy, Tony lacked self-restraint. This was as much due to circumstances and early background as it was precipitated by the child-oriented fantasy. Many men have extensive fantasy lives that they never act out in real life. However, very few *non*offending men have sexual fantasies about children. Consider the following scenes for their erotic value:

• You are in a public rest room, and a little boy asks you to lift him up to the sink so he can wash his hands. As you do so, he presses against your pelvic area to be sure he won't be dropped.

• An eight-year-old girl is taking a bubble bath. She soaks for a while, then begins to wash herself carefully. From head to toe, she takes her time in lathering up every part of her body.

• Two prepubescent girls are having a slumber party. They are next to each other in a double bed. The blanket is pulled over their heads, and they are whispering and giggling.

Most of us would find these rather commonplace and uninspiring. To the child molester, this is the stuff of his fantasy world. While the rest of us are mooning over John Travolta or Farrah Fawcett-Majors, the child molester is most stimulated by visions of children.

## A Useful Profile

*The Personality of a Child Molester: An Analysis of Dreams*, by Alan P. Bell and Calvin S. Hall, gives us more insight into the fantasy world of the child molester. This book is the extensive study of one offender, Norman, and the 1,368 dreams he recorded over a 3½-year period. Bell and Hall also investigated the circumstances of Norman's waking life through letters and interviews.

Norman came from a home very "typical" for the early background of a child molester. He felt a definite distance from his father, who seemed to prefer Norman's sister. At first, Norman didn't understand this, but through the logic of a small child, he reached a conclusion that would have lasting effects on his development. To Norman, the most obvious differences between his sister and himself were their bodies, so, concluded Norman, the father prefers the sister because of her body. Consequently, Norman developed an intense desire to see his sister's genitalia, to discover what was so powerful. But Norman's family was strict, so this was easier wished than actually accomplished. A heightened interest in the differences between the sexes is normal in a boy between three and six years old; however, this unsatisfied interest continued throughout Norman's life and became an obsession.

As Norman grew older, he did not make friends with boys his own age. He consistently relied on his mother for companionship and guidance. Norman felt very different from boys his own age, as he describes in this quote:

> I felt I was much deeper in thought than other boys. I was more serious. Maleness seemed to be equated with lightheartedness, and it was difficult for me to act that way. In fact, whenever the other boys acted sarcastic or flippant, I'd feel a surge of anger toward them. Whenever I was in a group of boys, I was afraid they would ridicule me. I felt I couldn't communicate because I did not know how, though I had deep thoughts I wanted to communicate.[40]

Conflicts that troubled him throughout his life and contributed to incidences of child molestation began very early for Norman. He had no desire to integrate himself into the adult world—particularly the adult *male* world.

> I used to try to prove I was a man. My mother wanted me to be more aggressive, but I couldn't pull it off. I finally came to realize that so-called masculinity was a false goal. Aggressive-

ness and competition—where do they get you, anyhow? *It takes too much energy.* So what if you win? It's a matter of being tops over nothing. You may be the victor, but it doesn't mean anything. Besides, reason is more important than power. Look at the dinosaur. [emphasis added][41]

Not only was Norman unwilling to become an adult male himself, but also he generally saw all adults in a negative light. In comparison, he was much more comfortable with children.

The child has no false self; the adult does. The child participates; the adult is an onlooker. Children are more curious; the adult leaves well enough alone. The child is not cynical like the adult. Consciously I'm attracted to the innocence of youth the way I used to be. I guess I'm searching for my own childhood by approaching children.[42]

Norman speaks for many child molesters in his statements. As adults, some offenders live a childlike lifestyle. Norman, as an example, lived with his mother well into his thirties. He received a subsidy from the state, so, therefore, someone else was supporting him. Norman believes other adults are intrusions into his own childlike world. On the few occasions when Norman did have sexual relations with other adults, he always put himself in the passive role.

His dream life is equally as revealing as his waking statements. Bell and Hall found that Norman dreamed about his mother and sister in much greater frequency than the average male. In these dreams, he saw himself as a small boy in a nuclear family. Not surprisingly, Norman dreamed about children four times more than the average for men. And his dream patterns were closer to the norm for children than for adults.

Norman molested both boys and girls, and his dreamlife was also polymorphically perverse. Through his treatment, Norman began to fantasize about a new adult woman friend. Bell and Hall were reluctant to predict the likelihood of Norman offending children again; however, a relationship with his woman friend was the first step to changing the attitudes *and* behavior reflected in his fantasies.

## Aggressive Offenders

Perhaps we dread the aggressive offender more than any other. The stereotype of the horrific crime of sexual violence against our children rivals the dirty-old-man vignette for prominence in our minds. We can somewhat openly discuss the stranger-in-a-car-with-candy ploy, but sadistic sexual abuse is the unspeakable.

We are not paranoid or silly in our fears. Glancing at newspaper headlines, we notice that the only incidents of child molestation receiving major coverage are sex-murder cases. Further heightening our fears is the fact that the most sensational sex murders of adults (Speck, Boston Strangler, Hillside Strangler) involve women victims, whereas sex murders of children (Corll, Gacey) involve *boy* victims. Thus, in our minds, three taboos are broken: sexual abuse of a child, sadism, and homosexuality. This is quite an overload for any rational understanding we might have of the crime. The larger picture of nonviolent child molestation of both boys and girls never sees the light of day in print, while the rape murders of little boys are front-page copy. No wonder we believe that most incidents of child molestation are violent.

The reality of reported cases is that less than 10 per cent involve physical violence.[43] We cannot be totally reassured by this statistic because so many cases go unreported. However, incidents involving violence are *less* likely to be covered up. Chances are better that the child would tell someone about the crime or the aftermath of the violence; bruises and the like would be apparent to adults, who would then report the crime. The reasons many people give for *not* reporting a crime of child sexual abuse (friendship or family ties with the offender, for example) would not be so durable when faced with a visibly injured child. So it is most likely that far many more nonviolent offenses go unreported than violent cases.

There is reason, beyond the statistics, to believe that violent offenders are in the minority. Remember the motivation of the child molester: He is seeking affection and control by "persuading" the child to enter into a sexual relationship. He must believe the child is a willing, giving, even enthusiastic participant. If the child resists or cries, most offenders will stop the sexual advance and move on to another potential victim. The offender is not going to obtain the intimacy he wants with a screaming child. Violence spoils the ambiance.

The contrast in the violent offender's perception of his victim to the nonviolent offender's perception is marked. A. Nicholas Groth describes the nonviolent offender:

> Such offenders appear to desire the child as a love object and typically describe the victim as innocent, loving, open, affectionate, clean, attractive and undemanding. They feel safer and more comfortable with children.[44]

And at the other end of the spectrum is the aggressive offender:

> Such offenders describe their victims as weak, defenseless, helpless, unable to resist, easily controlled and manipulated. They feel stronger and more in charge with children.[45]

There are two basic types of aggressive offenders.[46] First is the offender who has a low tolerance level for resistance. With little impulse control to speak of, he cannot afford to forego an accessible victim at hand. If the child is co-operative, then he will not resort to any form of violence, but if he encounters resistance, he will try threats of violence and verbal intimidation.

> I wasn't going to take any lip off that little nerd, so I threatened him with a knife. [twenty-six-year-old offender]

And if the child still resists in spite of his threats, the offender will become physically aggressive. He does not want to hurt the child, but the offender cannot tolerate defeat. This particular victim has been chosen, so one way or another, the child will co-operate.

The second type of offender is the sadist who intentionally uses violence in the commission of the crime. In fact, his sexual arousal pivots on the suffering and humiliation of the child.

> That man kept on asking me, "How does it feel? How does it feel?" I was crying too hard to say anything so he'd hit me some more. [nine-year-old victim]

He uses *more* force than necessary to overpower the victim, and not only does the violence have erotic value for the offender, he also desires to punish the child for being a victim. This twisted "logic" is in direct opposition to the nonviolent child molester, who rationalizes his offense by insisting he wants a "buddy."

Self-hatred is at the bottom of the sadistic offender's methodically planned offense. Hurting the child is an almost ritualistic purging of his own inadequacies.

> That kid was so weak and sniveling, he didn't deserve to live. If they hadn't found us, who knows what would have happened to the little weirdo. [thirty-year-old offender]

His choice of victim, according to Groth, is a reflection of his own feelings of weakness:

> In some way the child symbolizes everything the offender hates about himself, thereby becomes an object of punishment. The victim's fear, torment, distress, and suffering are important and exciting to the sadistic pedophile, since only in this context is sexual gratification experienced.[47]

By nature of violence, we might assume this offender is more spontaneous, but this is not true. The offender has most likely fantasized and masturbated to this scene of violence prior to the actual crime. Aggressive offenses are *more* often premeditated, and the offender may have a long history of fantasizing about strength and power with sexual overtones, perhaps beginning with torturing animals. The victim is not a child who unluckily stumbles across the offender's path during a fit of uncontrollable rage.

> I was really into little redheaded girls, and I'd fantasize about them all the time until finally I had to have one. But they are really hard to find, especially after you hurt them, so whenever I can find one, I take her picture first so I can have that later. That's the nice thing about pictures—they never grow old even though the kids do. [thirty-four-year-old offender]

Aggressive offenders are more likely to choose strangers for victims, and, of course, there is little chance of an ongoing relationship. They perceive their victims as expendable items that exist as means to their emotional ends. They do not want a relationship with the victim, or with anyone, for that matter. Although most child molesters do have an adult sexual preference, aggressive offenders are the least likely to be aroused by adults.

Alcohol is involved in approximately 60 per cent of aggressive child-molestation offenses; this is twice as often as for nonaggressive offenses.[48] In his pursuit of violence, this offender is more likely to attempt intercourse or some other form of penetration.

The entire lifestyle of the aggressive offender reflects his self-hatred and callousness toward other people. He earns a larger portion of his livelihood from criminal activity than the nonviolent child sexual abuser. There is little difference between the attitude of the armed robber ("Give me money") and that of the aggressive offender ("Give me sex"). The aggressive sex offender believes he is entitled to both, without question, and everything exists merely for the *taking*. Void of any sense of consequences for his consumption, he cares nothing for his victims.

Why should I think about other people's feelings? Who ever thought anything about me? If I need something—well, that's all I need to know. I just go ahead and take it. [forty-year-old offender]

He delights in defying numerous taboos and thinks of himself as a desperado. He gains his only sense of identity from acting in a way that alienates and repulses the larger part of society. As one therapist states:

There is an element of grandiosity here—"No other guy would do that." For many offenders, freedom, autonomy and identity are found only in the unconventional and offensive.[49]

He will try anything once for "kicks," including new and different ways of molesting children.

Aggressive offenders' victims are older than the average, and those who choose girl victims over twelve years old have strong ideas about the "rightness" of what they are doing.[50] Pursuant to the double standard, they *choose* the girl because she is vulnerable and accessible and then use violence to punish her for her availability. They discount the right of any young girl to refuse them sexually, and once through puberty, all girls are considered "fair game."

Those little girls in their tank tops—trying to look like Farrah Fawcett-Majors even though they are still in pigtails. If they've got enough to show under a tank top, then I'm gonna look. [twenty-eight-year-old offender]

Approaching an adult woman would be too threatening to his feelings of inadequacy, yet the offender explains away his "mistake" of molesting a postpubescent girl because of her "adult" appearance. He maintains he was confused and really believed she was over eighteen.

In all forms of child sexual abuse, we find that sex is not the major motivation. Other problems, sometimes not too far from the surface, motivate the crimes; it is not a matter of unmet sexual needs. Nowhere is this more apparent than in aggressive offenses.

We often use sexual terms or actions to communicate our feelings. "Making love" is a term of intimacy and closeness. "You look foxy" connotates affection or playfulness. "Screw you," a very sexual term, is used to express hostility.[51]

The aggressive offender is the personification of the "Screw you" message. His sexual behavior—the violent molestation of children— is his way of communicating his message of anger and worthlessness to the larger world. The sex act is secondary to his need to humiliate and control the victim and at the same time to offend society. Fortunately this type of offender represents a small minority of child molesters.

## Same-sex Offenders

We traditionally think of child molestation as something done to young girls by adult men. Some victims are boys, but we have no *unbiased* statistics about the incidence of boy victims of child molestation.

Protective agencies tell us that only one victim in ten is a boy.[52] It is an educated guess that cases of boy molestation are more underreported than cases of girl molestation. Prison studies, on the other hand, report that three of every ten victims are boys.[53] There is a large gap between representing 10 per cent of the victims to representing 30 per cent, and some colleagues interviewed believe boys are *equally* (50 per cent) at risk as victims.[54] There are many reasons for the discrepancies.

Reporting is skewed because the boy victim may never tell anyone about the incident. Feelings of self-perceived culpability, pride, fear, or confusion may keep him from asking for help.

> I sort of understood what this guy was asking me to do, but not really. I figured the reason it had happened was because I wasn't supposed to be playing there. I'd promised my parents I wouldn't, and I didn't want them to say, "I told you so." [twenty-five-year-old past victim as a small child]

> He got me just that one time. I didn't want anyone to think I was a queer, so I just stayed away from the pool and never told anyone. [ten-year-old victim]

If the child does tell his parents, they might not report the incident, believing exposure will further traumatize their son. Certainly they are as outraged as they would be if their daughter were a victim, but concern over the boy's healthy sexual development is paramount.

> If we made too big a deal out of it, I was worried it would become something he'd never forget. I didn't want it haunting him, so we just transferred him to a different school, never talked about it, and hoped he would get interested in girls when the time comes. Something like that can turn you off forever. [father of young victim]

Often the parents, when told of their son's encounter with a child molester, mistakenly label it as a "homosexual approach." They react very differently than they would if the same man made an identical approach to their daughter. When their son is involved, the offender is considered gay and the approach is homosexual. Disgusted and fearful of the "homosexual approach," the parents overlook the fact that the man was approaching their son as a *child*, not as another male.

When he told us about that guy hassling him on the bus, offering him money to do things, we made sure he never rode the bus again. I couldn't believe it—someone asking a nine-year-old boy to do that. I guess you can't be too careful about those gays. [father of a potential victim]

The parents never reported the incident as potential or actual child molestation.

When they do report, and if the offender is apprehended, his chances of going to prison are greater than if he had molested a little girl. In society's mind, boy molesters have broken two taboos: child sexual abuse and homosexuality. And the molester's defense is limited: The story of the ravishing, seductive little *boy* does not work as well as the "Lolita made me do it" rationalization. The offender has less of a chance to explain away his offense, and in double jeopardy for having offended society, the few boy molesters who go to trial are more likely to be found guilty and receive substantial prison sentences.

Boy victims' average age range is twelve to fifteen years old, which is older than the average girl victim.[55] In two thirds of the cases, the boy is molested by a friend or acquaintance.[56] His one-in-three chance of being molested by a stranger is slightly higher than the girl victim's one-in-four chance. The offender is often found in child-care roles: baby-sitter, activities leader, teacher, or church or school person. Boy victims are *not* more in danger of violent offenses.

Many offenders choose boy victims, first and foremost, because they want to have sex with a child, and individual circumstances dictate that boys are the most accessible children. For some, premeditation—especially the desire not to get caught—leads them to boy victims. Convenience rules their choice:

I molest boys because they don't get pregnant. [thirty-four-year-old offender]

When I want a relationship with a kid, I like to get to know them first. It takes a long time to figure out if I can trust them. If I hang around a bunch of girls playing volleyball, as an adult male, I stand out like a sore thumb. But if I'm around a bunch of boys every day, playing baseball or something, nobody thinks twice about it. [twenty-two-year-old offender]

Parents are the problem, you know, they are always checking up on the girl, making sure they know where she is. With boys, there isn't that hassle. The parents assume he can take care of himself, they don't check up, and it gives me more time to work with. [thirty-seven-year-old offender]

As with any molester, individual needs or personal history determines who is the desired victim:

I wish someone had been a friend to me when I was a boy his age—do the kind of things I do for these boys. Teaching someone about sex is really important and I'm just glad I'm here to do it. [twenty-five-year-old offender]

Anyone can push a little girl around, tell her what to do. They are easy victims. Now, little boys—they have a mind of their own and to get them to go along with you is a challenge. [forty-two-year-old offender]

I pick up boys because I was a boy. [thirty-six-year-old offender]

For some, there are specifics of sex with boys that are more attractive than sex with girls:

I used to like girls, but they aren't as sexually curious or spontaneous as boys. Girls are less discreet. Boys are more sexually free, you know, less hung up. [twenty-nine-year-old offender]

I look for the most sexless-looking kid I can find. It's all the mess of adult sex that turns me off, and boys smell less than girls. [thirty-year-old offender]

Boys are better because they are like women without all that nagging and whining. They still have high-pitched voices, no hair yet, their skin is so soft. It's all the sensuous things without any of the hassles. [thirty-year-old offender]

Opportunism is the predominant feature in the varied reasons given for choosing boys. The other common theme is that the of-

fender is choosing a *child* instead of an adult. To the offender, boys
are more child than male. As stated before, the majority of child
molesters do have an adult sexual preference, which they may
choose *not* to act on, or will be sexually active with *both* adults
and children at the same time. Given this situation, it is important
to understand that few boy molesters express or act upon a homosexual adult preference. Simply, most boy molesters are not gay.

Society in general tends to have two views on the relationship
between homosexuality and child molestation. On the one hand, we
seem to believe that all homosexuals are innate child molesters. If
they can't find a boy to molest, then they will molest a girl. Any
child will do. On the other hand, some of us might believe that
very few child molesters desire sexual relations with boys, but those
who do comprise the entire population of homosexuals. The facts
strongly dispute both views.

From 15 to 25 per cent of boy molesters are married at the time
of their offenses.[57] In Kinsey's overall study on human sexuality,
he found that only 3 per cent of the homosexual men in his large
sample were child molesters. This is a far *lower* percentage than
the projected percentage of offenders among heterosexual men.[58]

Two additional studies demonstrate the paradoxes of boy molesters whose adult sexual preference is *not* for men. The first experiment showed a series of landscape slides and a subsequent series
of nude-girl slides to a group of nonoffending heterosexual men.
The same series of landscapes followed by a series of nude-boy
slides was shown to nonoffending gay men. Not surprisingly, the
heterosexuals were neutral to the landscape slides. However, they
were notably aroused by the nude-girl slides, and the gay men remained neutral to both the landscape and the nude-boy slides.[59]

The second study administered a measurement of heterosexual
orientation to three groups: same-sex child molesters, opposite-sex
child molesters, and nonoffending heterosexuals. According to the
Edwards Personality Preference Scale, the same-sex child molesters
had the *strongest* heterosexual orientation of the three groups.[60]

The majority of same-sex offenders report being repulsed by
homosexuality.

Sex with kids is good, even sex with women is O.K., but sex

with another guy is *really* unnatural. [twenty-four-year-old offender]

Same-sex offenders do not identify themselves as homosexual, and in fact, many have never had sexual relations with an adult man.

Once this guy came up to me on the street and propositioned me, and I hit him, knocked him right down in front of everyone. [twenty-eight-year-old offender]

Above all, same-sex offenders are gratified by sex with children; somewhere in their development they decided boys were preferable sex objects to girls, but rarely does this decision reflect on their adult preference. If the issue was as simple as desiring sex with another male, same-sex offenders would molest each other. Given a choice between sex with an adult male and sex with a child, the same-sex offender would choose the child as a sex partner.

As we might imagine, gay men are as perplexed by and disapproving of the sexual abuse of boys as many heterosexual men are condemning of girl molestation. The rejection of an adult relationship in favor of sex with an unknowing, malleable child makes no sense to *any* healthy adult, regardless of sexual orientation.

I love men because of the specialness I find in that relationship, the give-and-take, the sharing, the choice we both exercise to both be with each other. I can't even stand emotionally immature men, let alone children. [thirty-year-old gay man]

The same-sex offender is no different from any other child molester; he strives to be equal with his victim. The child is desired for his or her compliance and lack of expectations. Considering the offender's childlike state of mind, to deem his choice as analogous to a sexual relationship between two adult men is akin to saying that Tony and Sam were "gay" when they masturbated in the woods.

The furor over child molestation as a "homosexual problem" is unfounded. It is curious that although opposite-sex offenses are anywhere from twice as to nine times more prevalent, girl molesting is never discussed as a "heterosexual problem."

In addition to the terms "heterosexual" and "homosexual" to describe adult sexual preference, we need a third category. A child molester is neither heterosexual nor homosexual; he is a *child* molester.

## Child Prostitution

Each year, at least one million American children run away from home.[61] An estimated 40 to 60 per cent of these children will be involved in child pornography and/or prostitution.[62] The use of children for these "enterprises" is a variation on an old theme: the sexual abuse of children.

Some leave home because they were victims of child sexual abuse, and their lifestyle on the streets leads to further victimization. For those who left for reasons other than sexual abuse, indoctrination into the street life will provide them with their first incident of child sexual abuse. As we consider the roles of the customer and the pimp, we find that they are, in fact, offenders. Child prostitution is not an "alternative lifestyle" available to "loose" kids looking for easy money. Pimps and customers use confused children who have few, if any, resources for daily survival. The entire industry of child prostitution and child pornography is dependent upon the imbalance of power, knowledge, and resources between the adults who make the money and the children who are the victims.

Induction into pornography and prostitution is almost ritualistic and differs little from the enticement the "neighborhood child molester" uses to gain access to victims. It begins when the child arrives in a large city, such as New York or Los Angeles. As he gets off the bus, he doesn't quite know where to begin. The stress of whatever drove him from home combined with the confusion of this new environment is very apparent as the child is spotted by a "runner" who works for a pimp. The runner offers to buy his new prospect a meal, then eventually provides a place to stay and advice on how to make a living in the city.

> At first I thought this guy just liked to help kids. I felt lucky that he saw me in the bus station and came over to help me. I don't know what I would have done otherwise—later I learned

he worked for the pimp I got mixed up with. Some friend!
[fourteen-year-old girl prostitute]

It is no surprise when the thirteen- or fourteen-year-old boy cannot find a job. The "runner" will "help" him look some more and insist the boy continue to stay at his place for free. Depression sets in, and although the child might not feel comfortable "crashing" with the runner, the child does not have enough money to live on his own and he has no other choice.

To combat the depression or perhaps under the guise of a "good time," the runner might introduce the boy to drugs. Chances are he has experimented with light drugs, such as marijuana, before, but now he has moved on to bigger and better highs. The drugs and/or alcohol help relieve the despair he feels in his new life.

I left home because I didn't think things could get any worse. I really thought there "was no place to go but up," but two weeks in that city, with no job, no money, nothing to do, depending on this stranger for everything, well, that was definitely down. [fourteen-year-old boy prostitute]

"Feeling good" under the influence of drugs does not help him get a job. Eventually the runner offers the boy an "easy way to make some money." Perhaps posing for a child pornographer is the proposition, or a passive involvement in prostitution with one of the runner's "trusted" customers.

The way I got into this was easy and painless. I just had to pose with my friend who helped me when I came to the city— but then the money really wasn't good enough, so I went on to do more. [thirteen-year-old boy prostitute]

Living in the city costs more money than children can usually make as pornography models. If a drug habit has been acquired to help blur the emptiness of the boy's life, then even more money will be needed. This necessitates moving into new areas of the industry: street hustling, bar hustling, or becoming a call boy.

And so his "career" begins. The boy who came to the city to escape an intolerable home situation has been defeated by lack of resources and social services. He becomes a prostitute, an option that probably had never crossed his mind before.

Covenant House, in New York City, is an agency that tries to affect that option whenever it can, providing food, shelter, counseling, health services, and whatever else is needed to five thousand children each year. Over two thousand of these children, ranging in ages from twelve to eighteen, are involved in child pornography and/or prostitution, and a staggering one thousand of the kids are under fifteen years old.[63]

The agency is located in Times Square, across the street from some of Broadway's best theaters. It serves the "Minnesota Strip" (named after the plethora of Midwest runaways working as prostitutes in the area), a ten-city-block area, including Eighth Avenue in the lower Forties and the arcades and bars along Forty-second Street. The "Minnesota Strip" is a disconcerting scene, dominated by adult women prostitutes contrasted with crowds of boy prostitutes, who outnumber girl prostitutes two to one.[64] New York City children comprise 55 per cent of Covenant House's caseload, 35 per cent are out-of-state runaways, and the remaining 10 per cent are New York State children.[65]

Why the children leave home offers us clues to why they become prostitutes. Studies report a range of 40 to 70 per cent incidence of prior sexual abuse for girl prostitutes.[66] There are no statistics about prior sexual abuse of boy prostitutes, but we can safely assume it is a factor in some cases. Having already been abused, what would a child have to lose receiving money, used for daily survival, for something that has already been done in the name of parental authority or "friendship"?

The full range of societal and family problems also contribute to the child's exit from home: problems in school, chronic boredom, no jobs, alcoholism, or physical abuse in the home. One Covenant House staff member noted that many of the children are "throwaways," forced out of their homes because of economic considerations:

> It is not unusual to see a kid "thrown out" of his or her home because the family can no longer care for them. Often these kids come from broken marriages or poor families where the

welfare allowance is woefully inadequate for a single mother to feed and care for her children. I've heard a mother say, "I love Johnny and I want him but I just can't afford to keep him." Johnny, the oldest, finds himself on the street, no home, no school, no skills. His parent, faced with overwhelming odds in this society, is forced into circumstances beyond her control. Johnny becomes the first casualty. Times Square—his new battleground.

Child prostitutes do not come from the ranks of street hoodlums or conspicuous "bad kids." They may have been delinquent to the extent of truancy and petty crimes, but their behavior was more of a transient indicator of their family problems than an antisocial lifestyle. Many runaways make the conscious decision to become prostitutes rather than push drugs or steal. They just want to survive; they are not interested in "ripping anyone off." Prostitution, they conclude, doesn't hurt anyone. Unfortunately, they cannot afford to recognize that prostitution is hurting *them*, but the priority is not self-enhancement; the reality is daily survival at the least cost to other people.

I thought about pushing drugs, but I know how that goes, how many kids get into heavy using, and what it does to their lives. I was having a hard enough time. What good would it do to give someone else a hard time too? [sixteen-year-old boy prostitute]

Stealing increases the chances of police involvement, whereas child prostitution is relatively "safe."

I don't want to steal because if I get caught by the cops, I won't make it in jail. I have to sell myself to get by. [sixteen-year-old boy prostitute]

All they have to sell is their bodies, which is no minor asset. In a culture that promotes sex with children, the pimp can make a lucrative career out of brokering this "hot commodity."

Where and how the child sells his body is complicated. He can be placed anywhere along a hierarchy, depending on his age, attractiveness, intelligence, visibility of drug involvement, and his "luck."

Child pornography is sometimes, but not always, the child prostitute's entrance into the hierarchy. It is often part of the induction process, used to "desensitize" the child to sexual exploitation, but the money is not consistent enough in pornography to provide a total livelihood for a child living in the city. As Father Bruce Ritter, founder and director of Covenant House, states:

> These children cannot go home, cannot find jobs nor take care of themselves. First they are approached to pose in the nude and it is a quick progression to engage in sexual acts for movies or in strip joints along Eighth Avenue for a hundred dollars for four performances.[67]

Some children can afford to work *only* as pornography models, never needing to "diversify" as a result of financial pressure. They live at home and their parents are their agents. In 1974, a suburban Long Island couple ran an ad in *Screw* magazine offering two hundred dollars for one day's nude shooting of girls aged eight to fourteen. Numerous parents answered the advertisement, ordering their daughters to pose for the photographer.[68] For the children working without the "benefit" of agent/parents, it is a very small step from pornography to real-life enactments of sex acts through prostitution.

The bottom rung of the prostitution hierarchy is the street hustler. He or she concentrates on one-time contacts, providing the requested sexual activity as quickly and as painlessly as possible. With girl prostitutes, the procurement is fairly direct and is often handled by a pimp. She has little or no veto power over what is requested of her. Boys, on the other hand, free-lance more, working either the streets or arcades. Often negotiations are carried out as the potential customer buys the boy a meal. They agree to the price and specific acts of the encounter.

The street hustler commands the lowest price so she or he either earns less than other prostitutes or has to turn more "tricks" (customers) to survive. Newness to the city, lack of familiarity with the business of prostitution, young age, unattractiveness, or an obvious drug dependency would account for a child beginning as a street hustler.

The next stratum is the bar prostitute. The child must *look* old enough to get into a bar or strip joint, or to be able to work in a disco or nightclub as busboys or occasionally waiters or waitresses and procure customers. The bar hustler makes more money for the same service provided by the street hustler. Contacts may be occasional and one-time, although there is more of a chance for a long-term working relationship between customer and prostitute. The contact process is very similar to the heterosexual singles-bar pickup. Not only do the children look older, but also they are probably attractive and less likely to have a noticeable drug habit. They may or may not have a pimp.

The highest position in the hierarchy is call boy or call girl. These children cater to special clients, make the most money, and have, by far, the best chance of earning their livelihood by the servicing of one customer. Especially attractive and flexible (in the sense of being willing to perform the more bizarre sexual requests) children become call boys or call girls.

The people who control and procure these children are not called "pimps." They are called businessmen. One New York businessman has a ring of over a hundred call boys whose clients are the upper echelons of New York society, including entertainers, sports figures, and other businessmen. He was convicted of procurement and his sentence was five years' probation.

No matter what level of the hierarchy the child is working at, girl prostitutes are far more likely to have a pimp than boy prostitutes. Because so many of the girls come from destructive home situations, with few or no healthy relationships with men, they are more vulnerable to the emotional security and protection the pimp has to offer.

I know lots of people don't understand my pimp, but he's the best to me—no one has ever cared as much about me. [fourteen-year-old girl prostitute]

Girls also feel they need the pimp's "protection" from both customers and police. The pimp presents himself as the father figure, able to "choose" customers who supposedly won't hurt her and willing to bail her out of jail if arrested. The typical teen-age girl prostitute believes she needs this type of guardian.

He's gotten me out of trouble with the cops or during tricks lots of times. I know my pimp isn't too far away from me on the street. [sixteen-year-old girl prostitute]

The pimps pretend to provide a family. The names they give themselves smack of this ludicrous ostentation. Note the many sugar derivatives in their names: Cotton Candy, Sugar Daddy, Poppa Bear, Sweet Honey, and Chocolate Drop. We might expect a person as exploitive as a pimp to have a name like the Grand Inquisitor or Bad News, yet all of the names imply warmth, sweetness, memories of childhood, and, above all, benignness.

A pimp with two or three children is called a Popcorn or a Macaroni pimp. Those who have many more child prostitutes working for them are called Macks or Players. No matter how many children they exploit, the pimps insist they provide an important service to both the children and society.

I always tell my kids, "Daddy will take care of you. . . ." It makes them feel real good. No one else ever said that to them. [Times Square pimp]

No one ever gave *me* the kind of affection and guidance I give these girls. Most of them never had it so good. [West Coast pimp]

To further their hold on the girls, pimps manipulate the children's already poor self-concept by convincing them that prostitution is all they can do.

My pimp used to tell me, he said for my own good, that I really wasn't talented or skilled enough to do anything else so I should just stay with him because I was good on the streets and safe with him. [fourteen-year-old girl prostitute]

Some girls get married and others get good jobs. For me, it's like my pimp says, I was born to be on a street corner. [thirteen-year-old girl prostitute]

Boy prostitutes, on the other hand, generally work independently of a pimp. The patriarchal values of our society once again have a profound influence. Boy prostitutes are considered *not* to need as much protection, nor are they as easily allured by the pimp's promise of eternal love. Boys in general are less predisposed or conditioned to turn their hard-earned money over to someone else, and boy prostitutes are no exception.

> Boys just aren't worth the trouble. They can move on easily and they don't follow orders as well as girls. Too much of a mind of their own—my investment is much better with girls. [West Coast pimp]

> Guys can handle trouble on their own. What would I need a pimp for? I get more business than I need just hanging out in the arcades. [fifteen-year-old boy prostitute]

A boy prostitute can "learn the business" by watching or befriending another boy prostitute, and, in fact, sometimes older, more experienced prostitutes will operate as a Popcorn pimp, controlling one or two younger boys. Because there are so many boys vulnerable to prostitution, and so many *new* runaway boys arriving in large cities every day, if a boy prostitute drifts away from his pimp, he can easily be replaced.

The pimp's desire to control and exploit is *not* only a reflection of his sick psyche; child prostitution and pornography are big business. The *lowest* published estimate of the yearly gross of the Times Square sex industry is $1.5 *billion*.[69] Experts in the field believe it must be much, much higher, and their projection is confirmed at least by the sale of one book as an example. *Where the Boys Are*, a catalogue of where to find boy prostitutes in thirty-five major cities, sold seventy thousand copies at $5.00 per book.[70]

Who are the men who buy these books and solicit the services of child prostitutes? Although a hefty portion are white, middle- and upper-class "family" men from the suburbs or traveling on business, child molestation masquerading as "an odd evening out on the town" knows no class, racial, age, or occupational boundaries. There is no one profile of the customer of the child prostitute.

It is interesting to note that most boy prostitutes have contempt for the men who are their customers, regularly referring to them as "gays," "fags," or "queers." Of course, the child prostitutes do not understand the distinction; their customers desire sexual relations with a *child*, not another male. Some boy prostitutes will not agree to any form of penetration, as a way of keeping their masculine image intact.

Dyed-in-the-wool child molesters also have very few kind words for the customers of child prostitutes.

> If you have to pay for it, it isn't worth having. It's second-class sex. Not having a relationship with a kid but still sleeping with him is wrong. [thirty-two-year-old offender]

Any competent child sexual abuser should be able to cajole or threaten a child into co-operation; laying down cold cash takes the sport out of it.

While the pimps and businessmen and organized crime count the customers' money, physical and emotional scars compound on the children earning the billions of dollars. A high rate of venereal disease and drug usage among child prostitutes is assumed. One social worker who works with bar prostitutes observes chronic depression as a major problem:

> In leaving home, they have lost a parent. It is like the parent had died and the child is going through the grieving process. They have a lot of sadness, sense of loss and some anger at the situation which they turn inward on themselves. Any child will have a lifetime of lovers, but she has only one chance at a parent.[71]

A strong sense of camaraderie comes out of these common feelings. Child prostitutes look out for each other, and for many, the affection they give to each other is the only sense of family they have ever known.

> I work the same place every day. I can't stand the work but the other kids on that part of the street are terrific. It's pretty much the same kids every day, and we really notice when someone suddenly isn't there anymore. [fourteen-year-old girl prostitute]

Child prostitutes speak the same language. According to one Covenant House staff member, words like "despair," "doubt," "confusion," and "pain" are prominent in the child prostitute's conversation:

> A lack of control over the situation seems to be a common theme. Often they say, "When will someone help me?" or "When will it all end?"[72]

For a few it ends in murder. Approximately two hundred prostitutes in New York City have been murdered over the past three years; at least five of them were child prostitutes.[73]

Covenant House has successfully reunited twelve hundred children with their families.[74] Other child prostitutes become adult prostitutes, or are "kept" by one customer in an ongoing service.

Boy prostitutes have shorter careers. When the boy loses his "boyishness," his greatest asset (childhood) is gone. Some move down to the Bowery or pursue other lifestyles to support their dependency on drugs or alcohol. After five or more years on the streets, crime may not seem as reprehensible as it did when the child first shunned "ripping someone off" as a way to make a living. What would we call what has happened to him for the past five years? The life expectancy on Skid Row or "on the road," using crime as a source of income, is not very long.

According to caseworkers in the field, a child needs to receive intervention and services and try to make a healthy transition by age sixteen for the most positive future. A constant connection with caring adults is needed throughout adolescence. In this respect, as in many others, the child prostitute does not differ from any other teen-ager.

The connection between child molestation and child prostitution is clear. Consider these two situations:

> A businessman pays a fourteen-year-old boy who lives on the street twenty-five dollars to fellate him.

> A swim coach requires a socially alienated fourteen-year-old boy to fellate him before he allows him to try out for the team.

Is there really any significant difference? Both adults have enormous power over the children, yet one is called a customer and the other is called a child molester. Both children believe their emotional or

physical survival depends on pleasing the adult, yet one child is
called a "hustler" or "bad kid" and the other child is called a
victim. We do not believe that the average fourteen-year-old possesses the skills or the judgment to venture forth into a full-time
career, but we often think of the child prostitute as *choosing* the
street life for the money or the glamor. How is it that the average
fourteen-year-old is *just* a teen-ager, but the boy prostitute, at the
same age, is a self-made man?

First the child is possibly victimized at home, which can lead to
prostitution. The induction into the sex industry is a slight variation
on the process used by neighborhood child molesters. Time and
time again, the child prostitute services the customers' urges for sexual relations with a child. Customers and pimps of child prostitutes
satisfy their needs and enhance their egos through servitude rather
than through tricks or threats. The process is one of capitalism
rather than manipulation, but the result is the same: Another child
is sexually exploited by an adult.

## Impact on the Victim

Child-molestation victims rarely are the stars of contemporary
dramas. When we do see a movie concerning the sexual abuse of
the child, it is generally told from the victim's point of view, as
an adult in-patient in a mental institution. She will probably never
be "cured." Or the story is of the older man falsely accused by a
conniving little girl who lies about this sort of thing just for the
fun of it. He is a broken man—his life capriciously ruined. He is
so down and out, he doesn't even hate the sleazy little girl who
did this to him. That is our job, as the audience.

These sporadic misportrayals of the impact on the victim are
neither accurate nor helpful. Every victim of child sexual abuse
needs sympathetic, professional intervention, even if it is just one
visit to a social worker to clarify that the child is not responsible
for the crime. Anyone who has spent any amount of time around
children is amazed at their resiliency—we can't remember the time
when we, too, were like that. Victims who do not receive any services may have long-standing problems, but few vanish to back

wards of mental institutions for the rest of their lives. Unfortunately, this is what immediately comes to the minds of many parents of victims.

Sexual abuse *does* have an impact on the child. The degree of impact can be measured by several variables.[75] These variables, interfacing with each other, will affect the severity of the child victim's feeling of disruption. Quick and responsible intervention goes a long way to alleviate the impact.

The first variable is the relationship between the offender and the victim. Common sense tells us that a crime committed by a total stranger is less likely to be as traumatic as sexual abuse by a trusted and loved parent. Yet, we must be careful of our assumptions in this area. The offender may have at one time been a stranger to the child, and may still be a stranger to the parents, but over the course of the molestation the child established a relationship with the offender which, in the child's mind, was built on trust and love.

> I kept on trying to get my parents to understand that Charlie was my friend. They didn't know him but they wanted to get him fired at his job in the school. I didn't want that, because then Charlie wouldn't have any food to eat. [eight-year-old victim]

So we must assess the depth of the relationship according to the child's definition, not the parents' or that of other authorities.

The duration of the sexual abuse is another important variable. There is a difference between the child who was "felt up" once in a movie theater and immediately told the manager, and the child who is molested for six months by his baby-sitter so he can stay up late on school nights. This is not to minimize the one-time incident of sexual abuse. However, many times we make the mistake of treating the one-time incident not with concern, but with the horror of a mass murder. For the child, the one-time incident is probably an unpleasant experience they would never want to go through again, but it is not an integrated, ongoing part of their existence.

> For weeks after the assault, my parents kept looking at me with this really anxious look. They stayed around me a lot, waiting

for me to have a nervous breakdown, I think. I was really into this science project and just kept on working on it. After all, it was just this creepy guy on the bus—it wasn't that big of a deal. Finally my parents got over it—but it was a long time after I did. [adult victimized as a small child]

Children who have had to live with regular sexual abuse are more impacted, as their survival becomes connected with the abuse.

The third variable affecting the child victim is the type of sex play involved in the molestation. Victims of penetration, sodomy, or other offenses against children that culminate in physical injury will, of course, be visibly impacted by the injury. If mutual masturbation, exhibitionism, or less physically injurious forms of sex play were involved, the younger child may perceive them as a "game" and not be visibly upset. While on the one hand, we should make no assumption about how any given form of sexual abuse will affect the individual child, we should not impose our *adult* interpretations (and resultant emotions) of the sex act on the child.

My parents were real religious, and they didn't believe in oral-genital sex, like it was against Church doctrines and all. When they found out that was what the baby-sitter had done to me, they freaked out. I thought it was really odd—that's why I told them about it—but at six years old, I didn't think anyone had to go to hell over it. [adult victimized as a small child]

As discussed in the earlier section on aggressive offenders, the victim of both physical and sexual abuse is most impacted. Two separate dynamics—that of the sexual abuse and that of the physical violence—combine to create a traumatic situation for the victim.

It was just that one time, but I think the beating scared me more than his making me suck his thing. I knew I'd live through that, but when he twisted my arm behind my back, I wasn't sure I was going to live through it. [adult victimized as a small child]

When I was in the hospital, they were stitching up my face, where he had hit me so hard. I forgot to tell them about the sex part until later. I was more worried about my cut-up face. [eleven-year-old victim]

In all cases, it is wise to have a trained physician examine the child victim and reassure the child that his or her body hasn't changed or been damaged because of the sexual abuse. With the victim of physical violence *and* sexual abuse, it goes without saying that sensitive and thorough medical attention is an absolute must. This type of victim might benefit from some long-range intervention to deal with a wide range of feelings—from helplessness to anger—resulting from the offense.

For the longest time, I had dreams about hurting him. Not even doing anything sexual—I just wanted to hit him back, to make him fall down, to break *his* nose. [adult victimized as an adolescent]

The fifth variable affecting the impact on the victim is the child's age and developmental level. Parents are sometimes amazed at the calmness of their five-year-old child who has been molested by the baby-sitter or the neighbor. They are waiting for the authorities to arrive, and the child entertains herself playing with Tonka toys. When the police arrive, she might be more intrigued by the fancy car and peculiar uniforms than she is interested in talking about what went on with the offender.

I remember how I really weirded everyone out. They sent a policewoman, thinking it would be easier for me to talk to her. I told them I wasn't going anyplace with a policewoman—it was a policeman or nothing. [adult victimized as a small child]

Not understanding the offender's actions, the victim has no particular feelings about the incident. This is not to say that child molestation isn't harmful or shouldn't be stopped; however, younger children need not always be visibly traumatized by sexual abuse. On the other hand, an older child who has an understanding of sexuality might know that what has happened is wrong and feel violated as well as responsible for the crime. The child's perception of the offense will vary with many circumstances, but we should not demand trauma from a child too young to display adequately the disdain we think she should feel.

The last and perhaps most important variable is the reaction of the parents or other important people around the victim. There are many components to this, and experts agree that this is the single most important factor in preventing the abuse from becoming a life-destroying event.

Do the adults important to the child (significant adults) believe the child? Is her statement about the molestation immediately accepted or is she questioned before believed?

> I told my parents about it right away. I expected them to believe me and *do* something about it. He lived in the neighborhood and I was scared of him. They asked me a thousand questions—because they had just given me a rinky-dink lecture on the birds and the bees, they thought I was making it up. They never did anything, and I never forgave them for it. [adult victimized as a small child]

Many children don't tell about the abuse because they fear no one will believe them.

Unfortunately, some of us still believe children lie about child sexual abuse to be vindictive. In false reports (which are very small in number), we most often find one *adult* filing a report in behalf of the child, accusing the other adult when there has been conflict between the two adults. A few parents will dismiss the child's complaint about sexual abuse as "confusing fantasy with real life." Young children speak from their own experience—they don't have the sophistication or the motivation to fabricate an accusation. Children can and should be believed. They do not have extensive sexual fantasies involving adults.

Some parents go to great lengths to test the child's veracity, such as ordering the child to confront the accused in person with the parents as witnesses. Inasmuch as the denial systems of child sexual abusers are extremely strong and well developed, this type of scene can only add to the child's trauma.

> My parents dragged me over to my coach's house. I was screaming and crying the whole way. He was the last person I wanted to see, but they were intent on this big confrontation. Of course he denied it—said I was trying to get him into trouble because I didn't make the team. My parents weren't too bright anyway, and they believed him. I don't know which was more

traumatic—the molestation or that scene. [adult victimized as a small child]

Do the significant adults reassure the child they will take care of her and protect her? Many victims fear being rejected or abandoned by their families because of the abuse. Not wanting to make trouble, they keep the secret. They also fear the offender's retaliation, which may have been an expressed threat.

He told me that if I told anyone, he'd come and do the same thing to all my little sisters. So I thought I'd better warn my sisters about him. My littlest sister went space cookie, and she's the one who told Mom. Not me, I would never tell. [ten-year-old victim]

The adults need to assure the child that they still love her, that she is not a bad person because this has happened, and that they will do everything they can to ensure her safety.

How much energy do the significant adults put into blaming? Do they enter into a vigilante movement against the offender?

My parents had a big neighborhood meeting in our house. They told everyone what had happened over at church. Then those parents told their kids, who teased me. I was really sorry I'd told anyone. [adult victimized as a small child]

This can have a backlash on the child, increasing the trauma because the child will believe *she* is responsible for the terrible things happening to the offender. Many times children are in the wrong place at the wrong time when the offense happens. She has been warned not to be with a certain person or to go to a specific place. If the offense is perpetrated by this person or happens in this place, the child is likely to interpret the molestation as punishment for disobeying the significant adult.

I don't know how many times I was warned about that guy, but I was fascinated by him. He never did anything—just sat there in the park. So I figured he was safe. It turned out he wasn't, and I was only five at the time. I was sure my parents told him to do something to me if I ever went near him, so he was just

teaching me a lesson. It was years before I told. [adult victimized as a small child]

She should be reassured that while you are not happy about her
disobeying you, she did not deserve to have this happen, the offender was very wrong, and you forgive her for her disobedience.
In other words, don't blame the victim.

Significant adults also blame themselves—they should have
watched the child, told her more about sexual abuse, not trusted
the offender, etc. As terrific as hindsight can be, it is of no good
whatsoever to the child victim. She will feel responsible for the
significant adults blaming themselves. Self-blame can be as misdi-
rected and inaccurate as blaming the victim. The responsibility lies
with the offender, no matter how precarious a situation the child
was in. Many other men would have encountered the child in that
situation and *not* molested her. It is important to keep this in mind.
The clarity that comes with insisting that the responsibility lies with
the offender will help minimize the impact on the victim. She needs
to be sure that child molestation is *his* problem, and she is not
changed or degraded as a person because of his problem.

Do the significant adults let the child ventilate her feelings about
the incident? This is very important if the child is to place the abuse
in its proper perspective and not be ruled by it. Adults make two
mistakes in this regard. First, they sometimes talk incessantly about
the offense. Their theory is that if it gets all talked out it will go
away. In a matter-of-fact manner, they will repeat the story to
neighbors, relatives, anyone who will listen.

For a couple of months after the molestation, my father was
obsessed with it. Everywhere we went, he'd point out the adult
men. Was that the guy? he'd keep on asking. I got so sick of
it, I'd just say "no," without looking at the man. [adult victimized as a small child]

It was the talk of the neighborhood for weeks—especially after
they arrested him. I was a star—I got more attention than anyone else in my neighborhood. [nine-year-old victim]

Although the adults' intentions might be helpful, the incident takes
on larger-than-life proportions for the child victim. The victim

learns that mentioning the offense is a sure-fire way to get attention, and it takes on a life of its own. Or the victim may feel overpowered by the incessant discussion, and take on feelings of greater trauma than she felt previously about the offense.

The other common, though well-intentioned, mistake is to tell the child it is all over and not to think about it. Natural questions that child victims have for perhaps six months after the offense are squelched. If the molestation can't be talked about openly, the child reasons this must be something *really* bad, like Godzilla or the boogieman.

Anytime I asked a question, everyone would say "Now, that happened a long time ago—it's all in the past. Just pray to God that it never happens to you again." I didn't want to pray. I wanted some answers. [adult victimized as a small child]

Having been directly involved in this terrible thing, the child concludes she must be terrible. Her natural curiosity turns into self-doubt—a very undesirable effect. If the child had broken her arm or lost a pet, the parents would be more open to her questions, allowing her to work through her feelings and learn from the experience. It is, unfortunately, not as easy for some parents to participate in the child's process of integrating a traumatic experience like child sexual abuse.

It is not uncommon for significant adults to change the routine of the child after an incident. Although some precautions might be needed to enhance the child's safety, it is best to maintain normal schedules. One study showed that 25 per cent of the parents of victims wanted to move out of their neighborhood after the sexual abuse committed by a person outside the family was discovered, while only 11 per cent of *their children* desired to move.[76] Major changes in meal, recreation, or sleep patterns are unsettling to children under normal circumstances. When the disruption follows the sexual abuse, the child concludes the offense is something that will rule her life. If she believes it can change how her entire family operates, it will have a stronger impact.

One common routine of the family that should be preserved as much as possible is the normal expression of affection. Perhaps at first the child victim will not want to be held and kissed, but on the other hand, perhaps this is what the child wants more than anything. Ask the child—don't make assumptions. If we stop hugging our child or kissing her good night because we assume this will bring back memories of the offense, the child can easily misinterpret this. She could conclude that you are punishing her for the offense; she isn't worthy of affection; or she might equate all normal affection with the offense.

> All of a sudden, they stopped kissing me or hugging me. They still did that to my younger sisters, and it really hurt me. When I tried to hug them, they were O.K., but I didn't want to take the initiative all the time. When I grew up, I asked my parents about it, and they told me they didn't want to scare me. But that is exactly what *pushing* me away did. [adult victimized as a small child]

While we need to respect whatever needs for distance the child expresses, we also need to be clear that normal family expression is healthy and has *nothing* to do with the offense.

And, finally, the impact on siblings is an often forgotten but critical aspect of sexual abuse. How do the brothers and sisters feel about the victimization of the sibling? Did they find out in the chaos that followed the discovery, or were they told calmly, as a preventive measure, so the offender cannot abuse them as well? Do they have a previous relationship with the offender and feel confused or ambivalent about what is going on? Were they witness to the abuse? Do they feel guilty because they were not able to help or protect the sibling/victim?

> It was hardest of all on my brother. We were playing together when this man came up to us. When he grabbed me, my brother ran away to get help. But it all happened so quick, by the time he came back with my mother, it was all over. He always thought it was because he couldn't run fast enough, but no one ever talked to him about it. [adult victimized as a small child]

These are all integral questions to minimizing the long-range impact on the child. Again, trained, sensitive intervention can't hurt. It can only help the parents and the child deal with a difficult situation that must seem, at times, out of their control and totally over-whelming.

One study found that 43 per cent of the children showed no *overt* reaction to the sexual abuse.[77] It is important to understand the concept of overt. The child may have had many internal reactions that she chose not to share with those around her. Often we mistake withdrawal for "dealing with the assault" or "forgetting all about it." Some people go one step farther and conclude that because the child shows no outward trauma, the offense never happened. Especially here, the intervention of a trained social worker is important. The child's outward display of emotion has no bearing on her veracity. She perhaps needs help in expressing whatever feelings she has about the offense.

Victims of child sexual abuse display different *behaviors* in response to the offense and the variables discussed above. For the younger child, or for a child who has poor communication with significant adults, the child's unusual behavior may lead to the discovery of the offense—that is, she can't or won't tell anyone about the sexual abuse, but behavioral changes indicate something serious is happening to her.

As we discuss some of the behavioral changes, keep in mind the continuum of child sexual abuse. At the one end we have a one-time offense, and the child tells the significant adults immediately. On the other end, the child has been abused repeatedly, has told no one, and even though the abuse has stopped, continues to be silent. The specific problems of any individual victim will be influenced by where he or she is on that continuum. Symptoms could also change from what they were *before* the silence was broken and *after* the discovery of the offense.

Some of the behavioral changes children manifest during and/or after the molestation are:

- loss of appetite
- changes in sleep patterns
- nightmares
- unprovoked crying spells

- bed wetting
- refusal to go to school
- fear of strange men and/or strange situations
- fear of a specific person or situation
- fear of playing alone
- running away
- social or emotional withdrawal
- clinging to significant adult
- changes in fantasy life (dealing with victimization or violence)
- taking excessive numbers of baths[78]

These symptoms are self-explanatory and are combined in different victims. Without sensitive intervention, the symptoms can become part of the child's personality. With support and intervention, they can serve as warning signals to the child's trauma and be worked through to minimize the damage of the offense.

Nowhere is it written that all child-molestation victims need to be victims their entire lives. Although the offense is probably one of the least constructive events of the child's life, it is not the last word. A child cannot deal alone with the masses of questions, confusion, shame, guilt, feelings, and behavior changes that can follow the offense. With the help of her or his significant adults, and the guidance of trained helpers, the offense can be put in its proper perspective: The child was the victim of another person's problems. This is not a reflection on the child or the parents. The child can grow up normally if it is understood that she or he has not changed into a bad person because of the offense.

# INCEST

## In Our Own Backyards

Most of us have some preconceived notions about where incest can be found. We would like to think it is a problem far away from our own communities and something that just doesn't happen that much. Unfortunately, incest happens often and can be found everywhere, although we do not know exactly to what extent.

The statistical data on incest are unreliable. Many states have different definitions of incest. Some states include distant cousins in their definition, while other states address the statutes to immediate blood relatives only. And there is much disagreement about how step- or adoptive relatives should be prosecuted. These skew any recording of incidence. In addition, much of the general public is confused as to *where* they should report a case of incest. If a concerned person does not trust the police and does not know of any social-service agencies where help is available, the case may go unreported.

Of course, there are cases where the appropriate reporting agencies are known, but individuals choose not to report. Because incest occurs within the confines of the family, there may be great pressure on the victim to "leave it alone"—to deal with it as a family problem. Families fear public disclosure. A victim often fears that reporting sexual abuse will bring on judgments against her. The child may feel that people will accuse her of enticing her father or other offending relative into the relationship. The parents fear loss of job, imprisonment of the offender, and being ostracized by the community. Basically because most families prefer to keep incest a secret, very few cases are recorded.

Where there are treatment facilities or responsive law-enforcement agencies, we find dramatic changes in reporting rates. An example of this can be found in Santa Clara County, California, which has a pioneer program in treatment of incestuous families, the Child Sexual Abuse Treatment Center. According to a 1973 census, the population of Santa Clara County was 1,159,500 people. In 1974, the Child Sexual Abuse Treatment Center handled 180 cases of incest. In 1977, 600 cases were reported to the Center.[79] As we can see, this is a substantial increase over the estimated rate of 1 to 9 cases per million population.[80] Even so, the staff at this program feel they are seeing only the tip of the iceberg. With more resources and treatment programs for incestuous families, they feel there would be even more dramatic rises in reported cases of incest.

We have no clear statistics on the distribution of incest across social classes or economic brackets. American folklore places incest with "hill people." However, they are no more vulnerable to incest than any other subculture or community of people. The incidence of incest is overwhelmingly represented outside of the Appalachian Mountains. Still, it is difficult to say which types of communities experience the greatest problem. We *do* know that virtually no social class or community has escaped the problem. As Sandra Butler says so well in her book *Conspiracy of Silence: The Trauma of Incest*, "Incest is relentlessly democratic."[81]

Again, the source of our best statistics is the Child Sexual Abuse Treatment Center in Santa Clara County.[82] In a sample of 300 families referred to their program, the fathers' occupations were professional, semiprofessional, and skilled blue-collar. The average income was $13,413 per household. The racial breakdown of the 300 families also was consistent with Santa Clara County's racial composition. White families comprised 76.8 per cent of the referrals, 17.5 per cent were Mexican American, 3.0 per cent were Oriental, 1.7 per cent were black, and 1.0 per cent were "other." No one racial group was disproportionately represented.

Few other studies examine the racial or occupational breakdown of incestuous families. Those studies that do provide us with some information about where incest happens are often geared to investigate the incidence among welfare recipients, families participating in prosecution, or offenders in prison. The reporting, prosecution, and incarceration processes in these crimes are definitely selective. Working-class offenders have a higher rate of conviction for all crimes. Because they do not have money for high-powered attorneys, or enough knowledge of the system to "beat the rap," they often are the sources of statistics or the subjects of studies. It would be misleading to conclude that incest is a lower-socioeconomic-class problem.

Because incest has been taboo for so long, it is easy for us to become complacent in our lack of knowledge. Like rape, we assume it will never happen to us. Surely there are not incestuous families in my neighborhood.

> When I read it in the paper, I was sure there was some kind of mistake. They were so quiet. And their kids were such good baby-sitters. [neighbor of incestuous family]

Of course, no incestuous father is active in "my church."

> He was an usher every Sunday. Very reliable, dependable—especially nice to the older parishioners. Didn't seem like the type of guy to do something like that to kids. [minister of church attended by incestuous father]

And definitely no incest victim attends "my daughter's school."

> When she told me why she wouldn't undress in gym, I was suspicious. Then she showed me the marks on her breasts. If it hadn't been for the gym situation coming up, we may have never known. She was so quiet, we just thought she was introverted. [school nurse]

The community attitude that rejects the possibility or ignores the reality is fostering the bases of incest—secrecy and isolation.

Because father-daughter incest accounts for 90 per cent of reported cases, the major portion of this chapter will be addressed to this phenomenon.[83] Other forms of incest (sibling, father-son, mother-son, etc.) will be examined separately, although much of the dynamic is common to all types of incest.

## Poor Self-concept: Where It All Begins

When the parents in an incestuous family first marry, they are afflicted with a lack of self-esteem. They look to each other to meet their needs; neither adult has self-confidence. Each believes the other is needed to complete his or her own self-concept.

> I'll never forget our wedding—we had just graduated from high school. Everyone was there. It was like a fairy tale. We promised always to be together and that we would never need anything else but each other. How was I supposed to know that wasn't enough? Ten years later he would "need" our own daughter. [twenty-eight-year-old wife of an incestuous father]

Without the spouse, each is only half a person. Marriage and family are seen as constituting their niche in life—they never will be alone again.

For a while, they do fairly well at meeting each other's needs. To this end, they are socially isolated, and have few friends. They believe having friendships with other adults is beyond their capabilities, so all of their energy goes into the marriage. Little or no outside interests are developed.

> When we were first married, I joined this bowling league. But then my husband complained because I was gone one night a week. I felt my marriage was more important, so I quit. After a while, I just wasn't very interested in anything. [thirty-two-year-old wife of incestuous father]

The desperate, all-consuming clinging to each other is due, in large part, to the deep-seated belief that *they have nothing to offer* other adults. Not wanting to risk rejection and being unable to face feelings of inadequacy, they invest everything in each other. Most of us recognize this as an unhealthy situation. The marriage did not create the poor self-concept in each of them—that was created and nurtured long before they met each other.

The woman may have been an incest victim herself and inherited all of the self-doubts and fears that go along with victimization. As a woman in American society, she is not given much encouragement to feel good about herself. She has probably been taught that her role is to be incomplete until completed by marriage. She may even be proud of her lack of mastery over her own environment.

I was never interested in school, or jobs, or other things like

that. I think some women are born to stay at home and just
be a wife and mother. I'm sure I'm one of those women. I don't
even care to learn to drive. [thirty-five-year-old wife of an incestuous father]

She honestly believes it is in her best interests to marry this man
and surrender her identity to him.

The man, on the other hand, suffers from his own brand of self-
doubt. Studies show the father's family background frequently includes incidence of sexual or physical abuse; desertion or depriva-
tion of a father figure; general lack of warmth and understanding;
broken home and leaving home at a young age. He sincerely believes the best role for him is to marry and take on full responsibility
for a wife and children. He wants to provide the kind of stability
in his family that he never had. It becomes his whole "life."

There was nothing else I'd rather do. Being at home, watching
TV, having my family around me. It was all I knew. I didn't
like my job. I wasn't good at sports. I hated to travel. At home
I could make a difference. I was somebody to the wife and
kids. [thirty-two-year-old incestuous father]

Not sure he has what it takes to be successful, he cannot let anyone
know what he fears. He is taught to compensate for feelings of overall inadequacy with outward displays of his masculine prowess
within a very narrow context—his family. He must be an excellent
breadwinner, a firm disciplinarian, the guiding light of his wife's
life. No matter how uncomfortable he feels in this role, no matter
how poorly his background has prepared him for this responsibility,
he must never let on.

We were in such bad shape financially. But I couldn't tell my
wife. She would want to go get a part-time job or something
stupid like that. I didn't want the hassle. So I just kept on bor-
rowing money. She didn't know it until I was sentenced to the
treatment program. [thirty-six-year-old incestuous father]

Seemingly free from self-doubt and able to handle *any* situation,
he is the center of his family's world.

It is inevitable that the marriage will be adversely affected by this pressure. The couple's unreasonable expectations of themselves and each other, combined with lack of communication, finally take their toll. By the time the festering dilemma becomes critical, they have had children. Still not believing in their ability to attract and maintain relationships with adults, they treat their children as peers.

## Role Reversal: Adult as Child—Child as Adult

The perception of children and adults as equals is a complicated and at times contradictory dynamic. The average age of the incest victim in America is eleven years.[84] The relationship, according to one study, lasts from three to five years.[85] Although some victims are infants, while others are in their late teens, the girl is likely to be approached around ages five to eight. Contrast that piece of information with the fact that the average incestuous father is in his mid-to-late thirties. An important part of the incest dynamic is that the father—while still being the master of his family's identity —sees himself as having a reciprocal, peerlike relationship with his daughter/victim. Of course, there are single incidents of incest that are never repeated, but generally, incest is ongoing.

The parents look to the children for the same satisfaction of needs, for the same completion of self-concept, that they once sought in each other.

My mom would tell me all about these fights she and Dad had. I never knew what to say. I didn't like it, but it looked like she really needed me to talk to. [thirteen-year-old incest victim]

Whenever things were bad at the factory, all I had to do is think of Lisa. She spent all her time at home with me. Even at five, she could make me feel better. She was the only person I ever looked forward to seeing. [twenty-six-year-old incestuous father]

At the same time, the father remains the supreme ruler in the family. No one is equal to him. The children and the mother operate on a more equal basis. They must look to him for their survival, direction, and identity. Other than this clear distinction between "father" and "nonfather," there is little other role differentiation.

In most American families, the rights and privileges of adults are clearly delineated from the rights and privileges of children. Adults look to each other for support and guidance. They do not use their children to define who they are. Adults are confident enough in their own social skills to venture out and make adult friendships. They do not invest *everything* in the family. And if things go wrong, it is not the child's responsibility to make it up to the adult.

In the average incestuous family, this is not the case. Every family member is on the same shaky footing. None of them are very sure of who they are, or how they fit into the rest of the world. Because the parents have so little going for them outside the family, the children are responsible for the parents' happiness.

> Mom used to tell me to take my dad his dinner when he came home from work. He always went right to the den and wouldn't talk to anyone, except me. He watched the news while he ate dinner. I was the only one that could cheer him up. Mom asks me to tell him things she doesn't want to tell him. [thirteen-year-old incest victim]

In a sense, the child exists to nurture the parent. The parent, feeling emotionally bankrupt, has little to offer the child.

A "trip down memory lane" may be part of the father's motivation for his involvement with his daughter. She might resemble her mother at a time when love was new and the marriage was everything to the father. He vicariously is a young man courting a beautiful, naïve, and giving woman. The important difference is that the daughter is not a woman—she is a child.

In this emotional "time machine" the father is not necessarily perceiving his daughter as another adult. It is more likely that he perceives himself as being much younger than he actually is. He and his daughter become the same age in some purgatory between childhood and adulthood. In contrast, the mother may be seen as the "big, bad adult." Afraid of her judgment, the father stresses the need for secrecy. It is quite analogous to two children entering a deserted house that they've been told time and time again not to go near. The father is telling his daughter, "We'll play this game together, we'll pull the wool over Mommy's eyes. Whatever we do, we can't let Mommy know." The differences between the mother and daughter cannot be denied; mother is an adult, and the daughter is a child. No matter how much the father wishes he was on an equal par with this "sweet young child," the fact remains that he is not.

> I remember how he treated us so differently. Around Mom, he was always so serious, always complaining about money. When he was with me, he was always planning fun things for us to do. It was like two different people. [fourteen-year-old incest victim]

As the child becomes older, the role reversal takes on another dimension. The oldest daughter "inherits" a disproportionate number of household duties.

> It started sort of gradual. I was in junior high, so I went to school later. That meant I got the younger kids breakfast and saw them off to school before I left. Mom wanted to sleep. By the time I was in high school, I was cooking all the meals. [seventeen-year-old incest victim]

Sometimes this is due to a disruption in the family. The mother decides to take a job, go to school, or her work hours change. Perhaps someone in the family is ill and she takes care of them. It might even be that the mother herself is ill or hospitalized. In the mother's absence, the daughter takes over part of the mothering role.

It should be made clear that the mother's absence is not the *cause* of the incestuous situation, nor should she blame herself for precipitating the onset of incest. In some ways, if she moves to interests outside the home, this is a healthy sign. If she had *not* temporarily left the home, the incest probably would have happened anyway. There are enough incestuous families where the mother has not left home to give us reason to believe that such a disruption is not necessarily a prerequisite to the onset of incest.

> The thing I still can't get over is that my mother was right there *in the house* while he was molesting me. He would wait until she went to sleep or was downstairs doing the dishes. [eleven-year-old incest victim]

of the daughter for such things. If he's not happy, why doesn't he get a divorce or have an affair? Anything is better than victimizing the daughter!"

The incestuous father believes differently. He takes Dr. Herman's and Ms. Hirschman's analysis of society's attitude literally. What happens within the family, in his mind, is absolutely no one's business. What to do with his children's lives is totally his prerogative.

When I'd question my dad about what he was doing, you know, if it was right, he would tell me, "You come from me— I made you, so you belong to me." It didn't make a lot of sense at the time, but I couldn't think up anything to say. [thirty-three-year-old woman, victimized as a small child]

As for divorce or an affair, these are not out of the question. However, they are very rare. Incestuous families seem to live by a very strict moral code. The source of this code may be religion, previous military experience, or even conservative political beliefs. The code stresses they are not to go outside the family to meet their needs.

I was working two jobs just to keep the family going. Where would I find the time or money for an affair? [thirty-year-old incestuous father]

All I did is work, go to church on Sunday, and spend time with my family. When would I ever meet somebody to have an affair with? [thirty-eight-year-old incestuous father]

The very integrity of the family depends on rigid adherence to this dictum. In the book *Betrayal of Innocence: Incest and Its Devastation,* Susan Forward and Craig Buck profoundly point out, "Adultery is *twice* forbidden in the Ten Commandments while incest is not even mentioned."[87]

If I'd had an affair with my secretary or picked up a girl in a bar—I could never live with myself—that would be cheating! [thirty-seven-year-old incestuous father]

If an extramarital affair is not considered a feasible solution, divorce is even less of a possibility. The self-concept of the man revolves around the existence of the family unit. This family is his kingdom. It is the only part of the world he rules. Without it, he feels he is nothing.

> I promised myself as a kid, I was never going to get a divorce. I would never cause the trouble my father had caused. [forty-six-year-old incestuous father]

> All of the aunts, uncles, everybody thought we were the model family. My wife and I never fought. The kids did well at school. We were well liked at church. I would never ruin all of that with a divorce. [thirty-six-year-old incestuous father]

To break up the family would be an admission to the world that he is a failure. It would be a revelation of the truth he already feels—that he doesn't have what it takes to be a man in this world. At any expense, he must protect those around him from this "truth." He must keep his feelings of inadequacy a secret from the entire world. Certain that his survival will end if the family falls apart, he makes a last-ditch effort to combat his feelings of worthlessness. He turns to incest.

## The Secret

It is obvious at this point that the continuation of the incest revolves around the child keeping the parent's secret. The safeguarding of the secret can make the difference between an incestuous incident and an incestuous *relationship*. Given that the child does not have the power, resources, or knowledge of the parent, it is very likely that the child will agree to keep the secret.

By keeping the secret, the victim does gain a sense of power that she did not have before the incest began. However, the sense of power is a double-edged sword. On the one hand, she recognizes that she finally has some "say" over her destiny. By keeping the secret, she probably feels she is single-handedly preserving the family. With the already poor self-concept common to most of these girls, a sense of being important is crucial. But on the other hand, she does not dare *use* her power. The father is still *more* powerful. He always reminds her that if she breaks the silence, the family will fall apart, she will be sent away, he will go to jail. In the last analysis, the only power she has is to expose the incestuous relationship. Not exposing it keeps the family together. Exposing it would mean the end to an unhealthy situation for the victim, but in the victim's mind, it would also bring on the end of her world as she knows it. It is a no-win proposition.

In pointing out that the victim has gained a sense of power, I am in *no way* implying that she instigated the incest in order to become powerful. Most victims are too young to think in these terms. They only realize their power *after* the father has initiated the relationship, met his needs, and introduced the secret into the relationship. Children, in their innocence, may not understand why other people shouldn't know about it.

I remember thinking, "If this is what people who love each other do, then why shouldn't I tell people about it?" [twenty-year-old woman victimized as a small child]

If this was how we show we like people, then why didn't my other sisters do the same thing? And why didn't I do that with my mother? I loved her, too. It took me a long time to figure it out. [twenty-six-year-old woman victimized as a small child]

The child has gained power only through the inappropriateness of her father's or stepfather's sexual activity with her—not a very reassuring situation. It does not bring real control, nor is it a power she can enjoy wielding. It is a secret burden shared with the adult, who has far greater power.

So a sense of helplessness emanates from being caught in a secret that seems too terrible to tell. She also may feel that telling would be fruitless—no one would believe her.

I tried talking to people about other problems, you know, my brothers being mean to me or questions I had about menstruation. No one ever listened—let alone helped. Even if I *did* want to tell—where was I supposed to go? [eighteen-year-old past victim]

He started messing with me for the first time while we were camping. I ran out of the tent and started running around the lake as fast as I could. There was nobody up there, so I thought to myself, "Who am I going to tell?" Especially since it was my father—who was going to believe it? So I slowly walked back to the tent. What else could I do? [thirty-seven-year-old past victim]

Once she agrees to keep the secret, the victim may feel she is drowning in quicksand. Remember, the average relationship goes on for three to five years. She may be confused, even frightened, by the continuing contact. Yet the offender has made it clear that her very survival depends on the continuation of the incestuous relationship.

It is not unusual for an incest victim to agonize over why this happened to her. She may feel she is the only person ever to be in an incestuous relationship. Until recently, there was so little news coverage or public information about child sexual abuse that this belief was reinforced by society's avoidance of the subject. She may look around at her neighbors, relatives, or other girls at school, and believe it is impossible that this could happen to any of them.

I would sit for hours on end and try to think of why this happened to me. I thought of every mistake, every lie, every bad feeling I had ever had toward another person. I thought I was being punished for something, but I couldn't think of exactly why. [eighteen-year-old victim]

I used to wish the situation on girls at school I didn't like. It made me mad. Why should they be happy, and why should I have to go through this awful thing with my stepfather? [fourteen-year-old victim]

The logical conclusion for her is, "There must be something about me that made this happen." The thoughts do not always revolve around issues of, "What did I do to provoke it?" More likely, she will think there is something innately wrong with herself that caused this to happen. "It didn't happen to anyone else, it happened to me, and there's a reason for that."

The obvious reason for the incest is that the parent initiated the relationship. But children more often look to themselves as the cause. There can be much confusion as a result. Small children often have their own secrets—fantasies of close and all-encompassing affection. A small child may want to be incredibly important to her father. She might want to be his "favorite" child. The child may approach her parent with these fantasies in mind. If what follows is an incestuous relationship, this may be an overload for the child's mind.

> I remember wanting to be close to him. I wanted him to teach me checkers, he was always playing it. That was all I wanted. [twenty-four-year-old woman victimized as a child]

> I was supposed to be his little girl. I just wanted more of his attention than my brother got. I thought maybe he would tell me stories or something. It took me years to figure out what that "game" was. [thirty-seven-year-old woman victimized as a young child]

> He was my mother's new husband. I wanted to show him that I liked him. I wanted him to stay a long time. I did whatever he asked me to. [thirty-year-old woman victimized as a child]

The child never intended the closeness and warmth to become sexual. Incest is an adult's interpretation of the child's wishes—an interpretation greatly colored by the adult's own needs. While the child did not provoke the incest or ask for a sexual relationship, the child *was* asking for *something*. In the tremendous upheaval and cloud of mystery around "the secret," the child may no longer be sure about what she did ask for. The normal, gentle fantasy of the child has been transformed into an adult version of sexual relationships. The child does not understand; she is sure she went wrong somewhere.

Some people may argue that the child *did* "turn on" her father with the intention of taking the relationship to another level. Again, this is an adult interpretation of a child's wishes. The thought processes of a child being what they are, she could have had a variety of *nonsexual* forms of relationships in mind. For example, she might have wanted uninterrupted time alone with her father.

> There were six kids at home—I always got lost in the shuffle. It was real important that Dad noticed me. [seventeen-year-old victim]

If she has been going through a difficult stage with her mother, monopolizing her father may be seen as a way to communicate her unhappiness to her mother.

> Every time my dad took me to a basketball game and he told her she had to stay home and watch the other kids, she would get furious. So I tried to get tickets to as many games as I could. [fourteen-year-old victim]

> My mom wouldn't listen to me. She was always too busy with other things. So I spent my time with him. At least he knew I existed. [sixteen-year-old victim]

No matter what the child's secret fantasies or motivations are, the adult is responsible for translating this mere wish into a sexual relationship. We do not attribute any other adult crimes to the reason that "the child wanted me to do it." My friend and colleague Florence Rush has a very illustrative example:

> Imagine a man and his daughter walking down the street, and the little girl saw a doll she liked in the store window. She points to that doll and says, "Daddy, steal me that doll." The father goes into the store, steals the doll, is caught and arrested. He stands before the judge, who asks him why he stole the doll. The father replies, "I stole the doll because my daughter told me to steal it." It is very unlikely that his daughter's request would be an excuse for the crime.

The analogy to cases of incest is obvious. In exceedingly rare cases, little girls do ask their fathers to fondle their genitals. Even if they do, it is the adult's responsibility to assess the short- and long-range potential harm. It is the father's responsibility not to do it. Little girls seeking affection, attention, or favor from their fathers with "niceness" are definitely not asking an adult to throw his better judgment to the wind and sexually exploit them.

The offender's perception of the child/victim consenting to the sexual activity is curious. Some nonoffenders agree with this belief—that children are naturally seductive and seek out romantic liaisons with adult males. Consider the concept of consent in this country. We legislate that children under sixteen do not have the skills to drive a car safely. We mandate that a person must be eighteen years old before she or he can exercise the power of judgment to vote or handle personal finances. Somewhere between the ages of eighteen and twenty-one, depending on the state, young adults mysteriously acquire the capacity to consume liquor responsibly—or so we hope. Our laws even go so far as to protect children from the sexual advances of adults. Crimes such as carnal knowledge, contributing to the delinquency of a minor, indecent liberties with a minor— all are there to ensure the child's healthy growth to adulthood. Why is it, when confronting the situation of a child sexually exploited by a family member, we ruminate over the distinct possibility of the child giving consent? This young person, who cannot yet legally vote, drink, drive a car, or sign a contract, suddenly knows his or her own mind about seducing an adult and has the wherewithal to accomplish this task. Only in incest are adults so generous in giving children credit for single-minded purposefulness.

Again, we find the child in the position of an adult. The child victim must bear the burden of the secret and take responsibility for what is so inappropriate that it must be kept secret. Not only is this blatantly unfair to the child, and in direct conflict with our culture's ideas about what childhood entails, but also incest totally disrupts the maturation of every individual victim.

## The Missing Childhood

There is no way a child can maintain normal rates of emotional growth and development while being subjected to an experience so disruptive and foreign as incest. The incestuous relationship creates disorganized development in the child. In some ways, her development is greatly speeded up. She has had many of the responsibilities of women twenty years older.

> I used to hear other girls complain about baby-sitting or having to do a few things around the house. I thought they were really stupid. I had run our house all by myself since I was thirteen. [sixteen-year-old victim]

She believes her role in the family, even the future of the family itself, depends on her acquiescence. She learns she can meet her needs for affection, attention, and daily survival by meeting her father's sexual needs. She never has the chance to develop other means of mastery over her environment. Progress in any areas of talent (for example, writing, music, public speaking, teaching) are suspended. She is taught to replace such talents with the role of lover. She is discouraged from putting time and energy into anything other than meeting her father's needs.

> I really loved riding academy. Then there wasn't any time for it. He said we didn't have the money—that I should drop out. I never did get back into it. [eighteen-year-old victim]

Could this be the daughter of the woman who quit the bowling league because her husband wanted her to? For the daughter, it is not a matter of preference. It is a matter of survival.

Already believing she is different from other girls her own age, the adolescent incest victim finds their concerns about clothes, grades, and rock stars childish and trivial compared to what she must cope with at home. She derives some semblance of good self-concept by believing she is more capable, more sophisticated than they are. In a sexual sense, she is far more sophisticated. She is yanked from the normal and gradual processes that many children happily go through and masters her environment, in a limited and perverse sense, quickly, after the incest first happens. Because she feels different, she does not participate with other children in the tasks of exploring her world and growing up.

A very unfortunate manifestation is the victim's inability to engage in age-appropriate activity. She is not comfortable going to a football game with a group of other girls. She is not interested in becoming part of the drill team after school. She cannot see herself fitting in with other kids her own age.

> All through school, I never asked anyone to my house. I was afraid they could tell. [thirteen-year-old victim]

> I hated those classes where we had to write something about ourselves, like what we did on vacation. We never did anything. I just didn't what people to know about me. [sixteen-year-old victim]

An incest victim who feels alienated from her peers can react in a variety of ways. Some girls handle the alienation by being aloof and withdrawn. School personnel would probably refer to this girl as a "very timid" child. Teachers may assume she will "grow out of" her chronic shyness. This type of girl typically makes good grades. She probably is very responsible for her age. Most of her energy goes into studying and taking care of her family. Being a "model child," she rarely attracts the attention to herself that the "acting-out" victims do. This isolation reinforces her poor self-concept. She believes she is not worth bothering with. The pain and confusion that culminate in her pulling into a shell are easily confused with mild temperament and maturity.

Another form of expression of alienation tends to attract much more attention. We see a large number of incest victims become involved in drugs, truancy, delinquent behavior, and sporadic sexual encounters. There are three reasons for this. First, this may be a way for her to expose the incest. It is not uncommon for cases of incest to be uncovered in juvenile court. An adolescent girl will be brought in on charges of running away, stealing a car, truancy, etc. An insightful and sensitive caseworker will probe into why she is involved in delinquency. Running away or involvement in delinquency that ends in removal from the home is one way to end the incest. The victim who has tried, unsuccessfully, to stop her father's advances may see a correctional institution as a viable alternative. Living "on the road" symbolizes the freedom she is so hungry for. Perhaps she still has concern about the family staying together; if so, she would prefer leaving the home, one way or another, to having her father leave.

Second, the victim may feel she is not worth much. She does not see herself as being adequate enough to make good grades, be a cheerleader, or work on the school paper. She doesn't want people so close to her that they might discover her secret. The label of "bad girl" fits with her belief in her innate evil as a cause of the incest.

Third, her development has been so skewed that age-appropriate activity may seem boring to her. Enveloped in a world of intrigue at home, she is certain that no other teen-ager would understand, and she feels she has nothing to say to them. Activities like making posters for a school game or toilet-papering the principal's house seem pedestrian and immature. So by engaging in dangerous, defiant, and sometimes illegal acts, she keeps pace with the abnormal atmosphere in which she was raised.

In some cases, it is very obvious that the parents have directly contributed to this confusion about age-appropriate activity. Because the parents probably married young, they may be closer in age to their children than most families. They may share the same tastes in music, films, sports. There are specific ways in which parents begin confusion about age-appropriate activity.

> I told my mother that I wanted those underpants with the days of the week on them for my tenth birthday. It was a big joke around school. The next thing I knew, my father went out and bought them. He gave them to me and asked me to model them. My mother thought it was real cute. [fifteen-year-old victim]

> When I needed a training bra, it was my father who took me to buy it. My mother was too busy. We had a real good time. [thirteen-year-old victim]

> While my mother was away taking care of my grandmother, my father and I had dinner by candlelight every night. We would feed the kids early, put them to bed, and have dinner ourselves. It was my reward for taking good care of the house. [sixteen-year-old victim]

If the father tells the victim that she is very beautiful, she may conclude her beauty caused the incest. As a result, she sets herself even farther apart from other girls.

> I got fat. If he did that because I was pretty, I figured he'd quit it when I got ugly. [thirteen-year-old victim]

At the other extreme, many incest victims dress in a very sophisticated style. This may seem to contradict the poor self-concept. If they do not like themselves, why bother with expensive clothing? And doesn't this set them farther apart from their peers? In many ways, the victim feels adult. By dressing in a style that is ten years ahead of her, she can *look* consistent with how she feels. Consistency, in the midst of the confusion and isolation of her life, is very important.

Specific forms of disorganized development go along with the age of the victim. For the prepubescent victim, one of the most dramatic negative ramifications concerns her expression of affection. Most of us are taught to knit a sweater, make a card, write a poem, give a hug to someone we like. Incest victims are taught to act out sexually if they like someone. The immediate connection is made between the *feeling* of warmth and the *behavior* of sexual activity.

> I was in my twenties before I figured out I didn't have to sleep with every guy who paid for a date. I used to think they were doing me such a big favor that I had to do something to show them I appreciated their going out of their way for me. [thirty-two-year-old past victim]

> I remember being really humiliated when I was about six or seven. I crawled in my uncle's lap. I started to do to him what my father taught me to do. I really freaked him out. He never let me near him again. I liked him a lot. I just wanted to play that game with him. [twenty-two-year-old past victim]

In later years, the victim may be sexually active as a genuine expression of affection. Unfortunately, this will be perceived differently by the men involved. Some may take this more as a sign of easy sexual access rather than affection. Such "misunderstandings" undoubtedly will cause pain and confusion for the victim. It is important for her to relearn other channels of affection that will not be so easily misinterpreted or taken advantage of.

The older victim probably understands the incest taboo. Because of her age and experience, she may not have made the simple equation that affection equals sexual activity. She knows better. For her, the developmental issues are different. The formula she may arrive at is *survival* equals sexual activity. She gives up her sexual privacy to live at home.

## Trust and Sexuality

As young girls, the victims were taught to trust their fathers. They looked to them for guidance, believing they would never do anything to hurt them. All of society reinforces the concept that fathers are wise, protective, and inherently good. But to incest victims, society has lied. Their fathers did not protect them—they used them. Their fathers were not wise and good. They involved the children in something they did not want or understand.

A sense of betrayal is prominent among incest victims, particularly if the victim was too young to understand the incest taboo. Perhaps she wasn't really aware of sexual relationships at that point. The adult told her, "This is what people who love each other do." As the child grows older, she learns the real meaning of the sexual activity and becomes aware of the adult's gross inappropriateness. Therefore she feels betrayed. She had looked up to and trusted this older person. She learns that his reassurances were monumental lies.

Sometimes the child has a sense that something is not quite right. If she challenges the appropriateness of her father's sexual activity, he will tell her her judgment is all wrong. Believing her intuition is faulty, and deferring to the father's wishes, she begins a pattern of ignoring her own feelings. One study uncovered a hefty incidence of other forms of victimization by others in adolescent incest victims' lives. Crimes such as rape, battering, or fraud are sometimes commonplace. The victim is more vulnerable because she discounts her own radar, which could have warned her that she was about to be a victim again.

Aside from victimization, when once again faced with a relationship that also implies mutual caring and maintaining each other's best interests, the incest victim may be cynical. What does she have to go on that tells her this time everything will work out? How does she know if this man is sincere, or if he is just using this rhetoric to use her to meet his own needs once again, with little or no consideration for her feelings? Can she afford to be hurt, to lose, to have her trust betrayed again? It is this type of questioning that often inhibits the past victim from venturing out into healthy adult relationships.

With the recent public recognition of incest as a widespread problem, we are finding many women in their twenties or older coming forth to talk about their victimization as children. Often the reason they begin to talk openly is that they are experiencing difficulty in their intimate relationships. The difficulty can take many forms. For some women, the incest may have left them sexually unresponsive. They are capable of feeling love for another person, but find themselves unable to express it in sexual terms.

> Sometimes I'll date a guy for a while, and I'll like him a lot. I want to be close, to be intimate with him. But most of the time I don't. I'm afraid he won't like me anymore or he'll think I'm too easy. It's hard for me to talk about. Usually they end up leaving. I guess all they wanted was sex after all. [twenty-eight-year-old past victim]

Other women fall into patterns of brief sexual encounters. As they get older, they are not happy with this pattern and wish to change. The message they took from the incest may be that they are capable of only short, demeaning, shallow sexual relationships.

> If I meet a man I like, I figure I'm going to sleep with him eventually, so why not just start right away and not waste any time? They all split on me anyway, so I try to have as much fun as I can. And never count on them . . . that's the key. [twenty-six-year-old past victim]

Because of their poor self-concept, they do not believe they are worthy of a relationship that is reciprocal, caring, or deep.

> Whenever some guy starts to like me, I get real nervous. What if they figure out what happened to me? Who would want to be bothered with someone with such a bizarre family? I generally get out before they start asking me all the personal-history stuff. [thirty-year-old past victim]

Confusion about trust and sexuality could cause her to repeat the dynamic. No victim intentionally marries a man who will victimize her children, yet statistical evidence shows that this frequently happens. The woman who has been victimized as a child has probably never had a close or intimate relationship with a safe, responsible, and caring man. Most of us learn about such a relationship from our fathers. This is not the case for the incest victim. Like any of us, she is most comfortable with what she knows. Also, she believes she does not deserve very much out of life. She does not have confidence that she could attract and maintain a relationship with a nonexploitative male. In fact, from her experience, she may not believe that any nonexploitative males exist.

> I never have met a man who wasn't in some way like my father. They all want their urges satisfied immediately. I don't think they are even aware that women have needs, too. [twenty-one-year-old past victim]

> After what I went through with my father, I decided never to trust another man again. I couldn't stand it a second time. You just can't trust them. [sixteen-year-old victim]

The sexual issues of past victims tend to be greatly sensationalized by books and television. Victims either become notorious prostitutes at age twelve, or they get married to an elderly man, move to the suburbs, and are frigid their entire lives. There is a wide range of women who cope somewhere between these two extremes. Nevertheless, there is one difficulty with intimate relationships that is fairly common. As one of the victims in my adolescent-victim group succinctly put it, "If you can't trust your own father, who can you trust?" Some victims can work out their distrust in their daily lives so that they are not suspicious of *all* men. Potential husbands, lovers, or close, intimate male friends may be in a different situation.

## The Mother's Role

When would a girl need her mother more than when she is being victimized by her father? For some victims, the mother is supportive and protective upon discovery of incest. Other victims are not so fortunate. The question of whether the mother knew or not re-

ceives an inordinate amount of attention in incest cases. While incest *is* a family problem and the mother's reaction to the daughter's
victimization is critically important, again the ultimate responsibility
lies with the father. He chooses to react to the circumstances of
his life by molesting his daughter. Yet the examination of the
mother's role in father-daughter incest is valuable. To say the very
least, the question is complicated.

The victim's perceptions of the role of mother help us to understand this Pandora's box. The daughter takes over the parts of the
mothering role that are mechanical in nature—making meals, supervising younger children, cleaning house. Although bonds of love and
protectiveness for the younger children may grow out of her care,
her perception of mothering usually does not include concepts such
as nurturance, guidance, or protectiveness:

> I was a much better cook than she was. She knew it too. It
> really bugged her. [fifteen-year-old victim]

> The kids came to me with requests for money or when they
> needed a fight refereed. I don't know what she thought she
> was doing. She sure wasn't doing much around the house.
> [fourteen-year-old victim]

The mother's role is perceived as fairly cut-and-dried—satisfying the
basic needs for food and hygiene, and little else. Her own mother
seems inadequate, unable, or unwilling to care for the family. The
child may see her mother as someone who has failed her father.
Most of all, the mother has failed the victim by not protecting her.

> If any man did to my daughter what that man did to me, I
> would leave him immediately. How can my mother stand to
> still live with him? [fifteen-year-old victim]

> You would think that my being a kid would mean something
> to her. Why doesn't she dump him? He's so gross anyway.
> [thirteen-year-old victim of stepfather]

Daughters, growing up in a radically different time from their
mothers, cannot understand their timidity. They are perplexed by
their mothers' subservience to their fathers. Although the daughters'
interactions with boyfriends closely parallel their mothers' interac-

tions with their fathers, they do not see the similarities. All the daughter realizes is that her mother is not able to take care of herself. She is not able to take care of her daughter. The daughter knows she does not want to be like her mother.

Chances are the victim's mother is nonassertive and defers judgment most often to her husband. As a result, the daughter may perceive women as weak, mindless, and not very self-sufficient.

She couldn't do anything right. If it hadn't been for me and my father, she would have just withered away years ago. [sixteen-year-old victim]

She did everything he asked her to do. When we wanted something, we went to him. It was never worth it to ask her. She'd just tell us to go ask him. [fourteen-year-old victim]

I used to promise myself I wouldn't have kids. I didn't want to be a rotten mother like her. [seventeen-year-old victim]

If the victim has no models of strong, autonomous, self-directed women, she may take on her mother's lifestyle without even realizing it. She has no example of someone saying that very important word—NO—to the father.

Some victims share the stereotypical attitude that women are to blame for the crime of incest. The father may have complained to his daughter about unhappiness in his marriage. The daughter may then blame her mother for making her father unhappy.

At first, my father and I talked a lot about my mother. I didn't like her either. She was never there. After a while, we stopped talking about her. [twenty-eight-year-old past victim]

If the daughter saw the incest as a way to relieve the father of his unhappiness, thereby avoiding the family's disintegration, she may also blame the mother for the incest. In the family's thought processes, father's unhappiness is mother's fault for not being a good wife.

Although the father is at least equally responsible for the marital problems, he does not explain this to his daughter. The problems are all Mommy's. Assuming that mother and daughter do not share the feelings openly, the daughter is vulnerable to the father's beliefs about the marriage. In some cases, the father will complain about the mother's lack of sexual responsiveness, citing that as his overwhelming need motivating him possibly to leave the family.

I never understood why he needed me sexually when my mother slept with him every night. But he said she rejected him, so he needed me. If she had been there for him, the incest probably would have never happened. [nineteen-year-old past victim]

Unfortunately, this logic is not necessarily sound. Many incestuous fathers have active sex lives with their wives *while* they are exploiting the daughters. Incest is not a simple matter of not being sexually satisfied by the spouse. The daughter is too young to understand why her mother might not be responsive to her father. She accepts her father's biased view of the mother.

In any family, there are normal mother-daughter tensions. Sexual competition, set up by the father, magnifies these conflicts a thousand times over. Even if the mother does not explicitly know the daughter is involved with the father, and no matter how unwilling the daughter is in the involvement, there are a myriad of issues that result in conflict. Both mother and daughter see themselves as being hopelessly dependent on this man for their survival. Both are incomplete people without him. Until the incest is out in the open, they cannot and will not help each other out of the trap.

I never will understand what was with my mother. I wasn't able to work or move away or anything like that. She could have done all of those things if she wanted to bad enough. I guess she didn't want to. [sixteen-year-old victim]

I wanted to say something to him. I really wondered about the time he spent alone with our daughter. I just had this funny feeling. But his temper—it frightened me so. I knew if I asked him about Holly, he would leave. And then what would become of the kids and me? [forty-year-old mother of incest victim]

How the mother reacts to the discovery that her daughter is an incest victim will have a large impact on the daughter's relationships with women. If the mother believes the victim and acts swiftly to protect her, this can be a very positive chapter in the relationship between mother and daughter. On the other hand, if the mother does not believe her, or chooses to maintain the relationship with the husband and have the daughter leave home, the effect on the daughter can be devastating.

Some mothers, for a variety of reasons, find themselves punishing their daughters after the secret is revealed. When the incestuous relationship has been going on for years, the daughter may have begun "acting out" (running away, stealing, truancy) in order to gain attention. The daughter generally did *not* do these things before the onset of the incest. Her actions emanate from a sense of helplessness and the need for someone to notice her plight and help her out of it. To the mother who knows nothing of the incest, the child may seem merely like a "bad girl."

> I tried telling my mother. Right away, she began reminding me of every lie I ever told as a kid. She said this was a lie, too. [fifteen-year-old victim]

> She said I didn't know what the truth was. All of the stealing I had done proved that. She wouldn't even listen. [fourteen-year-old victim]

> My mother started screaming at me—told me I was on drugs again. She said she would call the cops on me if I didn't stop saying those things about my father. [fifteen-year-old victim]

If the mother insists that the "story" about incest is just another troublemaking scheme, it is a particularly frustrating predicament for the child. The girl probably would not have been a "bad girl" if it had not been for the incest.

The mother might believe the daughter, but still choose to maintain the relationship with the husband at the daughter's expense. With more resources for women and more emphasis on assertiveness, mothers are choosing, in increasing numbers, to stand up for their daughters. Nevertheless, some mothers feel they cannot survive, emotionally or financially, without their husbands. Chances are that there are younger children still at home. In light of this, the mother cannot see divorcing or prosecuting her husband and supporting the family on her own.

I never even lived alone before. How was I going to support four kids? I wouldn't make it on welfare. What else could I do? I had no work skills. Not even a driver's license. [thirty-five-year-old wife of incestuous father]

My mother got a divorce. She was miserable. We never had what we needed. No way was I going through *that!* [twenty-nine-year-old wife of incestuous father]

This brings us back to the victim's original fear—that the family will fall apart. The mother, who shares the same fear, uses it as a rationalization to protect her husband and justify the removal of her daughter from the home into protective custody. The daughter's premise—"keeping the family together"—boomerangs on her to separate her from her mother.

Clearly it is the daughter, not the father, who needs the mother's protection. For some women, there is absolutely no question of what to do. Once they know about the incest, they sever their relationships with their husbands—possibly prosecute them—and stand by their daughters. There is no one type of mother who reacts this way. Perhaps she herself was a child victim and has dealt with that experience to the point where she is not immobilized by it and wants to give her daughter the protection she never had. On the other hand, the crime of incest might be totally foreign to her, and in her healthy rejection of the father's behavior, she sees only one course of action: to protect her daughter. Although this might entail some disruption to the family—the very event the daughter had hoped to avoid—there can be some healthy outcomes.

When I first called the police and pressed charges, my daughter was real upset. She kept on telling me that all she had wanted was for her father to stop bothering her—she didn't want him to go to jail. But I knew I was doing the right thing, and tried to explain that to her. It was rough going at first, but with me having to go back to work and all, we have gotten closer. We talk a lot more now, and she knows how bad I feel about it. I had to tell her a thousand times that it wasn't her fault. It will be O.K.—I didn't think so for a while, but now we both know it will be all right. [thirty-seven-year-old mother of a victim]

Women who take this stand deserve our respect and admiration. It cannot be easy. Removing their husbands from the home—even temporarily for purposes of therapy—means major lifestyle changes for their families. The mother's decision usually becomes public. Applauded by some for her courage, she may also be shunned by others for deserting her husband in his time of need, or for shifting all the "blame" onto him when she is perceived as the reason for the incest. Countless practical and emotional upheavals take place. However, if she and her daughter work together to forge a new life without the offender, this can be a constructive process for both the mother and daughter. Both learn mastery over their own environment.

I never thought I could hold down a job. I watched and learned from the other women at work, and now I can hold my own. [thirty-year-old mother of a victim]

I still get stuck with the housework. But it's different. Mom makes my brothers carry their share, and I'm not doing it with such a sense of doom. I do it because it has to be done. [sixteen-year-old victim]

Without the continued interference of the father, mother and daughter may become closer than they have ever been before. And the daughter has a strong role model of an evolving, self-sufficient, and caring woman.

Sometimes, without the daughter's exposing the secret, the mother suspects there is something going on between the father and the daughter. What is the mother to do next? Not feeling very confident about herself, she sees her options as limited. She has been taught to be supportive and nurturing toward her husband—to value her marriage above all else, even the children. Even though unquestioned loyalty to the father is what is expected of her, that is difficult under the circumstances. However, if she confronts her husband, then he points to this enraged, accusatory woman and says, "No wonder I turned to my daughter. Look at what I had to live with."

When I thought something was up, I talked to my mother about it. She told me I must be wrong—that my husband was too good a man. And did I want to lose him over such a silly suspicion? She made it sound like I had the problem for thinking it! [twenty-nine-year-old mother of incest victim]

I did say something to him. Asked him point-blank. I had gone through that as a kid, and no kid of mine was going to. Of course he denied it, but what was worse is that my daughter denied it too. She stood up for *him*. Later I found out he had threatened her, but then, it was all too weird. What could I do under the circumstances? [thirty-five-year-old mother of incest victim]

In the last quote lies another clue to the answer to the question of whether the mother knew what was going on. In many cases, we find the victims going to great lengths to hide the incest from their mothers.

My father told me it would kill her to know. She had been in the hospital twice that year. I loved my mother. I didn't want her to die. [eleven-year-old incest victim]

The way I figured it, it was none of her business. This was between my dad and me, and I'd get out of it when I left home. Besides, what was she supposed to do about it anyway? [seventeen-year-old incest victim]

In a few cases, the mother knows, without any overt disclosure, about the incest. The daughter's perception of her mother's state of knowledge is very important. When the daughter believes that her mother does know but takes no action to protect her daughter, the daughter is especially bitter. She may perceive her mother as colluding with the father in her victimization.

She must have known. He was always in my bedroom when she got home from work. As long as I kept up the chores, I don't think anything else mattered. [fifteen-year-old victim]

She was recovering from the operation. Even though she couldn't get out of bed, I could tell she had him figured out.

She sort of asked me about it a few times. She really never knew how to ask me straight out. [seventeen-year-old victim]

The reality is that very few mothers do know, though that is little comfort to the victim who believes her mother is aware of the incest and does nothing. As we have discovered, there are as many reasons for the mother's *not* knowing as there are individual mothers.

As mentioned before, an interesting aspect of the mothers' background is that they were sometimes incest victims themselves. The mothers may or may not be surprised to discover that their daughters are victims of the same crime. Recently I was consulting on a case with a local rape crisis center. The mother, a victim of incest herself, had called the police when she learned of her daughter's incestuous involvement with the stepfather. The daughter was confused and upset with her mother's calling the police and the rape crisis center. The mother told the social worker, "When this happens to *her* daughter, well, then she'll understand why I had to do this." Not, "*If* this ever happens to her daughter . . ." The woman assumed that incest was to be part of her potential granddaughter's fate as well.

In very socially isolated families, incest may not seem so out of the ordinary to the mother. She could even have the attitude that incest is part of life and must be endured. If a mother has this attitude, she will probably lend little support to her daughter. The mother may remember that she endured the relationship without telling anyone. She might resent her daughter seeking help by telling someone about the incest and "making trouble."

In a very few cases, the mother may feel so uncomfortable in her role as wife that she willingly surrenders part of the role to her daughter. Obviously, this reflects a serious lack of regard for the well-being of her daughter. Some women feel so overwhelmed by their relationship with husband and family that they believe they can do no better. In that context, the mother justifies (to herself) sacrificing the daughter to the father's needs. Obviously this will have a lasting impact on the daughter.

We can tell a lot about how a woman feels about herself by examining her opinions of other women. If she feels women cannot be trusted, are jealous, are not very good companions, etc., then she is, in essence, saying those very same things about herself. Due to guilt by association, she may be very uncomfortable with the fact that she too is a woman. Rarely do any of us make general condemnations of groups we belong to and mean them to apply to everyone else in the group *except* ourselves. By making general negative statements about women, the victim is making negative statements about herself. In the reverse, how she feels about herself will be multiplied and applied to all women. This process makes the world seem consistent. "If I am not O.K., then no woman is O.K." Through this thought process, the victim can gain some level of peace of mind.

## The Father's Denial

For many of us, the act of incest is linked with sexual intercourse. This is a myth. If you remember, the average age of the victim is around eleven years old. The average incestuous relationship lasts from three to five years, which means the victim is probably around eight or nine years old when the sexual activity first begins.

The involvement usually begins under the umbrella of normal "affection." The initial contact may be fondling. As the child grows older and fondling no longer satisfies the offender's needs, the contact may progress to various forms of mutual masturbation. From there, oral-genital contact may be introduced. Penetration or full sexual intercourse is often present in involvements with pubescent and adolescent girls, but not always.

Some fathers will involve their daughters in virtually all other forms of sexual behavior—but never penetration. The victims reported that their fathers used this technical abstinence to justify their involvement. As long as they didn't have actual sexual intercourse, the father believed he wasn't *really* "cheating" on his wife. In his own mind, the father would also avoid the label of an "incestuous father" or "offender" if he did not actually penetrate his daughter's vagina.

The entire time my father was having me masturbate and fellate him, he would give all of us daughters lectures about

> being virgins when we got married—because of our religion. He did everything to me but penetrate. [twenty-three-year-old past victim]

> Whenever I would tell him to stop because what we were doing was wrong, he kept on telling me what we were doing wasn't like "grown-up, married love." He'd tell me he respected me too much for that. [fourteen-year-old incest victim]

Certainly, the father who fondles his daughter's breasts, engages her in mutual masturbation or oral-genital contact is, in fact, an offender.

Upon discovery, fathers most often deny that anything inappropriate has happened. If the offender finally admits that there is something undesirable about what he has done, there are three general lines of defense.

First, it is the daughter's fault. She seduced him. Even if she is only eight years old, any man seeing her in pajamas night after night would have done the same thing.

If it is not the daughter's fault, then it is the wife's fault. If the wife had been a good wife and met his needs as her husband, then he wouldn't need to mess around with kids.

When the daughter or the wife are not found at fault, the offender's mother is blamed. If she had been a good mother and raised him right, then he wouldn't have been the kind of man who would grow up and molest kids.

The most common response of fathers when asked why they made sexual overtures to their daughters is, "I only did what she wanted me to do." When asked how he knew she wanted sexual activity with him, he replies with a variety of explanations: It was "the way she was dressed"; "she was always crawling in my lap wanting hugs"; "whenever I was alone, she would come be with me." Other explanations for his behavior are:

> I just wanted to teach her about sex. I wanted her to learn from someone who knew what he was doing and wouldn't get her pregnant. I didn't want her first experience to be with some careless, irresponsible teen-age boy. [thirty-six-year-old incestuous father]

I didn't do anything different with her than she was already doing with all those other boys. [thirty-one-year-old incestuous father]

I must have been drunk—sometimes I have these blackouts. Maybe it happened then. I don't think I really did it, but if I did, it must have happened when I was passed out. [thirty-eight-year-old incestuous father]

I was fantasizing about her, and all of a sudden she was there. I just couldn't help myself. [forty-two-year-old incestuous father]

Other, more bizarre, reasons were: "I was worried she was becoming a lesbian." "She gets cold very easily and I was just trying to warm her up." "I have a split personality and I don't know what happens sometimes."

Of course, the victim is painfully aware of this barrage of denial. Any self-doubts she previously had can be multiplied many times over. The "voice of authority" says it "wasn't his fault."

## Other Family Members

Brothers and sisters may not be aware of the incestuous relationship between the father and their sister, yet they are usually aware of some special relationship. They may not understand why, but they sense her hold on their father. She may receive special privileges, spend time alone with him, or be recognized as "his favorite." If this is the case, antagonism will develop.

He bought my older sister presents all the time. He took her places and got her out of early curfews. I remember thinking, "What has she got that I haven't got? What's so special about her?" I hated her for it. When she left home, I found out within a few weeks what had been going on. Only I wasn't willing to co-operate with him. I told my mom. [sixteen-year-old sister of victim]

Sometimes the father's treatment of the victim is not envied. They may see that their sister is treated differently by their father, but they are not anxious to change places with her. They notice that the father is quite jealous of her friendships and attempts to keep a close watch on her. They are aware that she is coerced into spending time alone with him.

> My sister couldn't even go out of the house. She couldn't even come do things with us. It was weird. The next thing I know, my dad is arrested because she said he did things to her. [fourteen-year-old brother of victim]

Professionals in the field sometimes carefully monitor the effect on male siblings once a case of incest has been uncovered. A good portion of the victims' brothers are probably not overtly aware of the incest. If the victim confides in anyone at all, she is more likely to choose a sister. But in the turmoil of discovery, the social worker is concerned about what consequences this may have on the young male's sense of self and his budding sexuality.

> I worried most about my brother. He was eleven when we went through prosecution. He didn't have any opinion about what our father had done. It just wasn't a big deal to him. [eighteen-year-old past victim]

As mentioned before, incest is found in many generations in some families. While the brother in a specific family may not have been a victim, he has been exposed to incest as a male "problem solving" technique. No doubt he is aware of the offender's denials and rationalizations. At the very least, this will have an impact on his view of women. Chances are good that he will glean his father's sense of prerogative concerning his supreme rule over the family. And, if the family is especially isolated, he may perceive incest as a normal part of life, thereby repeating the dynamic in his own adulthood.

Of course, some brothers are upset and behave in a protective manner toward their sisters, but this is not common. Because of the role confusion in the family, the brother has a more safe and valued position in the family. He has a lot to lose by rejecting the father's dogma of male superiority. He is not immune from the same poor self-concept that permeates the rest of the family: Where is he to obtain the strength to defy the father or challenge the family system? The section "Five Other Incestuous Relationships" will address the situation where the brother, as well as the father, is also involved with his sister.

The main issue for the sister of the incest victim is to avoid the same victimization. If she has envied her older sister's "camaraderie" with their father, she may be anxious to enjoy the same advantages. Very soon she will realize what the sister had to give up for those privileges. She probably has the same insecurities and fears as her sister. Even though they have so much in common, they might not have a close relationship. If they do, the older sister can, and often does, confide in the younger sister and afford her the protection she herself never had. This type of positive exchange not only stops the incest from continuing throughout the entire family, but also helps the victim to experience an important and healthy relationship with another female.

We must not overlook the impact of the extended family of the victim and offender. Grandparents, aunts, uncles, cousins, nephews, and nieces will all have opinions about the situation if they know about it. Victims report great amounts of pressure, as well as support, from the extended family. Usually the offender's side of the family rallies to his cause. They attribute his "temporary" lapse of good judgment to the victim's outrageous "seduction" or to the rotten treatment the offender received from his mother as a child. They will encourage the victim to drop charges against her father.

When a stepfather is the offender, the situation is even more complicated. The victim's steprelatives put in their two cents' worth. It is not uncommon for an offender to have a past history of child sexual abuse. Perhaps his family thought he was "cured" before he married again and acquired stepchildren. We have seen cases where steprelatives accused the victim of "making him go wrong again."

She was always getting in trouble. Couldn't expect much else from someone like her. Imagine, telling on her father like that —after all he'd done for her. That man worked hard for his family. [sister of incestuous father]

We told her she should tell the police she was lying. Her dad had a hard childhood. He couldn't help himself. He learned his lesson. We know it wouldn't happen again. Do you think she would listen to us? No, that ungrateful brat wasn't satisfied until he was in prison. [maternal grandparent of victim]

Extended families do not *always* know, because the incestuous family is usually very secretive. However, the extended family can be a resource for the victim after the discovery of incest. She may be sent to live with her grandparents while the father is being prosecuted. She may be able to confide in a favorite aunt. She may find that a cousin can reveal a history of her own victimization and encourage the victim to be open about her problems.

I felt real lucky to have my aunt there. I lived with her and my cousins during the trial. I guess they'll always be my family. I feel sort of guilty about—liking them better than my own family—but they were there when I needed them. [sixteen-year-old victim]

My cousin said the exact same thing happened to her—but she couldn't tell, so she was always there with me through everything—even the trial. That helped a lot. [fourteen-year-old victim]

Generally, the responses from the extended family are strong. They are either extremely supportive of the victim or of the offender. There seems to be little middle ground.


## The Way Out

At this point, incest may seem like a hopeless situation. The father needs to compensate for feeling rotten about himself. He sees family members as pawns in his quest to satisfy his emotional needs. The mother is overwhelmed by his needs. Unable to meet her own, let alone his, she abandons part of her role to her daughter. The daughter, sensing the unhappiness of her parents and plagued with feelings of helplessness, picks up the banner for the family. She will become involved with the father for a variety of complicated reasons. The main reason is that she feels she doesn't have much of a choice.

How does it end? In the vast majority of cases, the daughter breaks off the relationship. She becomes interested in boys her own age or ventures off to find a life of her own.

> As much as I hated what was happening, I could live with it. Then I met a nice boy in a class. We worked on a project together. My father became enraged and restricted me. I couldn't stand being in that house so much. I had to tell someone what was wrong. [thirteen-year-old incest victim]

> I couldn't even talk about liking another kid my own age. My father would get all hurt. Once he even cried. [fifteen-year-old incest victim]

Usually the daughter tells her father she wants it to stop. Her request is met with a barrage of threats and recriminations. Although the father considers his daughter a "lover," her ending of the "affair" is rarely met with the stereotypical, "I understand if you have to move on" sentiment of contemporary sexual liaisons.

He may threaten her with physical harm, the molestation of her younger sisters, or withdrawal of privileges or material support. He repeats his protestations that telling her mother would "kill her." He may make the observation that no one would believe her even if she did tell. After all, she is a "bad girl" (especially if she has been acting out as a way to stop the relationship) and he is an employed, upstanding citizen who has never attracted anyone's attention.

> He told me no one would believe me. They would think it was just another story like all the times I skipped school. He was right. [fifteen-year-old victim]

> He said my mother had been sick. She looked all right to me. But he said my telling her would "kill" her. So I told someone at school, instead. I just had to tell *someone*. [seventeen-year-old victim]

He may tell her to keep his secret and thereby save the younger sisters from the same involvement. Out of a feeling of helplessness and a sense of responsibility to protect her family, she may agree.

> When he used to bother me in the middle of night, he promised he would never do the same thing to my sisters. So I figured it

was better to be just me instead of all three of us. After I got married, my next youngest sister started running away a lot. I got suspicious. She finally told me the same thing was happening to her. [twenty-six-year-old victim]

As the oldest daughter leaves home, she may find that the father is turning to the younger sisters. We find this is the time when some victims choose to speak up. Feelings of protectiveness toward younger sisters prompt them to call a halt to the father's activity.

In spite of these pressures, many daughters persist in their own, less direct ways, until the relationship finally is severed. This may mean running away, moving out of the house, or telling the secret to a friend, school personnel, or a caseworker. She may back down later during prosecution or even refuse to involve the police. But the important point is that she begins to act in her own best interest —she begins to meet *her* needs. She needs to have this relationship stop and she does something to bring about its end.

Some daughters never tell. They live forever with the secret. Eventually, almost all victims realize the wrongness of what has happened to them. They do not share their father's sense of his "prerogative." For some, that realization comes about when they begin to see how other families live. As the daughter begins to have some friends through school, she becomes aware of how socially isolated her family is, how few contacts they have with other families. All of the family energy is centered inward, on each other. As the daughter moves outside the family circle, the parents will discourage her new friendships—the father may even be intensely jealous of them. But eventually, the daughter has a chance to see how other families live. She notices that her girlfriends are not responsible for their father's happiness. She sees other girls with far fewer household responsibilities. She watches the comings and goings of other people through her new friends' homes, which at first seem foreign to her. She used to think everyone lived as her family lives.

At some point, she perceives alternatives open to her. She is not locked in a hopeless situation. To best work through the resultant feelings of confusion, helplessness, and anger, she needs the help of a skilled therapist.

Group therapy is particularly effective in dispelling the belief that she alone is a victim. It is important for these young women to hear the amazing similarity of their experiences. Much of the pain and helplessness they felt in being "the only one" can be dissipated by hearing other women talk of the very same feeling, or the very same experience.

When I went to the group, I was nervous. And then I was surprised. I never thought anyone else's life could be anything like mine. One girl even had the same detective and caseworker! [fifteen-year-old victim]

When I finally told someone, I thought my life was really over. Just last week, someone came to the group. She felt the exact same way. We'll get her through it. [fifteen-year-old victim]

In my clinical experience, I have seen the incredible resiliency of incest victims. Their ability to give to other people enables them to reach out to each other and break the isolation. More important than knowing they are not alone, they must know they are not responsible. What has happened to them was very wrong, but it was not their fault. Life is not over for them. The positive traits that contributed to their vulnerability—their sensitivity, sense of responsibility, maturity, and caring for other people—can be channeled to shape a better life. The qualities that led to their exposing the secret —courage, indomitable spirit, and survival of the aftermath—only help to enhance their self-concept. The incestuous experience will always be a part of them, but they need not be ruled by it.

The victim who never tells has the same qualities. By reaching out to a helping person—even if it is many years after the incest has ended—she can work toward the life she deserves. It is most important that all victims understand that they are just that—victims —and never deserved what has happened to them. Without that understanding, within themselves *and* from all of us, they can be unfairly branded by the secret forever.

## Five Other Incestuous Relationships

Father-daughter incest accounts for at least 70 to 90 per cent of known incestuous relationships, depending on which study is quoted. The remaining 10 to 30 per cent is distributed among five other types of incestuous relationships. They warrant our attention because the incidence of any or all of these relationships could be much higher. Just as father-daughter incest is underreported, so are all other forms of incest.

There are some striking commonalities between the dynamics of these five types of incest and the dynamics of father-daughter incest. *All* victims believe their well-being depends on their continued victimization. However, some of the differences are significant. Keep in mind that none of the five other incestuous relationships have been studied as extensively as the father-daughter phenomenon. Still, there are some conclusions that have come out of clinical practice. The reader will notice that there are no average ages, composite psychological profiles, or numerous quotes. This is not a good situation. We need to start with what we know from the few victims who have broken the secret bond, and continue to explore this very important aspect of incest.[88] We would be doing our children a disservice to be aware only of father-daughter incest.

### MOTHER-SON INCEST

Romanticized and highly eroticized by the media in this country, sexual relationships between mother and son would seem to many of us as a not damaging incestuous relationship. He is seen as a supple, curious, but naïve miniature of the sensuous man. She is the sophisticated, all-knowing woman, oozing sexuality. They come together silently, and after his initiation to making love, they go their separate ways, without the hysteria or misunderstandings that go along with two adolescent virgins sharing a night of reckless abandon with each other. The difference is that she is the mother and he is the son. They had a previous relationship—maybe they were even friends. So they can talk about what happened, put it in its proper perspective, and cherish that special night forever. Everyone understands everything. There is no sense of rejection, no possessive jealousy. Mother-son incest is truly the all-American "get in touch with your feelings," personal-growth experience.

Nothing could be farther from the truth. Mother-son incest affects the victim every bit as much as father-daughter. Because the completion of the sexual act is under totally different circumstances, we assume mother-son incest is completely consensual and therefore not damaging. Father-daughter incest conjures up a visual image (erroneous as it may be) of the father lurking over the daughter's bed, preparing to force *penetration* on her. A mother cannot successfully lurk over her son's bed, thereby arousing him to an erection, then force her vagina onto his penis.

As with father-daughter incest, actual intercourse is rare in mother-son incest. The sexual activity more often consists of fondling and exposure. These take on rather subtle forms, such as washing the child's genitals to stimulation; the boy sleeping in the mother's bed past the age when that is appropriate; massaging the boy to erection; and undressing in the same room. Of course, it is totally proper for a mother to undress with her preschool-age child. Most parents use common sense about when such behavior becomes inappropriate. As the boy approaches puberty, subtle sexual activity with the mother can create havoc in his developing sexuality.

Role reversal once again is an integral part of the dynamic. The father in the family is usually absent. He may have died, he travels with his job, has divorced or deserted the mother, or is in the military service. In the father's absence, the son takes his place. He protects his mother, pretends to be a "little man."

I took my mother everywhere. It was really great. When we came home, I went into the house first and checked everything out for her. She had a hard time making decisions, so she talked everything over with me, even though I was only eleven years old. I felt real important. [twenty-eight-year-old past victim]

At first I was upset when my dad left, but then I did a better job of taking care of things, so I figured, "Who needs him?" [fifteen-year-old victim]

He senses his mother's loss. The son wants very much to help his mother to fill the void the father left. To this end, he may begin to sleep with her at night because she is frightened. Attempting to soothe the mother's feelings of rejection, the son escorts her about town. A quasiromance begins. They genuinely enjoy each other's company. The son enjoys making his mother feel better.

Subtle sexual activity is an extension of the emotional involvement. The mother, fearing the judgment of the outside world, swears her son to secrecy. She contends that no one will understand the depths of their love, the specialness of their relationship. The relationship is indeed special to the son. He agrees to keep the secret.

The dynamic of this secret is not much different from the father-daughter incest secret. The mother becomes very possessive of the son. Their relationship is so consuming it cuts him off from his peers. A grown woman is far more exciting than girls his own age. He has a full-time job—making his mother happy. He has time for little else.

The mother's needs are more emotional than sexual, but the situation is sexually charged for the son. He is approaching a time when his body is going through disruptive changes—many of which he might not understand. There is probably no father around to help him sort it out. As the boy begins to have wet dreams, he is socially isolated from his peers. Instead of dreaming about his first flirtation with a girl at school, he has the erotic material of his mother undressing. Although the boy does not understand these new levels of sexual excitement, he knows enough to feel very uncomfortable with sexual fantasies about his own mother. Being the center of her life is one thing, but actually sexually possessing her, as a grown man would, is often an overload to the boy's psyche. If there has been explicit sexual contact, the boy feels especially guilty. He believes he had to co-operate and *really* want the involvement for it to have been consummated. Unlike the girl victim, he cannot claim force was used. He does not see himself as part of a dynamic rather than a sexual pervert. He does not look at his mother's needs in the relationship—he only sees himself as grossly inappropriate. Overwhelming guilt results.

We do not yet know enough about how this guilt manifests itself in the boy's adulthood or sexuality. In individual cases, we have seen impotence as a ramification. As the boy is aroused by any other woman, he relates back to his sexual experiences with his mother. Guilt takes over, and he is unable to remain aroused. This guilt and frustration have taken, in some cases, the forms of misogyny, physical or sexual abuse of women, or self-destructive behavior. Obviously this is in marked contrast to the idyllic outcome of film and literature. The son, older and wiser, does *not* ride off into the sunset, a better lover of women all over the world because of his experience.

Our lack of understanding and our romanticizing of the older-woman-prepubescent-boy sexual liaison prevents us from taking this dynamic seriously. Often in our well-deserved concern for girl victims of crimes, we assume male children are never victimized; incest, if it occurs, is a worldly initiation by a generous older woman. However, the sex of the victim does not negate the differences in the power, resources, and knowledge between adult and child. Male children are not immune to the damage of exploitation of those differences.

### FATHER-SON INCEST

We know that approximately 10 per cent of incest victims are boys.[89] They are most likely to be victimized by their fathers. Here we see some dramatic departures from opposite-sex parent-child incest.

Previously, we have focused on a *family* dynamic. The lack of involvement or absence of a parent still contributes to the dynamic of the remaining family members. This is not the case with the father incestuously involved with his son. The father stands alone with his problems. He is more easily identified as a "disturbed person" than the father exploiting his daughter. This type of incest offender cannot hide his problems so easily. They are much more on the surface and usually more dramatic. In the few cases studied, some of the fathers are found to be psychotic.

Father-son incest is sometimes, though not always, violent. It may begin with fondling, mutual masturbation, oral-genital contact, or exposure. Often the boys are too young to understand the sexual nature of the activity. Like the father-daughter incest victim, if the boy questions his father about the appropriateness of the interaction, the wise and all-knowing father will reassure him that everything is just fine.

I was only five when my dad started messing with me. I asked him why Mommy wasn't bathing me and why he spent so much time drying me that way. He said she was busy and he wanted to be sure I was O.K. He said it was like the doctor giving me a physical. [twenty-five-year-old past victim]

Also like the victim in father-daughter cases, the not-so-naïve son may believe that his emotional and/or pragmatic survival depend on the involvement with the father. Such relationships can bring out the dogmatic side of the offender.

He never let me go out unless I fellated him. After a while I just resigned myself to it. I wanted to get a part-time job so I could save money and get away—but he wouldn't let me. So I just ran away instead. [fifteen-year-old victim]

He kept on telling me he would have me "put away" unless I did what he wanted. What did I know? I was just a little kid. I believed he could do anything he wanted. [twenty-nine-year-old past victim]

While most fathers demonstrate affection to their sons through shared projects, sports, or just plain talk, the incestuous father presents the sexual activity as his brand of affection toward his son. Many young boys, feeling there is something not quite right about the father's behavior, go along with it, believing it is the only form of affection they will ever know from him.

Father-son incest is still an enigma. Possibly it has not been studied very much because of the repulsion we have to the *thought* of a father sodomizing his son. Two taboos are broken here—first, the molestation of a child, and second, homosexuality. Homosexuality seems to be unimportant in the father's motivation. The father has feelings of inadequacy, anger, or is basically ill, and these motivate his approach of his son. Typically, the father is *not* a homosexual. No matter what the reasons for his involvement, the father sexually exploiting his son has not yet been as thoroughly examined as he should be.

The impact on the son is doubly complicated. Young boys growing up derive a large amount of their own identities from their fathers. Not only does the son/victim have to cope with sexual abuse, but also he is lost in terms of his identity. He may grow to hate his father because of the exploitation. Inasmuch as the son's own sense of self is not yet complete, hating his father is like hating part of himself. Self-destructiveness and loss of self-respect are certain results. In preliminary studies of boy prostitution (and some runaways), we find that many boys were incest victims of their fathers. The lack of esteem is compounded by inevitable confusion over sexual identity. Their primary sexual experience has been with a man (one who was supposed to guide and protect them) under at least subtly coercive circumstances. They never had the chance to flirt and grope as other prepubescent boys experiment and discover their own sexuality. The father's exploitation pre-empted that process.

### MOTHER-DAUGHTER INCEST

Mother-daughter incest is possibly the least reported type of incest. Studies show that 97 per cent of incest offenders are men. The 3 per cent that involves mothers includes mother-son and mother-daughter incest. There is no current report on which is more prevalent.

Once again, the strongest aspect to this dynamic is role reversal. The mother has great needs for attention and affection. She may or may not have a husband. She relies on her daughter for emotional support. The incest probably begins when the daughter is too young to understand the sexual nature of her mother's contact.

As the daughter grows older, she may be uncomfortable with the mother's needs. The daughter wants to become independent of the mother, as most girls do, but there is a special issue for this victim. She is consumed with feelings of responsibility toward her mother.

She knows that becoming more independent would, to the mother, seem to be rejection. In effect, the daughter develops strong protective feelings toward the mother. Because it makes her mother feel good, she continues to allow her to express her "affection."

Another common dynamic to same-sex incestuous involvements keeps the daughter attached to the mother. Like the offender in father-son incest, the offender in mother-daughter incest is likely to be conspicuously "different." Her personality problems go beyond the incestuous involvement. The daughter is aware of the community's lack of understanding or outright rejection of her mother. The daughter may not understand what is different about her mother, but the daughter knows there is something that sets her mother apart from other people.

> My mom drank a lot, would get real disoriented and lost. Sometimes the cops would bring her home, sometimes a guy from the bar. She had a real reputation. [thirty-four-year-old past victim]

The "differentness" of the mother is confusing to the daughter on many levels. It heightens the child's perception that her mother needs taking care of. The mother turns to the daughter for that care, and the daughter most likely is the only person around to do it, given the mother's label as "different" or even "bizarre." Yet the daughter looks to her mother in her search for her own identity. Most of us consider our mothers as the model of what we will be as adult women. When we become older, we see other examples of how adult women can be, and we modify our ideas. For the daughter/victim, very much tied to her mother and socially isolated, there is little opportunity to explore other ways of being. She is closest to her mother. This is not by choice, but she resigns herself to it because the mother's need is so overwhelming.

As the daughter grows older, she may become angry, repulsed, or even begin to hate her mother. Again, with so much of her identity tied up in taking care of her mother, hating this woman is tantamount to hating herself. She may try to escape the incestuous bond through self-destructive means. The relationship has untold effects on the victim's sexuality. In the mother's possessiveness, she has probably "sheltered" the daughter from normal sexual exploration appropriate to her age. Feelings of confusion and anger will have to be sorted out before the daughter can move toward healthy relationships.

### EXTENDED FAMILY-CHILD INCEST

In some families, incest can be found in consecutive generations. Grandfather-granddaughter incest occurs, the victim being the daughter of a woman previously victimized by her father. For the multigenerational offender, incest is more of a way of life than a solution to current problems.

Extended-family child incest also applies to uncles, nephews, aunts, nieces, and cousins. There are two criteria that are important in considering the dynamic. First is the age difference. Two cousins, close in age to each other, experimenting with each other on a summer vacation or a weekend visit, is not something to be considered harmful. However, a sixteen-year-old uncle bribing his eight-year-old niece into mutual masturbation is *not* part of the normal growth and development for either person.

Second, the living situation is important. If the relative lives in the home of the child and is a mother or father figure, then to all intents and purposes, the adult is in the parent role, and the relationship would parallel those described in the previous sections. On the other hand, if the child's contact with the relative is occasional, but sexual, the infrequency of contact changes the dynamic slightly. The imbalance of power, knowledge, and resources is still being exploited, yet the child probably does not feel that daily survival depends on the continuation of the incest. Bribes, innocence, or threats may be factors in the continuation of the incest.

Grandfather-granddaughter incest is the type of incest in this category that we hear about most frequently. Often the grandfather is living in the home and is relegated to the role of baby-sitter. If he does not live in the home, children may frequently be left in his care. In this situation, he has every power over the children that would be common to the father-daughter incest situation, plus a few other "magic spells."

The age of the offender distracts everyone. Older men in this society are thought to be nonsexual. If the grandfather is married, we assume whatever sexual needs he has are shared with the grand-mother. If he is widowed or divorced, we believe his sexual interest ended with the marriage. This logic in and of itself is faulty. Add the fact that incest has little to do with sexual needs and we have a situation where misinformation contributes to the potential for incest.

The grandfather experiences the same self-doubts as the inces-tuous father, magnified by the problems of aging. He is uncomforta-ble with the aging process. He does not feel as competent or powerful as he once was. If he has had to move in with his chil-dren, he may feel infantilized. It has been a very long time since he depended on anyone for his daily survival.

He may want companionship, yet fear rejection. His grand-daughter offers him affection. She will not judge him weak or make difficult demands on him. With her, he experiences free-flowing warmth that he has missed. If he has child-care responsibilities, he has easy access to her. She understands he has the authority of a parent, but he is more fun, because of his age and special attention toward her. It is a special relationship that can easily be exploited if the grandfather is so inclined.

Once the child realizes the inappropriateness of the grandfather's attention, she may try to terminate the relationship. If he refuses and she tells other people of his molesting her, she may find she is not taken seriously because of his age:

> I told my mother about my grandfather's "game." She told me he was sick and was going to die soon, so I should just try to stay away from him. [thirty-two-year-old past victim]

> When I was five, he started putting his hands down my pants. When I did the same thing to my brother, my parents wanted to know where I got it from. I told them my grandfather. He denied it. My parents thought I made it up. I heard them talk-ing—they said he was too old to do anything, anyway. [twenty-one-year-old past victim]

Many people are not willing to confront their own fathers about molesting their children. The usual rage against offenders is tem-pered by a lifetime of respect and obedience to the grandfather, coupled with the belief that he is a "harmless old man." Yet grand-father-granddaughter incest is just as much of a reality as father daughter incest. Until taken seriously and stopped, it carries every adverse effect as any other form of incest.

### SIBLING INCEST

Some experts believe that brother-sister incest is perhaps more widespread than father-daughter incest. Once again, there is virtu-ally no reliable information about the extent of this activity.

Whereas father-daughter incest can always be considered exploi-tative and unhealthy, there are more shades and degrees involved in sibling incest. As an example, two children, five and seven years old, experimenting sexually with each other, is a very different situ-ation from that of a five-year-old girl being fondled by her thirteen-year-old brother. In the first case, both of the involved children are at the same level of knowledge, resources, and power. In the second case, the older brother definitely has more knowledge than the young girl. As baby-sitter, older brother, perhaps even substitute father, he definitely has more power.

My mother was always telling me how lucky I was to have him as my brother. She never said anything about him being lucky to have me for a sister. Whenever he hit me or anything, my mother just assumed I deserved it. He was seven years older than me. I didn't understand what he wanted me to keep coming into his bed for, but I figured I owed it to him because he was such a good brother. [twenty-eight-year-old past victim]

We must not overlook the impact of understood *physical* power. A five-year-old girl is radically different in size and strength from a pubescent boy. Depending on the family constellation, the girl may feel she has few resources for dealing with the problem. If the boy is perceived as an "adult" in the family, and she as a child, then she will probably not readily venture to tell someone of the secret.

There are three forms of sibling incest: older brother-younger sister; older sister-younger brother; and same-sex incest. Again, ac-cording to the age difference, older brother-younger sister incest can parallel the dynamics of father-daughter incest. Generally, the older brother is intimidated by contact with peers, so he turns to his younger, less demanding sister to fulfill his needs for affection and sexual exploration. This is estimated to be the most common form of sibling incest.

In the case of older sister-younger brother incest, we also find the offender intimidated by her peers. Lacking the self-confidence to venture forth in a world of adolescent boys, she turns to her younger brother to satisfy her curiosity and emotional needs. There is an element of maternal preoccupation in older sister-younger brother incest. The sister has a protective attitude toward the brother. This extends from an exaggerated simple affection to sexually acting out.

Same-sex incest is the aspect of sibling incest that we know the least about. Some experts feel that same-sex exploration is normal and not harmful up to age seven. The difference in age, resources, power, and knowledge would be the most important variable. Where there is an age imbalance, depending on the sex of the siblings, the dynamic would parallel either father-son or mother-daughter incest.

In most cases of sibling incest, the victim is prepubescent, and terminates the relationship when he or she outgrows the innocence that was a prerequisite to his or her involvement.

Sometimes we find fathers *and* brothers involved with the daughter/sister at the same time. Not enough is known about this situation. Sometimes this is with the knowledge and encouragement of the father. The patriarchal, women-as-property mentality has been inclusive of two generations rather than one. This is a particularly devastating situation for the victim. On the other hand, both father and son might molest the female child independently of each other. The son shares in the father's sense of prerogative and imitates his father's manner of dealing with feelings of inadequacy. The victim knows no other circumstance. What kind of sense of the order of the world would she gain by being victimized by both her brother and her father? For her, being a victim becomes a way of life.

Returning to the original example of the five- and the seven-year-old playing doctor, it is important to understand the difference between normal sexual exploration and incest. As much as we would like to believe in childhood "innocence," most of us realize that sexual curiosity and exploration are very much part of the normal growing-up process. In my practice, I have experienced parents labeling a neighborhood five-year-old as a "child molester" because he plays doctor with the neighborhood girls. It is confusing and difficult, at best, for parents to discover siblings engaged in sexual exploration with each other. Yet, in some sense, it is not out of the ordinary. At a young age, they probably spend more time with the sibling—possibly sharing bedrooms and bath times—than with other peers. They like each other—most of the time—and share a variety of experiences, ranging from hatred and jealousy to love and comfort. Due to the process of bonding and the sheer volume of time spent together, chances are that curiosity will strike while they are together.

Susan Forward and Craig Buck set forth some ideas about the circumstances of sibling sexual contact that need not be harmful in their book *Betrayal of Innocence: Incest and Its Devastation:*

> Under certain, very specific circumstances, sibling incest may not be a traumatic, or even unpleasant, experience. If the children are young and approximately the same age, if there is no betrayal of trust between them, if the sexual play is the result of their natural curiosity and exploration, and if the children are not traumatized by disapproving adults who stumble upon them during sex play, sibling sexual contact can be just another part of growing up. In most such cases both partners are sexually naïve. The game of show-me-yours-and-I'll-show-you-mine is older than civilization, and between young siblings of approximately the same age it is usually harmless.[90]

Sibling incest that is exploitative can be as traumatizing as sexual abuse by an adult. As adults, we have a responsibility to react in a constructive manner to normal sexual exploration and to intercede in exploitative sibling relationships. In our conscience, we know the difference.

# TWO SCENARIOS

This section has presented the dynamics of incest and child molestation as they exist in American society today. The next section offers parents some ways to enhance their children's protection from the offender. In all of the literature on the prevention of sexual violence, little addresses itself to how the *offender* can prevent his crimes. After all, it is *he,* not the parents or the children, who is responsible for the crime.

The two following fictional scenarios are some suggestions on how offenders might curtail their desire to abuse children sexually. It is not meant to be a "how to" section, but it should offer us some clues. I have never met an offender who in fact did seek treatment on his own. This is one idea of how it *could* be.

### THE POTENTIAL CHILD MOLESTER

Rod is a thirty-two-year-old single man. He was married once, but his wife left him to return to her hometown and finish her education. They married very young—both before they were twenty years old—and although they once had wanted the same things, they eventually developed such different goals that they could not stay together.

Rod's goal right now is to be happy again. Ever since the divorce two years ago, he has felt anxious and unsettled. The marriage broke up with many things left unsaid—at least on Rod's part. His wife was quite explicit about why she didn't love Rod anymore. He was hurt and immobilized at the time. Sometimes he thinks about getting together with her, to tell her his side of the story, but then Rod thinks, "What's the use? It's over. She wasn't worth much anyway."

If she wasn't "worth much," Rod certainly spends a lot of time thinking about the divorce, which causes him trouble at work. There is a new training program for disadvantaged men in the construction company Rod works in. Rod finds this humorous because no one, in his mind, is more disadvantaged than he is. His father was killed when he was very young, and he helped his mother raise his younger brother and sister. No one ever gave Rod any breaks. Because of Rod's poor concentration, the new foreman was always on his back. He noticed the foreman was much more tolerant of imperfect work in the disadvantaged men. This led Rod to many hassles with the other men. He resented the special attention they got, blamed them for the trouble he was in, and picked a lot of fights with them. He usually lost, but Rod didn't care because it helped him to release some of the anger he always carried around with him. But he would wake up the next morning angry all over again.

Women were a major source of Rod's anger. He dated a lot—he is very attractive—but nothing ever seems to last for long. Rod has an image of the ideal woman, but all of his dates were repeatedly disappointing. They don't want the ideal relationship. They want to go to school, or buy a house, or do anything but settle down with Rod. One woman was saving her money to go on a camera safari in Africa. Rod lost respect for her and asked her, "What good is that going to do anyone?" She replied it would do *her* some good, and that is enough. Things sure had changed—when Rod got married the first time, there were plenty of women looking to settle down. "It's that stupid women's lib," Rod insisted. "Not only do they have a program for disadvantaged men, now they are talking about a program for *women* construction workers." Rod liked to rip down posters for Holly Near concerts.

Frustrated by his search for the ideal woman, enveloped in imaginary one-sided arguments with his ex-wife, and not doing so well on the job, Rod found himself with a lot of free time on his hands. One day, while he wasn't paying attention, Rod fell off a low scaffold. As a result he took a one month medical leave for physical therapy for a minor back injury.

With so much free time, Rod's feelings became more intense. Rod could identify his anger, but another feeling—one more elusive to Rod—prevailed. He had a gnawing sense of inadequacy and loneliness. What to do on a Saturday night was a constant source of worry to Rod. Even when he had a date, he felt unable to be a good

companion to the woman. He couldn't carry on a conversation, he
never knew when to "make the move," and his own neediness got
in the way of treating a woman right. He felt too anxious ever to
enjoy himself. Now on leave from work, Rod felt even more clumsy
and inadequate. And he still was angry.

Walking around the city, looking for some Holly Near concert
posters to rip down, Rod came across a playground full of kids playing baseball. It reminded him of something he hadn't thought about
for years. The coach of the baseball team was a very large, burly,
darkish person. He had a jovial laugh, and teased the boys. Rod
could tell the kids on the team genuinely liked him.

The coach, in turn, reminded Rod of the camp counselor he had
the one summer he was able to get free from his mother, brother,
and sister by getting a church scholarship to camp. His camp counselor took a liking to Rod, and together they went on special trips.
To a nine-year-old boy who had never known his father, the counselor's attention was important. Toward the end of the summer,
after sharing many new experiences and telling the counselor his
deep, darkest secrets, the counselor took Rod on many overnight
canoe trips—just the two of them. One night, after Rod had asked
the counselor some questions about sex that he felt he couldn't ask
his mother, the counselor molested Rod. He told Rod he wanted
to try something that would make him feel very good and he reminded him of all the other wonderful new things he had shown
Rod. The counselor performed fellatio on Rod and taught him to
do the same to him.

Rod was not entirely comfortable with the situation. This was
a form of sexuality he knew nothing about, but it just didn't feel
right to him, and he found the counselor's ejaculations very unpleasant. But the summer would soon be over, and Rod didn't want
to risk the friendship he had with the counselor. He was the best
friend Rod ever had. They wrote for a little while in the fall, then
gradually lost touch. Rod never received another church scholarship
to camp, and that was the end of the relationship.

When Rod looked closer at the coach, he realized the man really
didn't look like the counselor, but that realization didn't help. Rod
was already dwelling on the early victimization.

"That guy made a fool out of me," thought Rod. "It isn't fair, getting a little kid to do a queer thing like that, when he doesn't even know what it is. No wonder I have so many problems. It's probably due to that."

He wanted to find the counselor and tell him how he had ruined his life. Somewhere inside Rod, he doubted that the counselor would believe him. The counselor seemed to enjoy the sexual interaction greatly and was oblivious to Rod's feelings. Rod began to wish he had that kind of control over someone—that someone would perform so unquestioningly for him without any demands.

Just watching the kids play baseball seemed to soothe Rod's frustration. That day he introduced himself to the coach, and after watching them play for about a week, asked if he could help out during practice. Coaching helped pass the time and Rod felt in control—something he never felt at work or out on dates.

An attraction grew to one particular eight-year-old boy—he reminded Rod of himself at Kenny's age. A special relationship grew, and Rod found himself sexually aroused by Kenny. It started innocently enough—picking the boy up, hugging him, and swinging him in the air when he made a good hit—which was hardly ever. Kenny wanted physical closeness to Rod, and the closer Kenny got, the more aroused Rod became. Many times Rod flashed back on the summer with the camp counselor, forgetting the parts about not liking the sex. He remembered only how much the counselor enjoyed the relationship.

Rod always had masturbated quite a bit, but again was frustrated because the assertive women he dated didn't provide him with much material. He had pinup posters all over his room, but he grew tired of these. He went to a porno shop and saw a book entitled *The Boys on the Team*. Almost jokingly, Rod bought it and read it while he masturbated. Rod had happened onto powerful fantasy material. His contacts with Kenny and the good feelings that came from them strengthened his erotic responses.

Rod became close to Kenny's family. Kenny was raised by his mother and grandfather; his father had taken off years ago. Rod suggested he take Kenny on a weekend camping trip. Given the weeks of closeness between Kenny and Rod, the family was happy for Kenny to have this special chance.

Rod saw it as a special chance for him too. He no longer saw his own molestation in a totally negative light. After all, it wasn't the camp counselor who messed him up—it was women and their high-flung ideas about what they could do without a man—specifically him. The counselor had been Rod's teacher; Rod wanted to be Kenny's teacher too. He had fantasized about the weekend for some time.

Fear of rejection was at the bottom of Rod's problems with women. Although Kenny made Rod feel somewhat secure because Kenny made no demands, and Rod was less lonely when he was with Kenny than he had ever been before, Rod was still nervous about making his fantasies about Kenny come true. Rod needed to "test" Kenny first. Rod took off his pants when they both were in the tent. He walked around in the nude, hoping Kenny would seem curious. Kenny practically ignored Rod's parading, so Rod sat down next to him on his cot. He figured if Kenny became upset about his exposing himself, he could say it was an "accident" or a "misunderstanding" on Kenny's part.

Kenny's mom had done a good job of discussing sex with him. He didn't think Rod's prolonged nudity and approach were accidents. Kenny also knew what fellatio and mutual masturbation were, and no one was allowed to do those things to him. As soon as Rod sat on the cot Kenny became very upset. He cried and demanded to go home immediately.

Kenny's strong reaction to Rod snapped him back into reality. No longer identifying with the counselor, he now identified with Kenny. He remembered that being a victim was a helpless, scary feeling. Rod cried over his lost friendship with Kenny. He begged Kenny not to tell anyone—promised never to come around the baseball park if he didn't tell. Kenny figured his mother and grandfather had enough problems without this, so he agreed.

Rod had developed his fantasy life over months, and it wasn't going to disappear as quickly as Kenny did. He put his sex-siren posters back up, but they didn't compete with his vast collection of child pornography. Women were no longer outlets for his sexual feelings. Dating was a lost cause—Rod had spent so much time with Kenny and was out of touch with the bar scene. Besides, most of the women in the bars just wanted one-night stands. Rod was back at work, but things there had gotten worse—he enjoyed masturbating now more than ever before. The novelty of masturbation alone was wearing thin. Rod needed to act out his fantasies to get the same excitement. But the terrified look on Kenny's face stopped him from trying to molest a child. Still, what to do with all these feelings?

One of the few benefits of Rod's job was a good health-insurance plan. When he couldn't replace his child-molestation fantasies with any other material, and his general level of discontent kept on increasing, he decided to see a therapist. He and his wife had gone a few times before the divorce, and while it wasn't successful, it wasn't too unpleasant for Rod.

Rod did not tell the therapist about Kenny or his fantasies about children. He told him he wanted therapy because he was unhappy and depressed—he couldn't sleep well, he'd lost his appetite, his temper always seemed on the verge of exploding. At first, he talked about his feelings about his job, the disadvantaged men, his dating history, and his attitude toward Holly Near. They first worked on Rod's problems with authority figures and smoothed over some of the conflicts at work. Once Rod was able to deal with those situations more diplomatically, he talked about his feelings toward the divorce, how he felt about women, and what he wanted in future relationships. The therapist examined Rod's expectations of the women he dated in light of what he was willing to offer them, which wasn't much. Even though Rod had gained some insight into his adult relationships, that still didn't solve his problem of wanting to molest children. Rod felt more lost and alienated than he ever had before. Until he felt comfortable enough to talk about it in therapy, Rod worked overtime and stayed away from kids as much as possible.

The therapist knew something was going on inside of Rod, suspected it was sexual in nature, but wasn't sure exactly what the problem was. He asked Rod about his fantasy life. Rod felt comfortable enough to tell the therapist that he occasionally looked at child pornography. When the therapist was nonjudgmental about this, Rod decided to tell him about his own victimization. It was the first time Rod had ever discussed it with anyone.

Although Rod was glad he disclosed his childhood incident to the therapist, who was helpful, there was no change in Rod's feelings of loneliness that ignited his attraction to children. Finally, Rod told the therapist about Kenny. The therapist told him there were two good alternatives for Rod: He could join a therapy group of child molesters, meeting twice a week, or Rod could see a special-ized-behavior-modification therapist and work on diminishing his arousal to children as sex objects. Since Rod hadn't committed any crimes yet, he decided not to go to the group. Although he was concerned about his preoccupation with child sex play, he didn't see himself as an offender, and didn't want to be identified that way. To change his fantasy material back to where it used to be—focused on adult women—was a good goal in his mind. He wanted to continue to see his original therapist at the same time to talk about other issues.

Rod had made considerable progress in the behavior-modification program—he was highly motivated. He no longer masturbates to child-oriented material and has replaced that with adult-female ma-terial. The dating-life and work problems are not totally solved. In the meantime, Rod needed something to give himself a feeling of importance, of control over a situation—preferably something that helps him to feel better about himself, less anxious and depressed. The therapist suggested that Rod continue to avoid children and that he would do well with senior citizens. Rod now volunteers at a home for the elderly. The staff and residents like him; he is very helpful and generous with them. He feels he is making a big differ-ence in their lives—every bit as much as he impacted Kenny—so he feels better about himself.

### THE POTENTIALLY INCESTUOUS FATHER

Robert is an aerospace engineer who works hard for his wife and three daughters. Everything should be just fine with him—he makes a good salary, he's done well in a highly competitive field, his family is healthy, but all of this doesn't seem to be enough for him. He's not depressed—it's just that no matter how much he does, it never seems good enough. His standards for himself are so high, he always fails. Robert hates failing more than anything else.

His oldest daughter, Kathleen, is the spitting image of her mother, Betty, when she was younger. Robert looks on in amazement as his little girl begins to look more like a woman than a child. Kathleen also *acts* more like an adult than a child. Betty has taken a 4-to-11 P.M. job at an insurance company to help out with the household bills. While she is gone, Kathleen cooks dinner, tucks the younger girls into bed, and does some of the housework. Kathleen really doesn't mind those things—she likes her family and wants to see everyone stay together. Not so long ago, she was afraid the family might break up.

Betty not only took the job for the money, she also was anxious to be out of the house when Robert came home. He had high standards for her too, and nothing she did was right. She had never felt particularly good about herself anyway, so his nagging certainly didn't help any. She missed the kids, but they were getting older now, and she was home when they got home from school. Kathleen was an intense child, and very responsible. She was sure Kathleen could handle the extra household work. After all, Betty had done the same thing at Kathleen's age.

Robert now felt ambivalent about going home at night. He was glad that Betty wasn't there—that would end the fights. He thought it was much better now that Kathleen was running the household; as a twelve-year-old, she did a better job than her mother, and Robert felt a good job deserved a reward (even if no one rewarded him when he worked hard), so he would bring her small gifts and shower her with compliments about her looks. On the other hand, he didn't like being alone with the kids. It made him nervous, and all he knew how to do was tell them if they were good or bad. Eventually, Kathleen took the major responsibility for supervising the children.

He never really liked engineering, but he chose it as a profession after the war because of the potentially high earning power. He was right about the earning power, but for the past twenty-five years, he has hated the work. Robert's hobby is photography, and he is fairly good at it. As much as he would like to try to make a living at it, he is unsure about his talent.

To make the evenings go a little faster, Robert began to drink. He never got drunk—just enough to calm his restlessness. Since the fighting between her parents had stopped, Kathleen believed things were better at home, so she tried very hard to please her father.

She was also secretly happy her mother was working nights. Kathleen didn't much like her mother. Kathleen tried asking her mother questions about growing up, menstruation, dating, etc., but her mother always put her off. Kathleen felt stupid for asking the questions.

Kathleen found it much easier to talk with her father. One night, after all the girls were in bed, they were watching TV together. Staying up later than the other children was Kathleen's reward for all of her good work. She had a question about sex, and since her father seemed relaxed and was much nicer to her than her mother, Kathleen decided to ask him. She told him about the health lesson they had had today, and she sort of understood about the erection, but she didn't really see *how* the penis could go from being very small to very large, then back again. Stuttering and stammering, Robert tried to explain the physiology of erection but told Kathleen she should ask her mother.

Kathleen told him she had *no* intention of asking her mother *anything*. She complained that her mother never listened to her and piled all kinds of housework on her. She reassured Robert—she didn't mind helping him and the younger kids—but she resented her mother's absence. The camaraderie between Robert and Kathleen thickened. He kept his feelings about Betty's aloofness to himself, but he felt Kathleen understood the rejection and emptiness he felt. Instead of being father-daughter, they were two friends commiserating over the same problem.

For the first time, Robert felt sexually attracted to Kathleen. This unnerved Robert tremendously.

As time went on, he found himself increasingly attracted to Kathleen. The younger girls chided him that he liked Kathleen better than them. He tried to use his marriage as an outlet for his sexual feelings. That didn't really work—his wife wasn't very receptive to his newfound wealth of sexual feelings. She was busy thinking of how she could earn enough money to divorce Robert and be rid of his overbearing criticism forever. Even when Robert did make love with Betty, it didn't decrease his attraction to Kathleen—this was so much more than sexual feelings. Around Kathleen, he felt like a success. He didn't understand the erections, but they were persistent when he was around Kathleen.

Robert considered having an affair. Some of the women in his office had affairs, and from time to time they flirted with him. After a couple of clumsy attempts to ask one woman for a drink, he felt worse than before. She refused even to have a drink with him, and he felt foolish. Later, he rationalized, this was all for the better because if he and Betty ever did get a divorce, she could hold it against him and get a large settlement of money.

He tried to spend more time with the younger girls, and not focus so much of his attention on Kathleen. But Robert found he could not do this without Kathleen—the little girls were too demanding and he didn't know how to deal with them. He felt like more of a failure.

One night, he had a few drinks before watching television with Kathleen. She sat next to him and he put his arm around her, like he usually did. After a particularly difficult evening with the younger girls, Kathleen was more tired than usual. She fell asleep and her head fell down into her father's lap. Robert felt the erection beginning again. It would be *so* easy, he thought—so easy.

When Robert realized how easy it really was, he decided he had better do something about it. It was one thing to love Kathleen more than any other family member, and feel like a winner around her, but it was disconcerting to have sexual feelings about her. Suddenly, he suggested to Betty that they go see their pastor. Their family had been very involved in the church, and they liked the pastor. Betty was surprised—she had tried to get Robert to go with her many times, but he never wanted their personal problems to go beyond their family. If he was finally over his embarrassment, that was fine with her.

The pastor provided a way for Betty and Robert to talk about their problems without fighting. At first they talked about what was wrong with each other. Betty complained about Robert's sullenness, rigidity, and constant criticism. Robert complained about Betty's aloofness, her lack of sexual responsiveness, and he told her Kathleen thought she was a terrible mother, that Betty never talked with her. Once the conflicts were out in the open, they began to talk about how they felt and what they wanted to do about the future. Robert never discussed his sexual feelings about Kathleen, and the feelings did not go away.

Although the sessions with the pastor took the edge off the tensions at home, both Betty and Robert were still unhappy. The pastor suggested they become involved in more church-related family activities, so Robert and Betty could meet more adults and find that their problems were not out of the ordinary. "If he only knew," thought Robert. But the family was in a rut, totally consumed by its own problems. New activity was threatening, but at this point, Robert and Betty figured there was no other direction in which to go.

One of the activities they got involved in was mother-daughter functions. The club had field trips, luncheons, and guest speakers who talked about issues of communication and sex education—very timely for Betty and Kathleen. It was something for them to do, just the two of them—and with the club protecting Betty from her feelings of inadequacy about being a mother to a teen-age girl, Betty could bridge some of the distance she had put between Kathleen and herself.

Although the situation was improving between Kathleen and her mother, things were not much better between Robert and Betty, and Robert still had strong incestuous feelings toward Kathleen. He decided it would be best if he moved out for a while. This was an expensive proposition, but he felt he owed it to his family, particularly Kathleen. He and Betty continued to see the pastor and work out their differences. Eventually the entire family entered family therapy. The sessions helped them to talk openly and learn to trust each other. Robert visited the kids often and constantly reassured them that the separation wasn't because he didn't love them, nor was it necessarily permanent. Because of the relationship she was developing with her mother, Kathleen was less nervous about a separation than she had been months before.

Betty changed her work shift to the day. With Robert out of the house, there was no need to be away in the evenings. She took charge of many of the household chores, freeing Kathleen to participate in more adolescent activities than being surrogate housewife. As Kathleen became more of the child she should be, she appeared to be less of a woman, and therefore less sexually attractive to Robert.

The problem was still really with Robert in his perception of

Kathleen and his feelings of inadequacy, which resulted in incestuous urgings toward Kathleen. Slowly, he and Betty made some progress. It became clear to Robert that he would never be happy until he gave up some of his rigid values and standards. This was easier said than done, but because Robert loved his children and felt strongly about being a family man, he put his therapy to good use and began to change some of his old belief systems.

A major change came with his job situation when Robert started to attend night school in photography. He was greatly encouraged by his instructor's response to his work. Finally he found something he was good at *and* liked doing. He tentatively suggested to Betty that he might quit the engineering business, and after a little more training, start a portrait-photography business. Surprisingly, she was open to the idea—although she preferred that Robert first work in an established studio for a while. With the recommendations of his instructor, Robert found a photography job. It didn't pay as much, but Betty felt it was worth the end of his complaining about work as an engineer.

After six months on the new job and many, many more sessions with the pastor, Robert moved back into the house. Feeling better about himself and his relationship with Betty, he looked at Kathleen differently. She was now fourteen, and beginning the normal process of pulling away from her father. She no longer tolerated nicknames, insisted on being called Kathleen, and pulled back on the affection toward all family members. She and her mother shopped for dresses for her first boy-girl parties and dances. Kathleen was less willing to help around the house, insisting her little sisters could do more.

Robert looked at Kathleen—she was now his growing, sometimes difficult, beautiful teen-age daughter. Feelings of tenderness replaced feelings of arousal. He was finding in Betty and his new career what he had once thought he could find only in an intimate relationship with Kathleen.

# EXERCISES

## EXERCISE ONE     ADDITIONAL READING

To further your understanding of the crimes of child molestation and incest, I strongly recommend the following books:

Butler, Sandra. *Conspiracy of Silence: The Trauma of Incest.* San Francisco, Calif.: New Glide Publications (hardcover); New York Bantam Books (softcover), 1978.

Burgess, Ann; Groth, A. Nicholas; Holmstrom, Lynda; and Sgroi, Suzanne. *Sexual Assault of Children and Adolescents.* Lexington, Mass.: Lexington Books, 1978.

Rush, Florence. *The Best Kept Secret: A History of Child Sexual Abuse.* Englewood Cliffs, N.J.: Prentice-Hall, 1980.

## EXERCISE TWO     ORGANIZE YOUR NEIGHBORHOOD

Parents are tremendous resources for each other. Organize a neighborhood meeting to present constructive information on all crimes relating to children. Your local law-enforcement agency will probably be willing to give a lecture. Often local officers would like a chance to talk to parents, but they do not have the time or resources for community outreach. Ask for the following information:

1. *Statistics on child sexual abuse in your neighborhood:* incidence; circumstances; arrest rate; disposition of cases.

2. *Services for child victims:* Find out the location of the nearest hospital equipped to treat child victims. Get the phone numbers of the hospital and any existing sexual-violence crisis service. Ask if there is a victims' assistance unit in your local prosecutor's office and get detailed information on their services. Once you are familiar with the programs and have col-

lected important phone numbers, keep the information with other emergency information.

3. *How to organize a Helping Hand Program:* Ask your local law-enforcement agency about this program, and if you gain their co-operation, representatives from your neighborhood should meet with the school to institute the program. Large orange-and-black "hand" symbols are placed in the windows of homes where an adult is usually present. The adult should be interviewed by school personnel and neighborhood parents to be sure the adult will be responsible and knows how to intervene for a child in trouble. Then children in school are told that if they have *any* trouble (bullies, chased by animals, potential child sexual abusers) they can go to a Helping Hand house, and an adult will be there to help.

4. *Begin support groups for each other:* From your neighborhood meeting, begin ongoing talks about your personal experiences or problems in warning your children about child sexual abuse; share your sex-education concerns and situations; refer trustworthy baby-sitters to each other. Many neighbors have informal relationships that include these important sharing experiences; however, some new or isolated neighbors can get to know and help each other as a result of the neighborhood meeting if it is encouraged.

EXERCISE THREE    BABY-SITTER CHECK LIST

Sit down with the other significant adult or adults, if present, and formulate a check list/questionnaire to ask a potential baby-sitter. This does not need to be an interrogation, but thinking back to the section on adolescent offenders, what kinds of information do you want about the teen-ager who will take care of your child? Be sure to ask your child what he or she wants in a baby-sitter. Here is a beginning—each parent and child will add their own important considerations. Much can be gained from sharing lists with other adults:

1. Ask for references.

2. Talk casually about the adolescent's other interests. Do they all center on small children?

3. Inquire into *why* this teen-ager wants to baby-sit. How does she or he feel about children? Does baby-sitting fit into some long-range plan?

4. What do his or her parents think about his or her baby-sitting for money? Are they supportive and accessible?

5. Does the teen-ager understand emergency procedures? Has she or he had any experience in child-care situations where one of the children suddenly became sick or was hurt? Tell him or her what you would like him or her to do in an emergency situation.

6. What forms of discipline does the teen-ager use? How effective do they think bribes are? How often do they use them?

7. Give the potential baby-sitter some realistic hypothetical situations concerning your children. Discuss the best way to handle each situation.

# PART THREE[1]

---

## DISCUSSING CHILD SEXUAL ABUSE WITH THE CHILD

# INTRODUCTION

Not all crimes of child sexual abuse can be prevented. Any brochure, book, speaker, or class that encourages a parent to believe that he or she holds the power omnipotently to protect children from sexual abuse is irresponsible as well as inaccurate.

In the following section, various ways to warn a child about potential sexual abuse will be explored. If we understand the circumstances of the crime and impart that information to the child, the arena of potential abuse can be decreased. Through understanding some of the patterns of the child sexual abuser, nonvictim responses in a child can be developed. Much can be done to make child sexual abuse less likely in a child's life, but there is nothing we can do to ensure eternal safety. After all, that is the responsibility of the offender. Only when *all* offenders stop offending will *all* children be protected.

That is not a very likely state of the world, but it does put the responsibility for child sexual abuse directly where it belongs. Again, children are not responsible because they responded to the offender's manipulations. The parents are not responsible for the molestation because they did or didn't say something to the child about a potential incident. The offender made the choice to abuse the child sexually.

In teaching children prevention techniques, parents must be very clear about the offender's responsibility. As difficult as it might be, they must be honest with themselves as to how much they can do to keep an offender from abusing their child. In that frame of mind, parents can move ahead to teach prevention in the context of the real circumstances of the offense.

Even with a somewhat limited ability to provide a haven of invulnerability, parents are by far the best teachers of prevention of child sexual abuse. I did not write a book for children on this subject because the information needs to be repeated many times, and it is unlikely that children would read such a book more than once. I did not write a book for teachers or other child-care workers because the child's understanding and integration of the information depend upon trust and accessibility between the child and teaching adult. While these adults can be helpful, only the parent has an ongoing relationship with the child during the many years he or she might be a victim. In other words, no one can teach a child about the realities of child sexual abuse better than a parent. With whatever personal or societal limitations parents have, they *can* help the child be a nonvictim because they have the potential to reinforce, answer questions, and be continuing sources of strength and information for the child.

Knowing that you are the best person for the job, each reader/parent can take the knowledge of Part One and Part Two, go forward to Part Three, adapt all that you have learned to your own individual values and lifestyles, and begin the joint venture between parent and child toward a safer life. Although it is ultimately the offender who decides if a specific child is to be a victim, you and your child can make his decision very difficult, if not at times impossible.

## Looking at Other Forms of Survival Information

The time has now come to sit down and discuss child sexual abuse with the child. Giving children an understanding of child sexual abuse is really giving them "survival information."

Survival information is any warning or instruction we give children to ensure their safety. Some examples of survival information are:

"Dress warmly because it's cold outside."

"Eat your food, you need it to grow up."

"Watch before you cross the street. Look both ways and don't cross against the light."

"Don't play in the street after dark."

"Don't go near strange animals, especially squirrels."

"Don't pick up things on the street and put them in your mouth."

"Be very careful when plugging things in. You should never have wet hands when you're around an electrical outlet."

"Stay away from the pills in the cabinet. You only take pills that Mommy or Daddy give you."

"Don't play with matches."

"Don't accept rides with strangers."

Every parent can double or triple that list. In this part of the book, the phrase "survival information" is used many times. When you read the phrase, think of it as a positive way to enrich the child's ability to cope with the world. A warning about child sexual abuse is just one of the literally hundreds of pieces of survival information children hear every day.

The reason we give our children survival information is to provide them with the ability to recognize and cope with dangerous situations. If the warning is ominous and without constructive advice, only fear and confusion will be instilled in the child. The child may then become immobile when faced with a potentially dangerous situation. For this reason, all survival information should be presented in a straightforward and objective manner. With the subject of child sexual abuse, this is easier said than done, but, as much as possible, the atmosphere for these discussions should be similar to the emotional climate when discussing other things important to the child's continued safety (not crossing the street against the light, not swimming alone, etc.). If, in contrast, child molestation and incest are discussed in whispers or in a shameful and mysterious manner, the subject becomes something "nice people don't talk about."

To help the parent establish the matter-of-fact, unemotional climate, a review of how the family normally discusses other survival information is helpful. Some of the following questions may help to formulate the style of the many other warnings the child receives:

• What seems to be the best time of day to talk with the child about important things?

• What is the best place to talk with the child?

• Do I warn my child about things only as they come up or do I talk with my child about potential dangers in general terms?

• Do I talk with one child at a time, or are all brothers and sisters included?

• Does my child listen to the other parent or another adult better than he listens to me?

• Does my child come to me with situations she or her friends have encountered? Does this open up discussions?

• How often do I reprimand my child for asking questions or bringing up situations for which I feel he should already know the correct responses?

• Does my child seem to understand only after being rewarded or punished?

After we consider some of these aspects of our presentations on survival information, we will have a clearer idea of how to proceed to warn our children about potential sexual abuse. Remember, a warning about child sexual abuse is another piece of survival information, and it needs to be handled in the same style as other warnings.

Many parents believe they cannot discuss sexual abuse with their child without rendering the child suspicious and frightened of all people. Yet we warn our children to stay away from strange animals without worrying that they will be afraid of all animals for the rest of their lives. We caution them many times about the damage running in front of a car can do to them, yet we do not become concerned that they may never want to drive a car. Information about child sexual abuse does not need to have any more limiting effects than any other survival information.

Even if the parents are not totally satisfied with how they have discussed this subject with their child, the child is better off than if it had never been discussed at all. Even a nervous discussion is better than none at all. A child who is never warned of this reality, and is later victimized, may become distrustful and suspicious of people. The process of not dealing with child sexual abuse until *after* the child is victimized is a sure-fire way to alienate the child.

The best approach to the subject, of course, is to answer the child's questions about sex in the most simple and direct way possible, but this too is often easier said than done. Sometimes children ask us questions about sex or sexual abuse before we are ready with answers. Many parents, caught unprepared, don't know how to answer. Other parents, anticipating the discussion *they* have planned, give inappropriate answers.

We all know the story about the little girl who asks her mother, "Where did I come from?" The mother thinks this is the opportunity she has been waiting for to tell her daughter the facts of life. She goes into elaborate descriptions of sexual intercourse, the nine months of pregnancy, and the process of childbirth. When she is finished, she asks the little girl, "Now do you have any questions?" The little girl replies, "Yes. Where did I come from?" The mother is astounded. She answers, "But I just told you. Didn't you understand?" The little girl is exasperated at this point. She throws her hands up in the air and says, "Look, Susan says she was born in Cincinnati, and I just want to know where *I* was born. Where did I come from?"

In our anxiety about this subject, explaining too much is easy to do. We need to listen carefully to what the child is asking. Repeating the questions back to the child, in our own words, is a good way to gauge how well we have understood the questions. It is important <u>not</u> to give the child more information than was asked for. We need to respect our child's pace of learning.

Another frequent mistake is to put the question off. When we tell the child, "We'll talk about that later," or "Go ask your mother," this discourages the child. In the child's mind, the answer may sound more like, "We may never get around to talking about that," or "Don't bother me with those questions." Children need some form of immediate answer to feel that their questions have been taken seriously.

At the same time, the parents need to respect their own pace. It is perfectly natural to be uncomfortable with some of the candid inquiries children make. Parents need to know where their most effective level of operation is and then respect that. If you do not feel comfortable telling your child of three about some aspect of sex, then explain to the child what you can comfortably explain. After that, discuss the situation with other parents. Get some idea on how other people have handled similar situations. None of us are alone in this struggle to figure out *when* is the right time to discuss sex with our children. Gain some more information in order to be a little bit more comfortable the next time the child takes you off guard with a question.

The bottom line on this issue is that the parent needs to be aware of how he or she feels about the subject. Do some serious thinking about your attitudes toward sex, how well you can explain various aspects to your child and your values concerning sex education. If you haven't thought through some of these, you are apt to be confused when, all of a sudden, you are engaged in a conversation with a child about sex or sexual abuse. The child senses this confusion and believes she should be confused too. If the parent is uncomfortable, but *clear* about why he is uncomfortable, then the child does not take on the confusion.

For some parents, the child's question about child sexual abuse may bring up disturbing childhood memories. Some parents were victims of sexual abuse—from the single incident of being fondled by a stranger in a theater to an ongoing incestuous relationship. As hard as it is *today* for open discussions of these crimes, it was much more difficult twenty years ago. The parent's own victimization may be something he or she has not thought about until the child asks the question. Taken off guard, feelings of fear, confusion, anger, and sorrow are dredged up—perhaps all at the same time.

It is never too late to deal with our victimization. As an adult, the parent can contact the local rape-crisis or victim-service center to obtain counseling, or the parent can share the feelings with a close friend. However the parent chooses to deal with feelings about being a victim, it is important that some constructive process be pursued, not only for the purpose of enhancing the discussion with the child, but also for the parent's benefit. Victimization does not go away with time if it is not dealt with. Feelings die hard, and the parent deserves compassion and guidance every bit as much as the child. Once the past victimization is in the open, the parent will be able to discuss child sexual abuse more clearly and calmly with the child. More importantly, the parent will have finally received the positive attention he or she needs concerning the victimization.

Remember, *all* parents have something valuable to say about this topic. Sharing our experiences, our knowledge, and our mistakes can be very helpful. All of us have felt alone and overwhelmed by demanding situations. There are many demanding situations involved in parenting a child today, more than we like to think about. We can learn from and support each other.

## Setting the Tone

Now that we've put warnings about child sexual abuse into perspective with other forms of survival information and we are clear about the depth and range of our feelings about the topic, there are some other elements that need to be considered before we begin the task of sitting down with the child and giving warnings on sexual abuse.

Teaching the child proper names for *all* parts of the body (including genitalia) is extremely important. First, this removes the shame and mystery surrounding those parts of the body. The child learns how to react if someone on the school grounds is trying to break his arm. Violations of another part of the body should not carry an inordinate amount of fear or shame. The child's reaction should be as protective and spontaneous as in the school-grounds situation. If the child is as knowledgeable about genitalia as he is about other body parts, then activities affecting genitalia will not seem especially catastrophic.

Also, to be able to explain what has happened to her, a child needs to know proper terminology for genitalia. Many police detectives report being unable to take a statement from a child victim because the nicknames used for sex organs were so unique they could not interpret what had really happened. It is very traumatic for a child to want to explain what has happened to her, yet no one understands her because she uses family nicknames for genitalia that are not easily understood by other people. In order for a child to be clear about the act of molestation that has been committed against her, she must know the proper names for her body parts.

Parents make a game of teaching children the words for nose, eyes, ears, lips, fingers, etc. This helps the child's vocabulary, his speech, and his ability to conceptualize things. It does not seem reasonable that proper terminology is taught for all parts of the body except for the area from the navel to the knees, front and back. This part of the body, too, has specific names.

Along with the proper terminology, parents also teach the functions of body parts. Ears hear, eyes see, lips smile, and so on. There is no reason for the child not to know the functions of the penis, vagina, anus, buttocks, etc. What has been said about terminology applies equally well to functions.

Many years ago I had a client who was five years old. I would spend twenty minutes of each session alone with his mother. It was very important to this little boy to bring his mother and me cups of coffee during the session. We were concerned that he was really too little to handle two cups of coffee, but it was earth-shakingly important to him. One day, the inevitable happened: He spilled hot coffee on his hand. He began crying and one of the other therapists approached him and asked where it hurt. He pointed to his knuckles and said, "It's right here, the place that works like a hinge on a door, except that's not what you call it."

Obviously, the parent had done a very good job at familiarizing the child with his body and explaining in understandable terms what the functions of body parts were. He could describe them, though the word was missing.

It could be the most natural thing in the world for parents to name genitalia and explain their sexual and nonsexual functions in a matter-of-fact way while caring for their children. Most of us are not willing to sit down and have a special talk with our children to name genitalia in clear terms, but this really isn't necessary. The best way to teach children the proper terms for their genitalia is to do this along with other parts of their bodies, although bath times and toilet-hygiene training are particularly appropriate times. We often ask our children, "Did you wash your neck?" or "Did you reach behind your ears?" These are often-neglected areas of the body. We feel relatively comfortable asking our children if they washed in those places. Buttocks, penises, and vaginas are also hard to reach or sometimes overlooked in bathing. As we are asking our children if they washed their neck or ears, it is natural to ask, in a matter-of-fact tone of voice, if they also washed their buttocks. This process helps the child to be comfortable and familiar with genitalia. Those special parts of the body do not take on "larger than life" proportions. Genitalia are not to be feared or to be mysterious. This sense of ease helps to reduce anxiety that can surround warnings about child sexual abuse.

In many cases, the topic of child sexual abuse is brought up by the child with direct questions. But assuming the child has not asked about the topic, the parent must make a conscious decision of *when* to initiate this discussion with the child. This is a very individual decision; there is no right answer. Some variables to consider when making this decision are:

- How much time is my child spending without the direct supervision of her parents?

- How real is the danger of child sexual abuse for her?

- How verbal or articulate is my child? Could we carry on the conversation or exchange of information that is important in this discussion?

- How much interest has my child expressed in this subject?

- Has there been some incident or event in our community that warrants my bringing this up *now*?

For many parents, the answers to these questions add up to the answer, "I begin to warn my child about sexual abuse around four or five years old." There is a lot of room for variance among different families. And, within each family, the answer may be different for each child.

The initial discussion does not need to be complicated. Especially for the child of four or five, the explanation of what child sexual abuse consists of should be simple. The following example is a suggestion:

PARENT: "You know, Susie, there are some older people in the

world, people who are bigger than you, who have a hard time
making friends with people their own age. So they ask little
kids to be their friends. When they ask little kids to be their
friends, they sometimes ask the kids to do things like undress,
or they want to put their hands down your pants. Those are
things that shouldn't happen to children. If anybody tells you
to do that, we want to know about it right away. We want you
to say 'no' and come home and tell us."

CHILD: "But why would anybody want to do anything like put
their hands down my pants?"

PARENT: "Because they are mixed up. They want other people
to like them a whole lot, and they think that is the way to get
people to like them."

CHILD: "So why is it a bad thing for kids to do? Why should
I say 'no'?"

PARENT: "Because what that adult is asking you to do isn't good
for little kids to do with big people. There are other things we
don't want you to do, like driving a car or staying alone for a
long time. We don't let you do those other things because we
love you a lot. We want you to be safe and healthy. We want
you to grow up and be happy."

There is no need to go into elaborate descriptions of intercourse,
oral-genital contact, masturbation, etc. "Don't let anyone put their
hands down your pants" covers almost all possible sexual abuse.
Rules about undressing need to be very clear. The rules correspond
with the child's growing need for privacy. They are getting to an
age where they can bathe and dress themselves and should learn
to value that privacy and self-sufficiency. For parents who want
masturbation to be an option for their children, this is an excellent
opportunity to discuss it. "Nobody but *you* can put their hands
down your pants."

As for the motivation of the offender, this can be best explained
in terms of having "a hard time making friends with people their
own age." Children can sometimes recognize this difficulty in other
people. The explanation is nonsensational. It does not attribute child
sexual abuse to some advanced case of brain disease or overwhelm-

ing evil intentions toward children. And the explanation is true: In simple terms, offenders molest children because the offenders cannot meet their needs with adults.

This introduction should be presented in simple terms two or three times. Changing the words slightly may make it more interesting to the child. Stressing the aspect, "I love you and don't want this to happen to you" is critical. Once the child understands this, together you are ready to deal with more specific situations of child sexual abuse.

## Actually Giving Specific Warnings to the Child

Throughout this section, it has been stated many times that warnings about child sexual abuse should be treated like any other form of survival information. Perhaps we can adapt the warnings to the same format used in conveying many of the other types of information. This format is the "What if . . . ?" game.

We all play "What if . . . ?" games with our children. We probably aren't even aware that we are doing it—it is such a widely used tool in our culture. Consider some of the following situations. Examine how the "What if . . . ?" game fits into the learning process.

You and your small child are entering a large department store for the first time in the child's life. You take the child by the hand and say, "Now, what if we get separated in the crowd? It doesn't happen very often, but sometimes it does. What will we do then?" You talk it over with the child and decide together that he asks the saleslady to page you. He should wait there with her until you come to get him.

You are in a shopping center, and your child is going to take the escalator for the first time. You ask her, "What if, by mistake, I got on the up escalator and you got on the down? What would you do?" You and your child decide that she should wait at the bottom of the escalator until you come to get her. She should not try to come to find you.

Your child is going to take the bus downtown with some friends for the first time. The buses run rather irregularly. You ask your child, "What if you miss the bus? What will you do then?" She checks to see that she has enough money to call you if she misses the bus. You remind her to call, not to hitchhike or to accept a ride with a stranger.

Those are just a few examples of how "What if . . . ?" games can be used effectively.

There are many reasons why the "What if . . . ?" game is so popular. First, it is spontaneous. It is not a heavy command or a rigid instruction. "What if . . . ?" games, even though the parent has a specific answer in mind, represent some give-and-take between parent and child. Second, they allow the child to find her *own* answer to the question. In a relatively relaxed atmosphere, she can formulate her own game plan. This is excellent training for the number of decisions the child will have to make as she grows older. And last, "What if . . . ?" games are useful because they can convey the same message in a limitless variety of ways.

After the initial talks, I suggest you talk about child sexual abuse in more specific terms through the "What if . . . ?" games. The games should focus on *situations,* not on the person. There is no way we can effectively warn children about certain kinds of people. We need to warn children to stay away from certain situations (being alone with a stranger in a car, keeping secrets with adult men, leaving a friend's room and going to her older brother's bedroom alone) and certain approaches. In order to put the emphasis on the situation (and sexual activity) rather than the person, it is suggested that the "What if . . . ?" games be introduced in a hierarchy based on emotional involvement.

The hierarchy has four levels. It is best to use them in the order presented, one at a time, spaced over a long period of time:

## FIRST LEVEL: STRANGER-TO-STRANGER CONTACTS
Situations where the child has no previous relationship with the potential offender. The offender has no authority over the child, other than being an adult.

EXAMPLE:  "What if you were walking home from school, and

a man told you his cat just had some kittens. He invites you to go into the basement with him to see the kittens. What would you do?"

*SECOND LEVEL: ACQUAINTANCE CONTACTS* (PEOPLE YOU SORT OF KNOW BUT REALLY DON'T): Situations where the child knows the person's name, but really doesn't know the person very well. Because of the familiarity between child and offender, the offender has some influence. People in the acquaintance category might be neighbors, distant friends, janitors, bus drivers, or parents of friends.

EXAMPLE: "What if the janitor at school told you that you could earn a quarter by staying after school with him in the office? What would you say to him?"

*THIRD LEVEL: CHILD-CARE CONTACTS* Situations where the child has been left in the care of someone such as teacher, baby-sitter, relative, close friend, troop leader, etc. The offender has considerable influence because of being an adult, being familiar with the child, *and* having the parents' sanction to care for the child ("Do what the baby-sitter tells you to do.").

EXAMPLE: "What if the baby-sitter said you could stay up to watch the monster movie if you got in the bathtub with him and played games? What would you tell him?"

*FOURTH LEVEL: CONTACTS WITH PEOPLE THE CHILD LOVES* Situations with relatives, parents, or very close friends. These offenders are the most powerful.

EXAMPLE: "What if someone you loved a whole lot took you for a ride and wanted to put his hands down your pants? What would you do?"

The theme throughout these four levels is that someone is asking the child to do something inappropriate. It makes no difference who is doing the asking—the child's response should be the same. By beginning with situations where the child has no emotional investment with the offender, the child learns that no one has the right to touch him sexually or put him in potentially dangerous situations. As we move up to situations where there is more emotional investment, the earlier learning is clear, and the child focuses on the situation, not the person.

When the child gives a "wrong" answer to the "What if . . . ?" game, go back over the question and suggest a different answer. Try to get the child to offer a different answer. If it is an answer that would enhance the child's safety, then praise the child for figuring out such a good answer to the problem.

"What if . . . ?" games should include the participation of all important adults in the family, and children who are close to the same age. There is only one wrong answer, but many right answers for each situation. Children enjoy competing with each other for the right answer.

Families can actually enjoy creating a variety of "What if . . . ?" games. This could be a healthy attitude if the games are both realistic and specific.

Warnings must also speak *directly* to the point. We cannot assume that children are "getting the drift" if we dance around what we want to say. For example, a friend of mine told her children repeatedly never to get into cars with strangers. After two years of this repeated warning, she began to wonder if the children understood the danger she anticipated in the strangers-in-cars situation. She asked her children what they thought she meant by her warnings. The children replied that they assumed she didn't want someone to take them away from her and raise them. Although there were probably days when she did wish that someone would take them away and raise them, that was not the issue in her warnings. In the children's minds, the issue of child sexual abuse was not related to her warning.

Another friend of mine lived in a rural area where a series of child molestations had taken place. The friend's son was in the first grade at the time. His teacher sat all of the children down together and told them to be very careful of child molesters because they were sick in the head. That evening, this boy was boasting to his parents that he could recognize a child molester "a mile away." His parents were baffled by this and asked him how he would know. He replied, "You can always tell if he's going to be a child molester because he's got a bandage on his head."

This boy's experience was that when he felt sick from an injury, his parents would give him a bandage. He had combined his own life experience with the unclear, but well-meaning, warning from his teacher. Unfortunately, his sure-fire way to identify child molesters will not afford him much protection.

Both parents and teacher could have been clearer in warning the child. The explanation might have been:

> There is a man around your school who asks kids to take rides in his car. When the children get into the car, he touches their bodies in ways he shouldn't. He puts his hands inside their clothes or asks them to undress for him. We want to make sure that you know not to get into just anyone's car around school.

This would be an opportunity to remind the child that no one is allowed to touch him sexually, and if that happens, you want to know about it right away.

By telling the child that the offender is "sick in the head," the child is put in the position of making a judgment about whether a potential offender is sick. This is an unreasonable expectation of a child. Considering the fact that most children are molested by people they know (and they are taught that these people are not "sick"), it is easy to understand why the explanation about "sick" child molesters confuses children.

By following some of these guidelines, the parent should be able to keep the avenues of communication open on the subject of child sexual abuse. There is one other important element that should be included in the "What if . . . ?" games, and this is the common use of "the secret." It is crucial to warn children about the potential danger of entering into a secret pact with an adult. A direct conversation about the approach is warranted.

An almost sure-fire way to prevent incest is to include the father or stepfather in these preventive discussions. If the father tells the child in a calm, guiding way, "Never let an adult put his hands down your pants, and please don't keep secrets about that sort of

thing from us," the father has eliminated any chance he ever had
of successfully victimizing his children. How often have we told
our children not to smoke or use profanity, only to be forcefully
reminded of our admonishments when we light up or swear? The
same can be true for warnings about sexual abuse. If the mother
alone warns the children, the warning might not clearly extend to
adults who are part of the family.

As a supplement, the child should be taught the difference between a secret and a surprise. The difference is obvious. A secret
is *never* told—not even when threatened with torture or death. A
surprise, on the other hand, is most fun when it *is* told. The joy
of the surprise comes when a person finds out what everyone else
has known all along. Child molesters depend on the child keeping
a secret to keep the molestation going. They do not, however, encourage surprises!

Often we teach our children to keep secrets. We feel this makes
the child a good friend and confidante, a trustworthy individual.
Children can attain the same attributes by successfully keeping surprises quiet. Secrets are *not* a necessary part of growth and development. If the child can keep quiet about what his father is getting
for his birthday, then he is on his way to being a loyal and discreet
adult.

Alarms should go off in a child's head when an adult tries to enlist
him in a secret. The burden *never to tell* is too heavy for a child.
Some children won't tell about the incident of sexual abuse because
the label of "fink" or "tattletale" is more ominous than the violation
of their body. While the alternative of the "surprise" can be con-
structively used in the family, it cannot be effectively used by child
molesters. No offender is going to say, "We'll play this game until
your father's birthday, and then will we surprise him!"

## Understanding the Approaches
## and Circumstances

It is necessary for parents to understand the approaches and techniques used by offenders before discussing child sexual abuse with
their children. The approaches and techniques can vary according

to the offender's motivation, his relationship with the child, the age of the intended victim, and the environment in which the act takes place.

In this chapter we have classified the approaches as: *the shared secret; the special friend; the bribe; the threat;* and *the use of force.* A combination of these approaches may be present in any single instance of child sexual abuse. Also, there are subelements in each of these approaches that the reader will easily pick up, such as "the secret place," "the secret friend," and "the feelings of special friendship."

### THE SHARED SECRET

One of the more common approaches is for the offender to enlist the child in "the shared secret." Children are very vulnerable to this. In using this approach, the sexual activity can take place in relative security for the offender. The shared secret is used most often with the prepubescent victim. The secret may be "a secret place" where the molestation can be done, or "a special time" of the day (on the way home from school, or baby-sitting) when the molestation is planned to occur. In the majority of child-sexual-abuse cases, the shared secret is indeed the sexual activity itself. Generally, the child does not fully understand what is taking place. The offender tells the child the sexual activity is their own original "secret game." Because there is no pain involved and the child is not aware of the taboo against such "secret games," this explanation makes sense to the child. The "secret game" is common both when the participants are known to each other, or are strangers.

The motivation behind the offender's "shared secret" is transparent. It is, of course, designed to forestall or prevent discovery. As long as the child keeps the secret, the offender can operate in relative safety. Without this protection, the molestation cannot continue. So the secret is not only an approach, but it also serves as an "insurance policy" for the offender.

The shared secret is the central element in the following case story of a girl named Robin.

Robin was a six-year-old girl, fairly new to the neighborhood and school. Her family had recently moved into a new home from another town. She had also just started first grade. Robin was unhappy in her new home. There were few children in her neighborhood, and being very shy, she had a difficult time making friends at her new school. She missed her friends at the old school, but her parents didn't want to "listen to her whine" about how homesick she was.

Shortly after school began, she met an older man who lived in the neighborhood. He worked nights and was up in the late afternoon puttering around the house and garden. His children were grown and out of the home. His wife worked days, and over the years they had grown apart in their interests. He found his job of the past ten years routine, boring, and unsatisfying. He felt unnoticed and unappreciated.

He and Robin began saying, "Hi" as she passed him on her way home. He started thinking of how much she was like one of his daughters at that age. After a while, they had short conversations. He noticed she was always alone and began to look forward to her visits two or three times a week. During these visits, they talked about the pretty leaves and flowers and about school. Soon Robin was inside the yard with him and they would sit and talk before she left for home. They began to go into the house on dreary days and play the card game "Fish." This became a welcome time for Robin in her loneliness, and "Fish" became "their" game.

One day, the friend asked Robin if she would like to hear a story. When Robin answered, "yes," he told her to climb on his lap. Robin did not say "no," because she often sat on people's laps when they told her a story. She had been told by her parents not to sit on strange men's laps, but her friend was not a stranger. Before long, Robin's friend would tickle her when telling her a story. Then he began to pull up her clothes to tickle her bare skin. This soon led him to put his hands in her panties. Finally, he inserted his finger into her vagina.

He told Robin that this was their "secret game." She was not to tell anyone about it. Robin was puzzled by what happened to her friend's penis when they played the game. He explained it was part of the secret game especially for him. For a long time, Robin enjoyed the shared secret because it was exciting and she felt special. She felt no one paid any attention to her, except her secret friend.

One day, when Robin was helping bathe her baby brother, she

asked her mother why her brother's "thing" did not get hard. Her mother became upset. She tried to find out how Robin could know about or ever see a hard "thing." Robin refused to tell her the secret.

Thinking Robin had been spending her time at the supervised school playground, the mother called the school. The school personnel thought Robin had been going directly home after school. As calmly as possible, the mother then told Robin that she knew Robin was going somewhere after school and that she thought Robin had seen the hard "thing" there. Robin told her mother it was a secret and she had promised never to tell. It took much coaxing and reassurance that she wouldn't get in trouble before Robin would tell about her friend and their secret game. She felt terrible about telling the secret. Her mother tried to comfort her and reassure her, but it was a long time before Robin stopped feeling she had betrayed her friend.

Robin's parents called the police about the neighbor. Because Robin was too young and too upset to testify against her friend, the charges were dropped. Robin's family moved to another neighborhood.

There are three basic points of prevention in Robin's case, each equally important. Although none of them could have totally prevented victimization, the implementation of each point could have decreased the chances of her victimization.

First, it seems that communication had broken down in a number of areas. The school personnel and Robin's parents were not talking with each other about adjustment to the new school. Because Robin was so quiet, everyone assumed she was happy. If she had actually had other friends and activities to fill her after-school hours, she would have been less vulnerable to the enticements of the neighbor.

The school and the parents did not co-ordinate on Robin's after-school whereabouts. The parents assumed the school had custody of her. The school assumed she was going straight home. Both were wrong. The gap left a perfect opportunity for Robin to become a victim. The parents needed to be more clear with Robin about what she was to do after school. An absolute deadline for her arrival home would have been helpful. If Robin had wanted to visit with new friends, she should first come home, get permission, and then go about her activities. If this had been family practice, her parents could have met her new adult friend. Most parents would have decided, merely on the basis of his situation and the age difference, that he was not a suitable friend for her.

In addition, Robin was not talking with anyone else about her feelings of loneliness. For a variety of reasons, Robin didn't feel she could talk about these things, or think that anyone would help even if she did. Her silence created a vacuum that was filled by the offender's willingness to listen to her.

It is easy for all of us—parents, teachers, and other involved adults—to overlook children like Robin. Because she did not demand much, she did not receive much attention. But it was the responsibility of the parents to ask Robin how she was feeling about the new school. Surely they might have noticed that she never came home with enthusiastic stories of new friends. And most importantly, it was their responsibility to teach Robin to begin to ask directly for the assistance she needed in life. She had to be convinced she was worth that extra effort.

The second point of prevention comes from Robin's natural friendliness. None of us would want to change that in her. However, Robin had not learned the limits to healthy friendliness. She needed to know that it was all right to be friendly with an adult, but once he began putting his hands down her pants, she did not have to be friendly anymore. There should have been very clear lines of acceptable behavior from adults.

One way Robin could have learned this was through the "What if . . . ?" games. She might have been forewarned in the second level of "What if . . . ?" games—"people you sort of know but really don't." Perhaps the following "What if . . . ?" game would have stuck in Robin's mind and given her a way to refuse the secret.

MOTHER: "Robin, remember those talks we had about some grown-ups who find it kind of hard to make friends?"

ROBIN: "Yeah, like when you move to a new school."

MOTHER: "Well, I thought we would play some of those 'What if . . . ?' games again. O.K.?"

ROBIN: "O.K."

MOTHER: "How about this, Robin? What if you were playing at a friend's house and her big brother was reading you a story. He asked you to sit on his lap and you did. But then he tried to put his hands down into your panties. What would you do?"

ROBIN: "I would ask him why he was doing that."

MOTHER: "Well, I have a different idea, Robin. That is something that isn't right and I'd want to know about it right away."

ROBIN: "Should I ask to use the phone?"

MOTHER: "No, I'd want you to come home right away and tell me. Just tell him right away that you have to go home, and then tell me. Do you understand, Robin?"

ROBIN: "I think so."

As an extra precaution, her mother would need to review that type of situation again to be sure the solution comes readily to Robin's mind. When Robin had a clear and healthy reaction to the situation, the mother could make it firmer with a reward of praise or affection.

Considering the relationship the offender had with Robin, perhaps the appropriate "What if . . . ?" game would have fallen into the third level (child-care contacts) or, given Robin's lack of companionship, the fourth level (contacts with people the child loves). Yet the activity that was to be avoided (someone putting his hands down Robin's pants) would have been the same throughout the various levels of "What if . . . ?" games. The answer—to leave immediately and to tell her parents about what had happened—would also have been the same.

Going one step farther, Robin might have been more clear on those limits if she had known the proper names for genitalia. It could have been helpful if she knew that her friend's "thing" was a penis. If she recognized the penis as a sexual and private part of his body, she might have been uncomfortable about such close contact with it. As it was, it was merely a "thing" and of little consequence. By the same token, if Robin had understood that she has a vagina, also a very private part of the body, and that no one is allowed to touch it, she might have been more aware that there was something wrong with the "secret game."

The third point of prevention takes us back to the approach itself, "the secret." Robin and the offender had a secret friendship, a secret game, a secret time of day, and a secret place to meet. No aspect of the relationship was above-board. Referring back to the section on secrets versus surprises, what would have happened if Robin had understood that it was wrong to keep a secret?

ROBIN'S FRIEND: "Do you like that game, Robin?"

ROBIN: "Well, I don't know."

FRIEND: "That's our secret game—we made it up ourselves. We're the only people in the world who play it. It's going to be our secret. We don't want anyone else to play it."

ROBIN: "But I'm not supposed to keep secrets forever. Can we play it for a week then I'll play it with the kids at school? Maybe they'll like me then."

FRIEND: "No, Robin, you can't do that. It wouldn't be our secret game anymore. It has to be a secret. Just the two of us."

ROBIN: "But I can't keep a secret. Anything that is really neat needs to be shared. We just won't tell anybody about it for a while to make it even neater."

FRIEND: "Games can't be surprises, Robin. You don't want all those kids at school who won't talk to you to be playing our secret game, do you?"

ROBIN: "But I'm not supposed to keep secrets. And, anyhow, if it's a neat game, maybe they'll play with me more."

The offender's faith in Robin's ability to keep the secret would be considerably shaken. He would be throwing caution to the winds to continue playing that game with a little girl who had a natural enthusiasm to share it with the rest of the world. This healthy aspect of Robin's friendliness with the man, nurtured by her parents, could prevent any further victimization.

In essence, Robin was lacking in the necessary time and attention that should have been paid to her by the adults in her life. Careful instruction, continued interest in her, and reinforcement of survival information could have taken Robin a long way toward preventing the incidents.

### THE SPECIAL FRIEND

Closely aligned with the shared secret is the approach of "the special friend." Children of any age are vulnerable to this approach. A "special friend" exploits the child's sense of loneliness or isolation. Most of us feel misunderstood at one time or another. We feel we are standing alone against the world, somewhat inadequate, and not very well liked by others. This is a special issue for school-age children. "The special friend" approach uses the child's feelings of loneliness to begin the relationship. An adolescent girl who doesn't have many friends or dates is open to the promised warmth and fulfillment contained in a special friendship. The younger child, often at odds with his family and the world because of his struggles to become independent and to cope with school problems, also aspires to some closeness with another human being. No matter what age the child, this approach is effective only with children who feel alienated and out of touch with the rest of the world.

As in the shared secret, no one else knowing about "the special friend" is what makes the situation "special." In family situations, "the special friendship" can be legitimized by the child's love for the offender. Any misgivings the child may have about the rightness of the relationship can be dispelled by the authority of the offender, especially if the offender is a parent or a trusted older friend of the family. As stated before, it is not uncommon for the incestuous father to tell his daughter, "This [the sexual activity] is what people do to show their love for each other," or "I am teaching you how to love another person." The daughter may very much want to be loved.

Very often, the offender himself has overwhelming needs for closeness. He uses his authority and influence over the child to meet his own needs. Because he recognizes the similarity of the child's needs, he sees little wrong with the relationship. In fact, he may see "the special friendship" as highly desirable. The following case of Joe and Kim illustrates this concept.

Joe is the father of three daughters; the oldest is Kim. The family is socially isolated. Although they have a fair income, they seldom do anything to have fun together. Once a year, they make a trip "back home" to visit the grandmothers. Adult friends and visitors are rare. Joe and Ellen, his wife, do not share much of their lives with each other. Ellen has become increasingly dissatisfied with staying at home and having no variety in her life. She enrolled in a college course and is gone several nights a week. Frequently, she goes to study sessions on other nights. Joe, with a daytime job, does the baby-sitting.

When Kim was ten, she was taking on more responsibilities for running the house and caring for her sisters. Ellen would sometimes stay in bed in the mornings, leaving Kim to see the younger girls off to school. Ellen would praise Kim by saying, "Now keep on taking good care of your family."

Kim sensed that her parents were drifting farther apart, and sometimes thought that when her mother finished college, the mother would get a good job, move away, and never see her family again. But Kim had no one to talk with about this. She had no idea if her father worried about it, because he was such a quiet person.

Kim and Joe fell into a routine. Each night she put the younger girls to bed and then they would play Scrabble. Kim was hungry for attention. Joe felt that it would help Kim in school and, since she was such a help to him, he should somehow reward her.

But Joe, like Kim, was concerned that he and Ellen were drifting apart. He was lonely and felt something was missing from his life. He could go out in the evenings, leaving Kim to take care of the girls, but he didn't really want to go out. His job was secure and routine, and he appreciated that, but he had made no friends there.

He began to look forward to the evenings when Kim sat close to him watching TV. He felt best of all when she sat on his lap. The first time he had an erection with Kim on his lap, he felt confused and guilty. He started to take a few drinks in the evening and tried to put some physical distance between them. To Kim, this withdrawal was upsetting. She couldn't understand why they didn't sit together to watch TV anymore. She was afraid that she had done something to make him mad at her. Maybe he didn't even want her around anymore.

One night, after Joe had had a couple of drinks, Kim crawled up on his lap to talk to him. Joe held her very tight. He kissed her on the neck and placed his hand on her buttocks. Kim had seen Joe do this to her mother at times. She held him and kissed him back. After a few weeks, Joe noticed no repercussions from what had happened. Ellen hadn't said anything to him, and Kim seemed to enjoy the closeness. He decided there was no harm in it. In fact, Joe thought that he had never felt better in his life.

A few weeks later, Kim crawled up in his lap as she always did. That night, he put his hands inside Kim's panties. Kim knew that it wasn't right. Ellen had told her many times not to let the boys at school feel her that way. Kim asked Joe if it was all right for him to do that. Joe told her that it was all right because he loved her; the boys at school didn't love her, and that's why they shouldn't do it. He said that his touching her would make them both feel good. It did feel good to Kim. She was relieved that she had finally found a way to make him happy.

Eventually, the special friendship progressed to Kim's touching and masturbating Joe's genitals. This continued for the next three years, until Kim was about fourteen. Then a boy at school told her he liked her and they started to study together. Several times they studied at his house, and Kim grew very fond of his large, fun-loving family.

After she was around the boyfriend's family for a while, Kim began to wonder about her own. His family had a lot of friends, and many people were in and out of his house. The older children didn't have to take full responsibility for the younger ones. The parents took responsibility for the family and didn't seem to expect their children to make them happy. The father impressed her as being able to handle things around the house. At first, Kim thought that her boyfriend was just lucky—that he lived in a very special family. But when he introduced her to a few of his friends, she discovered that all of these families treated the kids differently than Kim was treated in her family. Unhappily, she decided it must be *her* family that was out of the ordinary.

Kim decided she no longer had to do everything to hold her family together. In three years, her mother had not left, and Kim was not so afraid of her leaving anymore. Kim was uncomfortable with continuing to be her father's special friend.

As Kim wanted to spend more time with her boyfriend, Joe became more strict with her. He took away privileges for minor infractions. Ellen became aware of the friction, but attributed the change to the difficult years of puberty. In a fight with her father, Kim told him that she didn't want his sexual advances anymore. Ellen overheard the fight. After much confusion and conflict, Kim entered a foster home, and Joe started psychiatric treatment.

Several points of prevention exist in the story of Joe and Kim. It is all too easy to say that it was all Ellen's fault: "If she had stayed home, perhaps none of this would have happened. Ellen's starting school offered an opportunity for the incest to happen." The personal problems that made the incest possible did not start when Ellen returned to school. They existed within the family and between the parents long before that; in fact, they began long before Joe and Ellen ever knew each other.

Joe had a great sense of inadequacy. He felt he was not smart enough, witty enough, or personable enough to make his mark in the world. He had never communicated well with anyone, including Ellen. He did not believe that he was good enough for Ellen, let alone any other woman. He found it easier to turn to others who were not his equals; this usually meant younger people like Kim. She didn't question or challenge him or make demands on him.

Ellen also was a troubled person. Like many of the parents involved in an incestuous family, she herself had been the victim of a brief period of incest. Because many of the victims of undisclosed incest carry around the feeling that they are unusual, they feel the experience is so unique that it cannot happen to someone else. Ellen's father had been a loud person who drank heavily and frequently abused his wife. Ellen had liked Joe because he was so different from her father. She never once thought that Joe could do what her father had done. Although she had told Kim not to let the boys at school play with her genitals, she did not get as specific as she wanted to and tell Kim that sometimes even family members might want to touch her sexually.

Maybe Kim's life would have gone differently if she and Ellen had shared a discussion as simple as this:

ELLEN: "You know, Kim, how we talked about those things you can't let the boys at school do?"

KIM: "Yeah, what about it?"

ELLEN: "Do you know why I tell you not to let them touch you that way?"

KIM: "I think so."

ELLEN: "I just wanted to make sure you knew. And I want you to know that other people besides the boys at school might try to do the same thing. And it isn't right for anybody else to touch you like that until you are quite a bit older and decide for yourself that you want somebody to touch you sexually."

KIM: "Who else would want to do something like that?"

ELLEN: "Sometimes men who have trouble with women their own age, or men who are around you a lot and start to like you in a certain way, or almost anybody, I guess. The point is, Kim, that it isn't just boys who try that sort of thing. For right now, it's wrong for anybody. Do you understand?"

KIM: "I guess so. But I don't understand *why* they'd want to do that."

Given the relationship between Kim and her mother, the above conversation is fairly realistic. Perhaps some of us would have spoken in plainer terms, but with at least the basics in this conversation, the warning about potential sexual abuse would have been generalized beyond the boys at school. If Kim had considered the possibility that other men might also act inappropriately around her, she might have been alerted to her father's advances. As it was, she was not protected from anyone other than the boys at school.

With their long-standing personality problems, Joe and Ellen may not have been capable of instilling good instincts and self-protection skills in Kim, but there are a few aspects of Kim's emotional growth which were important in preventing her victimization.

The role reversal between Kim and her mother is the most obvious. Probably unwittingly, Ellen transferred most of her "mother" duties to Kim. Without taking the next logical step, Ellen failed to see how close the roles of "mother" and "wife" are. By setting up Kim as "little mother," she was on her way to the role of "little wife." In Joe's mind, all wifely duties were included in that role.

Many families rely on the oldest daughters to supervise younger brothers and sisters, cook meals, and do household chores, but certainly most do not develop into incestuous families. In Kim's case, there might have been a less gradual transition into the role of "wife" if she had not had so many and such exclusive responsibilities. Perhaps if Joe had taken on some household chores and if the younger children had been encouraged to take more responsibility for themselves (cleaning their own rooms, setting their alarms for the morning, putting themselves to bed, etc.), then Kim would not have felt so overwhelmed. The enormous weight of all the duties undermined her already shaky self-concept. She did not think she was worth much. If she could not live up to her mother's expectation to "take good care of her family," then her poor self-image would be confirmed.

Kim was acutely aware of the problems between her parents and did not sense much effort on their part to resolve them. Therefore, she did not feel confident that the problems would be worked out. When Kim took on the cause to "save the family" single-handedly, she greatly increased her chances of being a victim. Both Joe and Ellen, it appears, were avoiding their problems. Some action on their part would have greatly reduced Kim's anxiety about the impending doom in the family, and discouraged her from feeling so responsible for the family's future.

By the same token, Kim had a very confused sense of priorities. She seemed to believe that she could, and should, make *everyone* happy. In that belief, she lost sight of what would make *her* happy. She did not learn from her parents that each of us is responsible for our own happiness.

Kim had great needs for affection. Within her family, expressions of affection were not appropriate for the age of the child. At Kim's age, she should not have been sitting on her father's lap. Playing Scrabble together was a good outlet for their caring for each other. It was a special time they shared with each other. This broke down when Joe did not restrain his needs for affection, and manipulated Kim's appropriate expressions of affection into a gradually more adult activity. At the same time, Kim did not seem clear about what were correct expressions of affection for a child of her age.

Lack of friends was an important factor for everyone in the family. Joe and Ellen might have had some adult friends to turn to for warmth and advice. If Kim's energy had been directed more toward kids her own age, she might not have been so wrapped up in her parents' problems. Without much knowledge about how other families functioned, none of Kim's family had any sense of where they were having difficulties. Everything seemed wrong, and nothing seemed like it could be fixed.

It is all well and good to make these observations after the fact. However, the chances of Kim's family recognizing some of these problems without outside help are not very good. Are there some tangible prevention tools that could have helped Kim?

We do know that Kim did receive some warnings about sexual abuse from her mother. It would have been very helpful to Kim if her father had been involved in that process as well. If Joe had participated in some version of the fourth-level "What if . . . ?" games (contacts with people the child loves) with Kim, he would have been less likely to use his authority to legitimize the sexual activity. Once he had told his daughter, "Even people who love you a whole lot aren't allowed to touch you sexually," he could not take those words back later on in life. After all, his power in the family outranked Ellen's. Even if Ellen had warned Kim about friends and possibly family trying to touch her sexually, her father's reassurance that it was all right probably would have carried more weight. His involvement in her training could have put up a natural barrier for the subsequent activity.

So Kim was a girl with many responsibilities who felt alone. All of us look to our friends when we are under stress. We gain reassurance, a different perspective, or even distraction when we are in difficult situations. Kim had no one to turn to. Her father offered her solace and friendship. Not knowing any better, and not feeling she had any other choice, she became his "special friend."

### THE BRIBE

The shared secret and the special friend are probably the two most common approaches in child sexual abuse. The bribe is often used by the stranger-child molester, but this approach can also be an element in incestuous situations.

The bribe is most effective with younger children, perhaps ten years old or younger. However, it is frequently used with older children. The offender has needs, sexual or emotional, that he wants met, and he sees the offering of a reward as an expedient way to accomplish his purpose. In doing so, the offender is relying on the child's lack of sophistication in understanding what is to be done in order to get the reward. Young children love surprises, and above all know what they like best at any moment in time. If the bribe consists of, "I'll get you what you've always wanted," it is most difficult to resist.

If the child is sophisticated enough to understand that he must perform sexual acts before he receives the reward, the offender depends on the child desperately needing that reward. In this situation, the offender has ironclad control over the victim.

The type of bribe varies, depending on the age and desires of the victim. Toys, food, trips, movies, things which can be satisfied and obtained immediately, are effective for younger children. Older children may accept a bribe of money, shelter, or clothes. They may see involvement in sexual activity as the only means available to survive.

In using the bribe, the offender wants to control another human being. He hopes the victim will focus on the reward, rather than the sexual activity that precedes it. The offender may not realize the fleeting nature of bribes. He will be forced to offer a bribe each time he victimizes the same child. Or he is forced to find a new victim for each incident.

The following case story of Charlie and Eric is not one of the dirty old man offering candy to a little girl. However, the approach of the bribe is evident.

Charlie is an eight-year-old boy. His parents bowl every Tuesday night and every Thursday night. They hire a sixteen-year-old neighbor boy, Eric, to baby-sit. Eric baby-sits for many people in his neighborhood. They agree he is good with children. Some of the adults, including Eric's parents, have commented about the strangeness of Eric spending all his time with the younger children in the neighborhood. But they know he is saving money for flying lessons and welcomes every baby-sitting job. Because he is always available, Eric is very convenient. As well as baby-sitting, Eric also takes the kids on trips to the park and movies.

Eric and Charlie like each other a lot. They play a number of games together. Sometimes Charlie's friends come over to play when Eric is baby-sitting. These are fun times for Eric. He likes the younger boys better than kids his own age. Eric's peers think he is "weird." He is not self-assured, and they make fun of him for his shortcomings. Girls at school are more interested in older, self-confident boys. They think Eric is too shy and serious.

Eric is inexperienced in matters of sex. He occasionally masturbates but is uneasy about it. He fantasizes about Charlie or his friends while he masturbates. Eric doesn't have friends his own age, so he doesn't know how much masturbation is all right or what other boys think about while they masturbate. He has tried to think about girls at school during masturbation, but that didn't work for him. Eric was sure that the girls didn't like him at all. The only fantasies that worked for Eric were about his younger friends.

At the same time, Charlie was curious about sex. He wondered what an adult's penis looked like. He wanted to ask his father, but had discovered such questions bothered him. A lot of things bothered Charlie's parents. He had heard them talking about how a child "ties them down" and how much they treasured their times with each other away from home. Charlie didn't feel especially wanted.

One day, Charlie asked Eric what a big boy's "thing" looked like. Eric said he would play a game. He would show Charlie his "thing" if Charlie would show him his. Both boys quickly pulled down their pants, exposed themselves, and just as quickly pulled them back up again. Both of them thought it a silly game and agreed not to tell anyone. But they did it many times again, mostly out of curiosity.

After a few more "showings," Eric was dissatisfied. He felt he wanted more in the game. As he thought about it, he knew he could get Charlie to do more if he gave him something. He also knew that Charlie liked him and obeyed him. Eric became impressed with his power over his friend Charlie. He could get Charlie to do whatever he wanted.

The next time Eric baby-sat, they played the game again. Eric told Charlie he would give him a quarter if he touched his "thing." Charlie agreed, although the money didn't mean much to him. He was more curious about touching the penis, but the money seemed to make it O.K. His parents had told Charlie not to accept money from strangers, but Eric was not a stranger. Eric was someone who took care of him, and Charlie thought of Eric as a friend. Touching Eric was like the other game. Charlie didn't know the difference. Eric did.

Eric was not satisfied with just Charlie touching him. He began to bribe other kids to touch his "thing." For some, he promised to take them riding in the car if they would "rub" him. He let one of Charlie's friends stay up late to watch television if the child would "hold his thing." Charlie knew about this, and was sad that Eric went to other kids, too. Charlie was unhappy, but didn't say anything about it.

One time Eric asked a boy to "kiss his thing." Eric promised to give the boy some ice cream. The child wanted the ice cream, but he knew he should not kiss Eric's "thing." He told Eric, "no." When his parents came home, he told them about what Eric had asked him to do. The parents told other parents for whom Eric baby-sat. Charlie's parents asked him about Eric, and Charlie told them everything.

In the case of Eric and Charlie, there were several points of prevention. A number of them revolve around the parents themselves. How many parents obtain references from their baby-sitters? All too often, the adolescent next door is handy, and who would think of questioning a neighbor's child about his ability or ideas about baby-sitting?

Certainly this is not a foolproof method of detecting a potential offender, but it can be useful. If the baby-sitter cannot provide any references, this is a good clue. Baby-sitters who work for a series of families (only a short time with each family) should be considered with caution. When children suddenly develop a dislike for a previously well-liked sitter, this should be investigated. The children themselves can usually give us an accurate and fair appraisal of the baby-sitter's skill.

In this case, the initial point of prevention could have been for Eric's parents and the neighborhood adults to question why Eric had no friends his own age. Why was he isolated from kids he went to school with? Why did Eric depend on his baby-sitting charges for friendship, enjoyment, and recreation? It would have been a different matter if Eric had had other interests and friends his own age *and* enjoyed spending time with the younger children. However, there was nothing in his life to balance his interest in the younger boys. This could have been a clear warning to parents. Boys like Eric are not *always* potential molesters. Yet their investment in the younger children overrides good judgment at times. Puberty and adolescence are confusing times for most boys. Total involvement with younger boys can present more temptation and stress than they can cope with.

The adults sensed that Eric was confused and withdrawn. They did not take the next logical step and wonder what Eric was confused about. The parents gave Eric a position of authority as baby-sitter and ready access to younger boys.

There was, also, not much attempt by the parents to ask their children how the evening had gone with Eric. "What did they do?" "Did they go to bed on time?" "Did they have a snack?" Consider why the parents did not question unexpected extra money their children had, tiredness of the children in the morning, the extra car rides. Those who sat up and watched late television with Eric must certainly have let it slip through play or chance comments about characters in the programs. If they did, the parents didn't look into it, because of their unquestioning assumption of the goodness of Eric.

Some very good pointers on prevention can be found in the family of the little boy who refused the bribe and told his parents. What made him different from the other children? Why did he avoid being a victim while the other little boys were caught up in Eric's bribes?

It seems the little boy had a healthy sense of self, which is important. Maybe he wanted very much to have the promised ice cream. Yet something stronger prevailed, and he rejected the bribe. The boy was very clear on what people had the right to ask him to do. He knew that what Eric was asking him to do wasn't right. That was all he needed to know. He acted to keep those limits intact. In doing so, he prevented his own victimization.

Taking the case one step farther, the boy also trusted his parents enough to tell them what had happened. By telling the parents, the boy prevented further victimization of the neighborhood boys. The parents must have instilled a strong sense of trust and open communication in their son. Because of this, the case had a less tragic ending.

The third level of "What if . . . ?" games—child-care contacts— is an important level. Baby-sitters, troop leaders, teachers, etc., sometimes are the people who molest children. The child needs to know that limits are important when dealing with those people as well. The following conversation with an eight-year-old child speaks to the point:

PARENT: "O.K., now that we've played all those other 'What if . . . ?' games, let's try this one. What if your mommy and I went to the movies, and we left you here with a baby-sitter. Now, it's almost time to go to bed, but the baby-sitter tells you that you can stay up if you take a bath with him. What would you do?"

CHILD: "I'd do what he says. You always tell me to do whatever the baby-sitter says."

PARENT: "I know we say that, and we want you to be good when the baby-sitter is here, but remember all the other things we have been talking about. What about undressing with people?"

CHILD: "I'm old enough to undress myself now and older people shouldn't go around undressing around me when we're alone."

PARENT: "That's right. You really understand that. Very good. Now, what does this mean? What would you do about this baby-sitter situation?"

CHILD: "I don't understand. Which is more important, being good for the baby-sitter, or not letting people do stuff like that to you?"

PARENT: "Which do you think is more important?"

CHILD: "I think not letting people do stuff to you is more important. No hands down the pants, and all that."

PARENT: "You are absolutely right. You remembered very well. So how are you going to answer the sitter if he says you can stay up late if you take a bath with him?"

CHILD: "I say, 'No, I don't want to do that,' and then go to bed."

PARENT: "Good. You're right. And what happens next?"

CHILD: "I go to sleep."

PARENT: "No, remember, this is the kind of thing Mommy and I want to know about right after it happens."

CHILD: "So I'd tell you when you got home."

PARENT: "Right; you sure are smart."

CHILD: "Do you think Susan would ever do anything weird like that? I mean, she never lets me stay up late anyway."

PARENT: "No, I don't think she would. But no matter who it is, it's important to remember not to do it. No one—no matter who they are—should ask you to do those things. And Mommy and I always want to know."

CHILD: "How come?"

PARENT: "Because we care about you a whole lot."

Maybe Eric's last attempted victim had a similar conversation with his parents. Something was different in his attitude. It might have been the parents' willingness to talk about child sexual abuse in nonstranger terms. Whatever the reason, the difference was crucial.

## THE THREAT

Elements of the threat are present in the other approaches. However, the threat can stand on its own as an approach. Most of us conjure up an image of threats against our bodies when we hear this word. This is not always the case in child sexual abuse.

The motivation of the child molester is to gain control and affection from the child. He can gain only control—not affection—with blatant threats of bodily harm. Many times the threat is introduced when the child says she wants to end the relationship (or "special game"). When the threat is the approach used to enlist the child in the sexual activity, many of the following kinds of threats are used.

"I won't like you anymore if you don't do this for me."

"You know your mother told you to do whatever I told you to do. What would she say if she knew you disobeyed me?"

"I won't give you your allowance anymore unless you do what I tell you."

"Why would you want to tell? You know no one would believe you anyway. I'll just say you're lying."

"You know this would kill your mother if she ever found out about it—you must never tell what's happened."

"Your mother told you never to come here. If you tell her what happened, then she'll know you disobeyed her."

Threats often are more emotional than physical in nature. Special attention should be paid to the last threat. Younger children are often told not to go places that parents feel are unsafe for them. If the child disobeys the parent, and subsequently is molested at that place, the threat to tell the parents that the child was in forbidden territory is powerful. Unfortunately, the child may think the molestation is punishment for disobeying the parent.

We must not forget the *implicit* threat that is present when the offender is much older, bigger, or more sophisticated than the victim. The approach of the threat is the discrepancy among power, resources, and knowledge put into action. Without the wide gap between offender and victim in these three areas, the threat is meaningless. It is the offender's ability to carry out his threat that makes this approach effective.

The story of Claudia and her uncle illustrates the approach using the threat. The reader will probably recognize other approaches as well.

Claudia is an eleven-year-old girl. She lives with her family and is a fairly happy little girl. She has many friends in the neighborhood. Horseback riding is her favorite sport. She rides with her best friend whenever she can.

She is relatively sheltered. Her parents have not told her very much about sex. The family is very religious and feels that too much sex education is unhealthy for children. No one in Claudia's close-knit group of friends talks much about sex either. They are just beginning to like boys; they all still like horses better.

Claudia gets along with her parents fairly well. One day her mother asked her how she would feel about her uncle coming to live with them over the summer. Claudia's uncle was in college. She didn't know him very well. The plan was for her Uncle Steven to come live with them and work in Claudia's father's business to earn money for school. He was twenty-two years old. The idea sounded all right to Claudia.

Uncle Steven worked nights. He was home with Claudia and the younger children during the day while the parents both worked. Steven knew a lot about horses, so he and Claudia became fast friends. The parents would let Claudia ride more if Steven was along to supervise. She was really enjoying having her Uncle Steven live with her. She began to treasure his friendship more than anyone else's.

Her friends all thought Steven was "cool." Before long, they were taking him along when they raced their horses on the beach, an area that was forbidden for horseback riding by their parents and the local parks department. Steven ignored the signs prohibiting horses on the beach. He raced with them down the deserted shore and crowded their horses out into the surf, where he splashed the girls with icy water. They screamed, begging him to stop, or their parents would "kill" them.

As Steven was driving Claudia back home one day, he stopped "to let her dry off a little more," and asked her if she wanted to do something special with him. Claudia replied that she wasn't sure and wanted to know what it was. He said it was to be a surprise—she should close her eyes and he would do it. "If you don't do it," he told her, "I won't like you anymore." Claudia felt very confused, but she was more curious than frightened. Steven had never done anything to hurt her, and she and her friends trusted him. She closed her eyes; then he grabbed her hands and pushed them down his pants.

Claudia didn't understand her uncle's game. She didn't like it—something about it made her feel uneasy. She asked him to take her home, and he did. When they got to the house, Steven told Claudia, "Now, don't tell your parents about what happened." Claudia asked him why not. He told her, "It would make them unhappy. And, besides, if you tell, I'll tell about the horses. And I'm an adult, so they'll believe me instead of you."

Claudia wasn't sure if he was right about that or not, but she was uneasy about what might happen if she told only her part of the story. She wished she hadn't trusted Steven.

During the next week, Claudia tried to stay away from her uncle. She wanted to tell her mother about what had happened, but she knew it would make her mother unhappy. Since it hadn't happened again, she decided there wasn't much point in making a lot of trouble. She still wasn't exactly sure what he had done. She was sure it was wrong, but she wasn't sure if it was worse than riding her horse on the beach.

Steven approached Claudia later in the week and told her he wanted to take her to her friend's house to go riding. Claudia said, "No, thank you" to him. Her uncle threatened to tell her parents that *Claudia* had asked first to play the game, and if he told first, he said, they wouldn't believe her, especially when they found out she had been disobeying them. Claudia decided it was time to end her uncle's control over her. That evening, she told her parents the entire story about Steven.

At first, the parents were confused. Steven denied everything and said Claudia was making it up to get back at him. He didn't want to take her to ride anymore, so she was getting even. After a lot of yelling and crying, the family decided it was best that Steven leave. The parents still keep in touch with him, but Claudia doesn't.

Again, in Claudia's case there are points of prevention. The approach of the shared secret was used in tandem with the threat. To some degree, Claudia, like all children, was vulnerable to this—especially in such a powerful combination. The legitimacy of the uncle-niece relationship complicated matters for her. At eleven years old, Claudia did not know enough about sex to recognize what her uncle's game was. It is good that she followed her instincts not to play the game again. However, it would have been less confusing to her if she had known the meaning of the game. She might have told her parents sooner, and might not have played the game at all.

Claudia was caught up in one of the most powerful aspects of the threat—that no one would believe her because she was still a child: "I'm an adult, so they'll believe me instead of you." In the last analysis, her relationship to her family and her natural aversion to her uncle's request motivated her to tell in spite of this threat, but it was not an issue about which Claudia was entirely clear. She would have told her parents sooner if they had reassured her that she *would* be believed. The idea that adults are somehow more credible than children is a potent tool of the child molester.

In practicing the "What if . . . ?" games, it is important to play games where the child is in a situation that has been forbidden by the parent. The following example illustrates this:

PARENT: "O.K., Claudia, what if I told you not to play at Susie's house anymore, but one day after school, she got a new record album and she wants you to come over and hear it. So you go over there without telling me and while you're there, someone bothers you. You know, tries to touch you in a way they shouldn't. What would you do?"

CHILD: "I would tell them to stop, just like you said."

PARENT: "Then what would you do?"

CHILD: "I don't know. I guess I'd either stay or I'd come home."

PARENT: "Would you tell me about it, Claudia?"

CHILD: "Of course not. Why would I tell you?"

PARENT: "Why *wouldn't* you tell me?"

CHILD: "Because you would get angry."

PARENT: "Well, I want you to know that it is important for you to come home and tell me. I might be a little disappointed or angry, but I care about you, and if something like that happens to you, I want to know about it. Understand?"

CHILD: "I still think it's a dumb idea to come home and tell you I did something you told me not to do."

PARENT: "Maybe it sounds dumb to you, but that's the way I feel. What happens to you is most important to me. We'll work out the problem about disobeying me. But I want you to know you can come and tell me things like that."

CHILD: "And I won't get in any trouble?"

PARENT: "I can't promise that. But I will listen to you and take care of you."

As it was, Claudia had some fairly healthy attitudes that prevented further victimization. But like any child, she was particularly susceptible when she felt threatened. The threat is meaningless if the child believes her parents will trust and love her no matter what happens. All threats play on the confusion in the child's mind about how much people care. When we stress that caring with our children, we help them to build defenses against the threat.

### THE USE OF FORCE

The last important approach in child sexual abuse is the use of force. Fortunately, this is a rare approach for most child abusers. Sometimes it may be part of the threat before the abuse takes place. Also, the threat of physical force may be used on the victim when the victim wants to terminate the relationship.

The motivation of the offender is clearly that of forcing his will on another human being. Generally, offenders who use force as the approach are not interested in an ongoing relationship with the child. They do not want to be bothered with the elements of persuasion or friendship we have seen in the other cases. Perhaps they do not feel capable of having a friendship—even with a child. In any event, they use their advantage of physical strength to exploit the child. The case of Billy and George demonstrates this.

George is thirty-three years old. He worked nights at the skating rink, checking out skates, doing maintenance work, and locking up. He also provided first aid when needed and stopped fights between kids on the floor. George enjoyed stopping fights. The kids do little fighting when he is around. Other than that, the kids don't pay much attention to him.

George doesn't like most of the kids at the rink and resents the money they seem to have without working for it. He cannot remember being able to enjoy himself like that when he was young. George's most prominent childhood memory is of an uncle who repeatedly abused him sexually when he was thirteen.

One thing George *did* like about the kids was his ability to boss them around. He knew he was *the* authority at the rink, and everybody had to do as he said. For some reason, the girls didn't take him seriously. Once in a while, they would make fun of him, call him "gruesome George," and blow cigarette smoke in his face. This would infuriate George. In fact, almost everything made him angry. George felt victimized by low pay, no friends, and a feeling of lack of control over his life. He made up for it by using his authority to make sure the kids could not have their way.

On Saturday night, George was in his usual angry mood. He was hoping there would be a fight to break up, but there wasn't. He was planning to get drunk at the tavern after work. Maybe a fight would break out there.

While watching the kids, he noticed Billy. Billy was thirteen and there by himself. Billy usually stayed until his parents picked him up. He was the last one skating at closing time. He took off his skates and was standing by the door waiting for his parents. Without thinking about it too much ahead of time, George made his move.

He called Billy over and said that he wanted help moving some benches. Billy was puzzled. George never asked any of the kids to help him. Why should he ask Billy? Billy couldn't see why the benches needed moving—they were always like that. Billy felt something was wrong and wanted to leave. But he knew George was bigger and could catch him. Besides, George was an adult and Billy didn't want to alienate him. Billy wanted to continue skating at the rink.

Billy thought it was silly to feel afraid. He had always been told to stand his ground and fight "the way men are supposed to." What would the others say if they saw him scared and running, especially if it turned out to be nothing to be afraid of? Billy decided it was best to do as George asked.

Once George got Billy inside the rink, George pushed him into a corner and forced anal intercourse on him. When Billy's parents finally picked him up, they could tell something was terribly wrong. He told them what had happened. After he had medical attention, the police were called. George was arrested and sent to prison.

Most readers will immediately recognize one important point of prevention: Why was Billy at the skating rink alone? Billy was at an age where children often insist on being left at public places alone. Although parents will warn the child of the potential dangers, children counter that no one will even notice they are alone in the crowd. And if someone does bother them, there are plenty of other people around to help.

After much pestering, many parents allow their children to go to the movies, the skating rink, the ball game, or whatever, alone. This is possibly against the parents' better judgment. In most instances, the child is safe. However, an exceptional case such as Billy's should cause parents to reassess this rule.

Children are not correct in their assessment of the situation. People *do* notice when they are alone. Often no one helps if the child is in trouble. It is easy for onlookers to assume the child is with someone who will soon give him the help he seems to be needing. Child sexual abuse is clearly a crime of opportunity. The child who is alone in a public place is not safe.

Once George had Billy inside the rink "to help with the benches," there was little Billy could do to defend himself. The point of prevention can be found in Billy's decision-making process. He had an intuition that George was up to no good, but he had not been encouraged to trust such an intuition. Billy heard a stronger voice that said, "Don't be silly. You're going to look like a sissy if you start to run. All he's asking for is help moving the benches."

The source of the voice that overruled Billy's first (and most healthy) impulse to run was his training as a young man. Billy was probably told many times to "face up to situations" or to "never let people know you're afraid." Unfortunately, this training made it much easier for George to victimize him. If Billy had been encouraged, at least by his parents, to trust his feelings and ensure his safety—no matter what other people thought—he would have escaped George's victimization.

This is not to say that Billy caused the attack, contributed to it, or was stupid for having acted the way he did. Indeed, most young men in our society would act as Billy did. There is strong pressure for them *not* to run away. A reassuring conversation might have helped Billy.

FATHER: "How did it feel to be out on that football field?"

BILLY: "I was scared when we started to tackle. I guess I don't like it too well."

FATHER: "What are you going to do now? Are you still going to play on the team?"

BILLY: "I guess so."

FATHER: "But why, Billy, if you really don't like it? Why would you go on, especially if you are really frightened?"

BILLY: "Because all the other kids play it. Maybe I'll get over feeling this way. I'm just being silly."

FATHER: "I don't think you're silly. If you don't like it or are afraid, that's all you need to know. It's all right with me if you want to quit."

BILLY: "But what would the other kids think?"

FATHER: "It's more important what *you* feel, Billy. There's nothing wrong with being afraid. We all are sometimes. What's important is to be able to do something so we aren't so afraid. You decide for yourself, and then do what you want to do."

As general as the preceding conversation was, it would have taken Billy a long way toward escaping George. Of course, it would have to be expanded and repeated, but the confirmation from the important people in Billy's life that it is all right to be afraid is critical. There are many cases of young boy victims who sensed from the beginning that something was not right with the offender. They knew what they wanted to do about it (run away, scream for help, say "no" to the offender's initial demand), but were unwilling to do so because it would mean "acting like a sissy."

It probably would have been very unwise for Billy to try to defend himself physically. Even if he were very well versed in physical self-defense and confident about what he was doing, Billy probably could not overcome George. In trying to do so, he stood a good chance of making George more angry. Just as many boys feel they cannot run from the situation, they also feel, once in the assault, that they must fight back. This is not a good plan of action.

Even in this use-of-force approach, there was a conversation that preceded the crime. There was an opportunity for Billy to escape. George is, of course, totally to blame for what happened. Nonetheless, it is a shame that Billy did not have a healthy sense of self. Running in the face of danger should be a legitimate option for all children.

## Keeping the Discussion Going

The child will not effectively learn warnings about child sexual abuse through one discussion. No matter how skilled and earnest the discussion is, it will not work. The discussion about potentially dangerous situations needs to continue at the child's own pace.

One way to be sure the conversation will continue is to solicit questions and feedback from the child. Ask the child how she likes playing the game. Does she feel comfortable talking with you about this topic? What is her favorite part about the talks? Ask her if she has any questions. Give her time to think of some questions and then answer them as directly as you can.

Another way to keep the discussion going is to ask the child to repeat back to you, in her own words, the warning you have given her. Let her "try it on" in her own language. That transfers the information from being a warning from you to being something that comes out of herself. It is important that children integrate warnings in their own style.

Repetition is one of the major principles in teaching young children. Older children and adults learn by relating new knowledge to something they already know. Young children do not have a fund of old knowledge; everything is new to them. It is necessary to repeat instructions to them over and over again, in many different ways and at many different times. As children develop and mature, learning becomes easier; they can reach back in their memories to find something to which they can relate. That is when knowledge comes alive for children. Until then, repetition is the key to learning.

It can be frustrating for parents to tell a child *anything* over and over again. And child sexual abuse is not the subject that most parents would choose for repeat performances. However, relief and variety can come into the teaching process by utilizing the child's daily experiences. Repetition can occur whenever there is any opportunity to reinforce the message.

As time goes on, the child will bring up questions on her own. Parents will not need to make up any more "What if . . . ?" games. Enough will happen in daily activities to give the parents an opportunity to remind the child about the warnings. Following are some examples of what those opportunities might be:

- Your eight-year-old son comes home and tells you that one of his teammates wandered away from team practice, and when the coach found out he was gone, the coach got very upset. The boy had gone to a local store to buy candy. The discussion could lead to many issues. Does your son understand why the coach was concerned, even though everything had worked out? Does your son understand that the coach was concerned about a lot of things, one of which was that a man might have taken off with the missing boy? How would your son have handled the situation differently if he had wanted candy at the store?

• There was an Officer Friendly presentation at your daughter's school. She comes home and tells you about the Dangerous Stranger. She wants to know how you can tell who is a stranger.

• You and your child are watching a detective program on TV. The plot concerns a fugitive who has a record of child molestation. The offender is now raping women, and the detectives are trying to find him. Do your children understand what a "prior record" is, and exactly what the detectives are saying he did in the past?

All survival information, including warnings about child sexual abuse, need repeating. Children rarely learn habits of dental hygiene without repeated reminders. Also, they are very able to exasperate parents by staying out after dark and not returning on time, regardless of the clear orders they have received. In the above situations, the repetitions come after the fact. We want to turn this pattern around for child sexual abuse. Repetitions come *before* the fact so it need never happen. To do this we have an asset in the child's curiosity, the desire to learn, and the developing sense of human sexuality (babies, body parts, etc.). The child can come to the parent with questions and situations about which he is unsure. It is vital that the parent takes each question seriously and makes full use of the opportunity to both teach and reassure the child that he does not need to become a victim.

Some parents become concerned when we talk of the importance of repetition in the child's learning. They believe repetition will instill fear in the child. Again, it is all a matter of the parent's attitude. If the parent is fearful and ashamed, then of course the repeated warnings will relay those feelings. If the parent is matter-of-fact and looks to the child for opportunities to repeat the warning about specific situations, then the message will be realistic and useful to the child.

## About Rewards

The elements of reward and punishment are crucial. Discipline and punishment, on a few occasions, may be good teaching devices. Punishment is *not* a good tool to teach a child about the dangers of child sexual abuse. Fear of punishment narrows the child's options in responding to the situation and adds to the atmosphere of mystery and shame surrounding child-sexual-abuse episodes.

In teaching the child about child sexual abuse, we feel that the best possible reinforcer is *reward*. Rewards are not limited to the giving of candy, money, or special gifts when the child learns the survival information. There are many effective verbal and physical ways to reward a child. A pat on the head, a smile, praise, hugging, and expressions of concern are all very important rewards. Each child reacts particularly well to unique types of rewards. The giving of love and the showing of concern are perhaps the most important rewards the parents can offer.

If a child reports on having handled a potentially dangerous situation in a way that ensured his safety, it is a putdown to the child to respond, "Well, you knew to do that anyway." It is helpful for the child to receive praise for doing what the parent has so painstakingly tried to teach him. When the child has done well, a remark like, "You did well and I'm glad you remembered our talks," is critically important to the continued healthy reactions of the child in those situations. I also suggest relating the praise to the child's sense of reality. A response like, "I bet you were scared, because I would have been, in your shoes. You did so well to leave that house," can open up new areas of discussion and sharing between child and parent. An extra reward when the child has successfully coped with a potentially dangerous situation is advisable. A simple reward like, "Let's go and fix your favorite dinner," can be immensely pleasing to the child.

Rewards help to quicken the learning process for the child. When a pleasurable experience follows the child's responding in a sensible and healthy way to the "What if . . . ?" game, then the child is more likely to return to the answer that earned him the reward. In other words, the "right" answer sticks in his mind.

By giving rewards, the parents encourage the child and help to instill the positive self-concept that is so vitally important.

## Advice from Offenders

Throughout this book, parents, victims, and offenders have spoken for themselves through many quotes. I believe this is far more valuable than professional interpretation alone.

Also throughout this book, child sexual abusers have been described as immature adults who have little or no sense of responsibility for their crimes. I felt it was important that offenders have a voice in the advice section, but the task of finding responsible and thoughtful offenders was not easy.

A. Nicholas Groth, Ph.D., is a forensic psychologist and the director of the Sex Offender Program at Connecticut Correctional Institution in Somers, Connecticut. I have great professional respect and admiration for Dr. Groth, not only as a therapist but also as an author of many articles and books on the psychology of the sex offender. I have met with the men in his group, and because they have been in treatment, and to differing extents each man has accepted responsibility for his crime, I asked them to share their prevention advice from their viewpoint as the adults who approach the child as a potential victim. Dr. Groth has synthesized the group's advice, and the group has approved the following statements as reflective of their ideas on what a parent can do to decrease their child's chances of becoming a victim:

1.  Establish a relationship with your child in which the child can feel comfortable in talking openly to you. Develop a sharing, caring, and trusting atmosphere so the child can bring his or her concerns or questions to you.

2.  Make a point of knowing any adults or older juveniles who are involved with your child, especially adults in some position of authority to them, such as teachers, Scout leaders, baby-sitters, and the like. Be alert to anyone who seems

overinvolved or overinvested in your child, or anyone the child may seem to try to avoid. Any contact that departs from the traditional procedures, such as individul overnights at the home of a Big Brother, a special field trip or a campout without most members of the Scout troop, an invitation to go on a vacation or trip alone with a single adult, and the like, should first be carefully looked into.

3. Be alert to any apparent behavior changes in your child—for example, if she or he does not seem to be herself or himself, or has physical complaints such as headaches or stomach aches regularly, or exhibits other signs of stress. Be alert to other clues, such as the child having money she or he cannot account for, or toys, candy, or other gifts—especially if this happens regularly. Investigate the basis for these observations.

4. Alert children to the risks of victimization and teach them how to handle such situations, how to be assertive with an adult. Inform them of their rights and the risk others may constitute to them. Tell them that people do not have the right to do certain things, and one of the things they don't have the right to do is to touch children's bodies in personal and private (sexual) areas or to ask children to touch them in such places or to expose themselves (undress) in the presence of children. Tell the children that they should be suspicious of anyone—a relative, friend, acquaintance, or stranger—who permits or encourages them to do things their parents do not approve of, such as smoking, or drinking, or looking at certain types of adult magazines, and to report this to their parents if it happens.

5. Most important, be sexually informed yourself and provide your child with a good sex education. If she or he is informed about human sexuality, an offender cannot capitalize on the child's curiosity to engage them in sex. Prepare the child for sexual development and encourage their school, church, library, and other agencies to reinforce such education to ensure its reaching the child. Don't be repres-

sive or punitive toward age-appropriate sexual activity. If children are behaving in sexually inappropriate ways, investigate the reason for this and correct them and/or the situation without punishment. A good sex education and preparation for this area of human behavior will also help counter the impact if sexual victimization does occur and reduce the risk of the child's conception of sex and her or his sexual values and attitudes becoming distorted.

6. Finally, in teaching a child about victimization, be sure to clarify that sex is not in itself bad or wrong, but that exploitation, deception, trickery, betrayal of trust, taking advantage of someone else *is*—whether this occurs in a sexual or a nonsexual way. The child isn't wrong for trusting or obeying an adult or bad for co-operating with what the adult demanded of her or him, and the child is not to be blamed. Sex is not bad, but it is not proper for a grown-up to take advantage of a child sexually.

The text of this book was written before I met the men at Somers, and their viewpoints were developed totally independent of any input from Dr. Groth and myself. Although I have developed *The Silent Children* from my perspective as a therapist, and the men formulated their advice from their experience as offenders, we have all come to many of the same conclusions.

Nothing in this book has been gospel; all advice must be adapted to each parent's belief system and lifestyle. The offenders have offered us another analysis, and while their advice is reflective of their experience and progress in treatment, it is not the last word.

The nonvictim personality has been a major focus in this book. I believe that if these offenders had themselves been raised with some variation of the family atmosphere of Part One, the information of Part Two, and the communication embodied in Part Three, *perhaps* they could have developed a non*offender* personality as well. It is apparent that the same conditions create both offenders and victims and that in some cases the same person is both.

# EXERCISES

## EXERCISE ONE    BODY LANGUAGE

Throughout this book, we have given the message that information about child sexual abuse is like any other survival information for the child and should be treated as such. The parent needs to strive for body language that looks like his body language during any other important discussion. This is often easier said than done. Our own anxiety about child sexual abuse can often affect *how* we say things. Children are very quick to pick up those differences. Because we want our children to be listening to the information we are giving them, instead of trying to figure out why we are acting so differently, we want to appear as comfortable as possible.

Some parents may not be conscious of changes in their stance, tone of voice, eye contact, etc. This exercise is an inventory of the different aspects of nonverbal communication. Suggestions are included to help change whatever the parent feels needs changing.

*Posture:* There are many forms of posture we can take while discussing child sexual abuse with our children. They range from standing over the child in an imposing manner to shuffling nervously and fidgeting. It is most uncomfortable for the child if the parent is standing over her. This can seem overwhelming. Sitting next to the child so that you are both at the same level is most desirable. Staying in one place is also important. If the child is sitting and the parent is moving around, it may be distracting. Movement may also contribute to a sense of confusion in the child.

The parent's posture gives the child an indication of how comfortably the subject can be discussed. If the parent is slouching or hunched over in a shamed or timid manner, or looking defeated, the child is more likely to adopt this stance for herself as well. On the other hand, a rigid or authoritative stance can inhibit discussion of the subject. If the child feels she is being preached to or given orders about potential abuse situations, she may tune out the information. If she is confused or has questions, she will be less likely to bring them up.

It is difficult to be relaxed while discussing this problem, but it is relaxation you should strive for. The parent who is comfortable with the subject will instill confidence and resourcefulness in the child. Again, the resources of other adults are important in overcoming our own uncomfortableness. Other adults can give us feedback about our posture when we discuss child sexual abuse with them.

Examine how you normally discuss survival information with your child. Do you all sit around the kitchen table? Do you sit on the edge of the child's bed after she is tucked in? Do you go for walks when you talk? Whatever the environment, it would be helpful if it is consistent with that of other survival-information discussions.

*Eye Contact:* It is important to look the child directly in the eye when discussing this subject. It is not necessary to maintain direct eye contact at all times; in fact, the child may interpret this as staring.

On the other hand, constant looking around or downcast eyes during the discussion of child sexual abuse does relay the message to the child that the parent is extremely uncomfortable. This is easily interpreted by the child as meaning that the subject is shameful or mysterious.

The middle ground—fairly direct eye contact—is important. Not only does it relay the parent's adequacy in dealing with the subject, it also reassures the child that there is nothing evil or foreboding about the topic. Also, direct eye contact with the child gives the parent an indication of how the child is reacting to the discussion. If the parents are looking around the room, they will not see how the child is dealing with the subject. Direct eye contact provides an arena for important discussion. For example, "Billy, I can see from the look in your eyes that you are confused. What is it that you are confused about?" The directness of eye contact can be one of the most important aspects of nonverbal communication.

It is understandable and not uncommon for parents to have a

difficult time maintaining eye contact with their child while discussing any sexual issue. Parents who normally have very good eye contact with their children may have problems maintaining good eye contact when discussing sexuality. Direct eye contact is difficult in such situations, with both children and other adults. For parents who wish to improve the directness of their eye contact, there are two suggestions:

First, you and another adult can practice direct eye contact with each other while discussing the topic of child sexual abuse. Discuss sections of this book, or plan how you will talk with your child. As you do this, try to maintain as much eye contact as you can. Give each other feedback about how the eye contact is matching what is being said, and let each other know when you have maintained a good degree of eye contact. It is important for each adult to appear comfortable. When enough is enough, let each other know. Trying this out with a supportive adult usually helps a parent become more comfortable while discussing the subject. As a result, it is easier to maintain eye contact during a similar discussion with the child.

The second suggestion is for those parents who still experience difficulty after practicing with the adult. Focus on a part of the face around the eye (eyebrows, nose, forehead). This serves the same purpose as direct eye contact and is definitely a better option than looking nervously around the room. In most cases, the person with you feels you are looking him directly in the eye.

*Tone of Voice:* Tone of voice can have the same impact on the child that the parent's posture or eye contact has. If the parent normally speaks in a well-modulated tone of voice, then discussing child sexual abuse in a whisper *or* in an angry tone of voice will confuse the child. The ideal here is a calm, controlled tone of voice.

This is perhaps the easiest aspect of nonverbal communication for which we can create self-awareness. When talking with our children, if our voice trails off, we can quickly correct that if we notice it. By the same token, an angry or anxious voice can also be corrected. Listening to ourselves very carefully is the clue to a constructive tone of voice with our children.

## EXERCISE TWO     PROPER TERMINOLOGY

Use a diagram to teach proper terminology to your child. After reviewing the names and functions of the genitalia, ask the child to explain the same to you. Correct any misconceptions or misinformation. This process should be repeated until the child is familiar and comfortable with the genitalia.

(NOTE: This exercise will consist of two simple drawings—one of a girl and one of a boy. All of the genitalia and other relevant parts should be identified, with proper terms listed next to the body part. Parents can do this or use a textbook with anatomical illustrations. The drawings are intended to be used by the parent to teach the child proper names for the child's body parts.)

If you have a difficult time with the proper terminology—particularly in saying the words comfortably—repeat the troublesome words to yourself many times in your mind while you go to work or do your household chores. Usually your discomfort is, in part, due to the taboo against saying the words. Repeating the proper terminology to yourself can break down the taboos.

## EXERCISE THREE:     ELEMENTS OF PREVENTION

With at least one other adult, read over the five case studies in the section on common approaches. Discuss and agree on what common trends or circumstances you saw in at least three of the case studies. Is there something you saw in all five case studies? We ask you to discuss this with at least one other person because there are different ways in which to look at any one case. We can all learn more by discussing these cases with other people. Also, we all have past experiences that can affect how we look at the cases. It is important to share those perspectives as well.

After you have identified some of these common trends in the case studies, discuss what steps you would take to prevent the incidents. Prevention is not possible in all cases. It is possible, however, to formulate some actions that might reduce the child's chance of being victimized.

It is not the purpose of this exercise to place blame on any parent for the child's victimization. We ask you to focus on *action* and tasks (for example, warning the child ahead of time, telling children about nonstranger molestation, talking with the child) rather than attributing the incident to poor parenting. No parent intends that his child becomes a victim. Unfortunately, it is relatively easy for parents to overlook certain aspects of this problem. By exploring the common elements in these cases, parents are encouraged to think about those many different aspects and what *action* they can take toward prevention.

## EXERCISE FOUR   "WHAT IF . . . ?" GAMES

Very few "What if . . . ?" games were suggested in the text. Now comes the challenge for the parent to provide realistic "What if . . . ?" games for the child.

The child's daily activity should be considered while formulating these games. To what types of approaches and under what circumstances is your child vulnerable? And remember the four levels. Each is equally important.

It is worthwhile to write down these games. Also, the "What if . . . ?" games should probably be different for each child. If they have different rules, different friends, different interests, their "What if . . . ?" games should be adapted to their particular situations.

## FIRST LEVEL   STRANGER-TO-STRANGER CONTACTS

1. "What if . . . ?"

2. "What if . . . ?"

3. "What if . . . ?"

4. "What if . . . ?"

5. "What if . . . ?"

SECOND LEVEL     ACQUAINTANCE CONTACTS
(People You Sort of Know But Really Don't)
1. "What if . . . ?"

2. "What if . . . ?"

3. "What if . . . ?"

4. "What if . . . ?"

5. "What if . . . ?"

## THIRD LEVEL     CHILD-CARE CONTACTS

1. "What if . . . ?"

2. "What if . . . ?"

3. "What if . . . ?"

4. "What if . . . ?"

5. "What if . . . ?"

**FOURTH LEVEL    CONTACTS WITH PEOPLE THE CHILD LOVES**

1. "What if . . . ?"

2. "What if . . . ?"

3. "What if . . . ?"

4. "What if . . . ?"

5. "What if . . . ?"

## EXERCISE FIVE    REWARDS

The purpose of this exercise is to give serious thought to defining the most effective rewards for each of our children. Few of us ever sit down to think about how each of our children reacts to rewards. Yet, again, for each child, the list of positive reactions will be different.

There are basically three areas of rewards. The first, and one of the most important, is affection. This can take many forms: hugs, kisses, pats on the head, tickling, holding hands, messing up the child's hair. Perhaps you and your child have a special way of physically relating to each other that gives the message that you care for each other. Think of three forms of affection that are important to your child. How do you reach out to her in a way that makes her light up or reach out for you in return?

1.

2.

3.

The second form of reward is verbal praise. What words hold your child's attention? What kinds of compliments mean the most? Are there any phrases or statements that have special meaning to both of you? When you want your child to know she is very special, what do you say?

1.

2.

3.

The third form of reward is material goods. This does not need to be extravagant. Material rewards that children often respond to are ice cream; rides in the car; a trip to the amusement park; certain kinds of candy; staying up late; an evening at the movies. Think of what is particularly important to your child.

1.

2.

3.

Material rewards should probably be reserved for special occasions. They are more meaningful if they are few and far between. Affection and praise, on the other hand, are most helpful if they are given freely between parent and child. Healthy doses of all rewards help to instill that all-important self-concept in the child. On a very practical level, rewards given for good reaction in a potentially dangerous situation or for coming up with a good answer for a "What if . . . ?" game help to reinforce the warning. We want to do as much as we can to make the message a part of the child's everyday survival information.

# PART FOUR

---

## CONCLUSION

This book was written to give parents information about the prevention of child sexual abuse. If the parent effectively teaches the child prevention techniques, then some of the circumstances surrounding *individual* offenses can be recognized and avoided. Although this procedure can decrease the child's chances of becoming a victim, other answers to the prevention of child sexual abuse are more far-reaching than the teaching process between parent and child. Our examination of this problem would be incomplete without considering the cultural influences at hand.

American society creates both offenders and victims. Child sexual abuse is the natural extension of the imbalances of power, knowledge, and resources among all of us and found in so many areas of our everyday life. Although I have stressed the individual responsibility of each offender for his crimes, it is important to recognize the support and rationalizations the offender finds in a culture that claims to be repulsed by child sexual abuse.

If the various forms of American communications media are reflections of our culture, then we are still, in spite of all efforts toward women's liberation, a nation that worships the blond, "stacked," not-too-bright goddess. The plethora of "tits and ass" or "jiggle" television programs and the abuse of sex in advertising bombard us with the same helpless, seductive, childlike object. The media do not encourage us to have sex; they encourage us, through sheer volume and overstimulation, to view women as things and to think of sex as something devoid of feeling or responsibility. Sexy women are everywhere, and they seem to be there for the taking. We tolerate, even encourage, men to ogle women's bodies and to treat the person of that body as a sex object. Yet that same man whose attitude toward women is that women exist for his entertainment and prerogative could very well be a father of young daughters. Why are we so surprised when his attitude culminates in the sexual exploitation of his daughters? After all, his girl/child is a female. How is it that he can demean and objectify all women in the world *except* those he has the most access to and the most power over?

Pedophiles seeking material for their masturbatory fantasies need not patronize pornographic establishments. Exposed buttocks of precocious four-year-olds abound in our magazines and on the nation's highways. There is no obvious connection between the sale of suntan lotion or dairy products and the sexual vulnerability of little girls, yet we buy (with great volume) what is sold with the alleged seductiveness of children.

And for those of us who do not ogle women or masturbate to fantasies about children, how do we explain the fact that we have idolized child actresses Jody Foster, Brooke Shields, and Tatum O'Neal in movie after movie about the innate eroticism of prepubescent girls? Adult actresses, less vulnerable and symbolically more demanding (in their personal relationships) than the child stars, cannot rival the box-office appeal of girl sex sirens. And the adult women who are winners in the pinup poster sweepstakes are often childlike in their appearance and gurgling in their sexuality.

Yet we are shocked when an individual man takes our unwritten rules about the sexual desirability of children very seriously and lacks the self-restraint to avoid acting out all that surrounds him. Offenders are *not* victims of a sex-crazed society, who cannot help themselves and therefore should be forgiven. Many men, exposed to the same hype of the child as malleable sex partner, avoid victimizing *real* children. However, the offender is not so out of the ordinary. He did not land on Earth from an alien planet, intent on eroding our society with what we abhor most. He came from among us, and while he should be held accountable for his crimes, he is also a mirror of our culture.

Americans have not always been so centered on the objectification of children as we are now. There have always been child sexual abusers, and perhaps there are more now than ever before. We do know that child pornography and child prostitution are proliferating. What used to be "women's work" is now also the lot of children.

The "work" is the product of the male-dominant paradigm. In this scheme, someone gets to be powerful (men), and someone else contrasts his power with subservience. Women may still be accessible for pornography or prostitution in the street and the sexual marketplace, but in the confines of our respectable institutions (marriage, family, and the workplace) women's roles are changing. Still, many people believe in that female-submissive paradigm; they believe in the inherent need of men to dominate their sex partners, to be the master of their castle, to possess the ultimate power of deciding other people's fates. As women are less available to be the providers of subservience, men will, rather than try to dominate each other, look for a substitute with the same qualities. Thus children are the ultimate "workers" for the pleasure of the dominant male. Every time a child is the victim of sexual abuse, the imbalances of power, knowledge, and resources are set in motion.

To suggest that women should "go back to our places" in order to protect our children from the same subjugation we suffered (and still suffer, to a large extent) is a form of sexual blackmail. The attainment of dignity and human rights is necessary for women. The same struggle is necessary for children. What both struggles have sorrily in common is the same oppressor. At least 97 per cent of the time it is men who have raped, battered, and generally oppressed women. Men are also the child molesters, incestuous fathers, pornography makers, pimps, and customers of child prostitutes.

Certainly men hold the vast majority of the power in this society, but women *do* contribute to our collective attitude toward children. As we are on the front lines of child-care work (mothers, teachers, nurses, etc.), we know that something has gone very wrong. Sexual abuse in our homes is not a happenstance occurrence. Runaway statistics soar each year. Teen-age pregnancy and venereal disease are epidemic. And somehow, men and women together have not been able to make a dent in these problems. Child sexual abusers are too often there to take advantage of our failures. As Trudy Peterson of Covenant House reminds us:

> If a pimp is meeting the needs of our runaways in our society, if he's taking them in and sheltering them, what does that say about us, as a society? These are not sluts and whores and fallen women. These are our children.[1]

In order to put the pimp out of a job, there are many facets of our national attitude that need examination and change. It is not enough to give cocktail-party lip service to the rhetoric, "Children are treated like property." We must go beyond this truism and engage in the hard work of looking carefully at our personal feelings about some crucial issues. If each of us changes an attitude and subsequent behavior, then the collective impact will be an improvement in a culture that has created a healthy climate for child sexual abuse. As each of us takes some responsibility for our own contributions to the mass confusion or hurtful belief, then we will be *doing something* about child sexual abuse. Our efforts, in concert, can change the complicated system that made child sexual abuse commonplace.

Much of what has gone wrong can be traced to adults' perceptions of children. We are not clear about what is an adult and what is a child. In incest, we know that the role reversal between the adult and the child is a key ingredient, and the incestuous family can be viewed as a slightly deviated microcosm of the larger society. Many children in the general population have the responsibilities of adulthood but none of the rights. At the same time, other children are kept as children, denied both the responsibilities and rights, far into what is considered adulthood. We have no meaningful ceremony or rites of passage from childhood to adulthood. At one time, completion of secondary school was considered such a landmark, but today many children do not finish school, while others go to school for years, well into their twenties, and remain supported by their parents. For some families, Bar Mitzvah or Bas Mitzvah or religious confirmation is a point of entry into adulthood, but the acceptance of these as meaningful entries into adulthood is out of the ordinary. We have no *uniform* gradation of rights and responsibilities in between the status of child and the overnight endowment of adulthood at age eighteen or twenty-one. This ambiguity is convenient for the child sexual abuser who contends that he and his victim are equals and, in fact, that the child (*à la* Brooke Shields and Jody Foster) seduced him.

At the crux of our inconsistency in regard to rights and responsibilities for children is the concept of consent. Not only are offenders unclear about what constitutes a child's consent to sexual relations with adults, but also society as a whole is unclear about the specifics of this question. In our confusion about when a child is a child and when a child is an adult, we often agree that a child can matter-of-factly consent or refuse.

Consent is based on information. In requests made by an adult to a child, specifically of a sexual nature, the child does not have the power, knowledge, or resources to consider the request, assess the consequences, and give valid consent. Yet we insist victims were precocious and seductive and knew what they were getting into. We believe that child prostitutes work the streets because, if given the choice between prostituting and working as a cashier in a fast-food chain, they *choose* to be sexually exploited. We believe the daughter who desperately wants her father to stay at home can set her fears aside, weigh all the possibilities for keeping the family together, and rationally decide to enter into a sexual relationship with her father.

Many times children *do* withhold their brand of consent, but because we as adults have such a tenuous understanding of what consent means, we interpret the child's response in our own self-serving light. Crying in fear does not constitute consent. Accepting sexuality as a "special" form of sought-after *affection* is not consent. Recognizing that daily survival depends on sexual involvement does not mean consent. Saying nothing at all is not expressed consent. Being under the influence of drugs or alcohol is not a valid condition of consent. Consent means that the person has the power, knowledge, and resources to say, "I know the consequences of entering into this, I know the alternatives, and I choose to do so." Few children, if any, would say that about sexual relations with adults.

Our laws offer no clarification. There is a wide variation in age of sexual consent among the states. Until 1972, an adult in Maryland could *legally* have sex with any child over seven years old, whereas neighboring states legislated an age of consent of sixteen or eighteen years old. The *damage* done by child sexual abuse does not differ from state to state, yet we have dozens of radically different legal definitions of that same harmful activity. In the early 1960s, the American Law Institute, in an effort to gain a consistent legal definition, recommended that the legal age of consent to sex be legislated at age *ten* in all fifty states.[2] Certainly we do need a uniform legal definition, but the sanction of adult sex with eleven-year-olds is hardly a step in the right direction.

Self-concept, individual and collective, is another area of the American mindset that needs examination in the interest of preventing child sexual abuse. Not coincidentally, poor self-concept is an underlying motivation among many types of child sexual abusers. Out of their lack of self-esteem comes an inability to connect with other adults and a refusal to risk vulnerability by asking for help with problems, sexual or otherwise. Victims often become victims because the self-degrading offender recognizes the same confusion and low self-worth in the child. Just as the offender can easily manipulate the concept of responsibility for his own life, he believes he can also manipulate the child. Too often the offender is right— the alienated child does not reject him. And if a child with a healthy self-concept is randomly picked to be a victim, the molestation can erode his emotional health if responsible intervention does not follow. It seems that no one involved in child sexual abuse—offender or victim—feels very good about himself or herself.

No one is born a child sexual abuser. We do not come into the world hating ourselves, and self-concept is not developed in a vacuum. We need the support, experience, and feedback of many people to learn about and subsequently feel good about ourselves. However, this is not easy to do in a country of isolated islands, either in nuclear families or disenfranchised individuals, where we rarely reach out, help, or share with each other. In this lack of a larger community, while everyone is "doing his own thing," it is easy for any one class of people (children) to be exploited. Who will notice or care?

The offender with his overwhelming sense of inadequacy will not share his life in any real sense with adults. The modern adult world is too threatening to him, so he stays to himself and takes comfort in children.

Members of an incestuous family believe they are nothing without this tight entity called a family. They consider it a conviction of shame or failure to look outside their family to the solution to their internal problems. Instead they become more deeply rooted in their own inequities, and no one is the wiser.

Literally thousands of children run away to cities each year. With few available social services and no one really watching, they find a "family" in the street life at the expense of their freedom and sexual dignity. We would all agree that this is a sad situation, but too often we shake our heads and say it's really the child's family's problem and none of our concern.

And many more children are the victims of child sexual abuse each year. In our isolation, we believe it happens to *other* people's children and we breed the very myopia and lack of support that make a young child vulnerable to the "friendship" of the offender. Although our double standards and isolation can culminate in "aberrant" forms of sexuality, sex is really not the problem. The issue here is our misunderstanding *and* abuse of power in the culture. Power and sex are closely connected; it is no surprise that corrupted power is acted out in sexual abuse and that the most accessible and vulnerable people will be victimized. As Judith Coburn explains in her brilliant essay on the sexual abuse of children:

> The issue here is not the exploitation of innocence, or even of sex per se. The central issue is power, which cannot be separated from sex. Even in some utopian, guilt-free state of nature, it's doubtful sex would ever become just some healthy bodily function. By its physical nature alone, sex is fraught with issues of control and surrender; between an adult and child, those overtones of power reach their extreme. Even for the most cynical sexual gymnast or the celibate, sex represents an act of vulnerability—a momentary loss of self—that can call up the deepest feelings of connection, transcendence or exploitation.[3]

Given the inevitable connection between power and sex, what do our societal misunderstanding of consent, our epidemic lack of self-esteem, the isolation of our personal experience, and our obsession with the dominant/subservient paradigm do to our dignity? Given that there will always be adults with a sexual interest in children, how likely is it, in our present state, that we can eradicate child molestation and incest? Child sexual abuse does not happen outside of our mainstream of values; it happens within our belief system. When our values no longer reflect an imbalance of power, resources, and knowledge, the silent children will no longer be silent.

# PART FIVE

---

## PARENTS
## WITH SPECIAL NEEDS

# INTRODUCTION

I have spent the past two years researching this book, and worked as a therapist in this field for five years before that. Yet no one book nor a single person can say everything there is to say about a subject as complicated and important as child sexual abuse.

Each parent will have different needs in regard to this book, and there are large groups of parents who face special considerations in warning their children about sexual abuse. I have chosen eight obvious groups with special needs and asked a person deeply involved with his or her respective group to read *The Silent Children* and offer some additional advice and insights. The following chapters are not meant to be a "how to" lesson for ethnic or other types of parents. Each chapter author is one member of a group, someone who is concerned and who has thought out some of the implications of the previous pages. Each chapter author offers a point of reference to other parents in similar circumstances. They do not intend to speak for all members of their group. Whatever the reader takes from these very special chapters must be adapted to his or her own family.

Although every chapter is aimed at a specific audience, it is my hope that all readers will continue on and read this section. I believe books are best used when they are shared and discussed. I believe we can learn more about and understand each other through the experiences the following mothers, fathers, and two sisters share with us. The purpose of their chapters is to begin the discussion.

L.T.S.

# Black Parents

BY DORINE BARR BRYAN

Dorine Barr Bryan is a doctoral student in sociology at Stanford University. She is married to a psychiatrist and has a six-year-old son. She read the manuscript and she and her husband discussed it.

The sexual abuse of children is a subject that most people find difficult to discuss or comprehend. Most of us feel that it is a random crime that we are powerless to prevent or do anything about. Considering this, I was intrigued by the opportunity to read a book which was written as "a book for parents about the prevention of child sexual abuse." Actually I was more than intrigued, I was hopeful. As the parent of a young child, I was interested in any information on this subject.

Even with those feelings, it was difficult for me to read this book. I have the same negative feelings that most people have. Most of us would prefer that this area did not exist. And I had a natural reluctance to read any material which would provide me with details. Fortunately, I overcame this and I was pleasantly surprised by the book. I have gained valuable information and insights. More importantly, the book has helped me to move beyond much of the emotionalism which surrounds this issue.

I was asked to read this book specifically as a black parent and to respond by pointing out differences for black children pertinent to the general statements the author has made. I find few differences that I would attribute to race *alone*. Rather, the differences I saw were due to differences in *economic* background. How many resources we had as children, have now as parents, and the values that go along with any class, all of these factors make more of a difference, in my mind, than race. However, we cannot ignore that black Americans have not had limitless opportunities to be of any economic class that they choose, so the differences I point out often have more to do with our economic status than our race.

I do have one specific point of disagreement which I feel is very important. Part One teaches us how to raise *non*victim children. This certainly is a large part of the answer to preventing child sexual abuse, and it may be a good idea in other areas of life, but as black Americans, we must face the fact that society may not warmly embrace a new generation of nonvictims. In a country that has been built on institutions like slavery and still discriminates against minorities, the ethnic "victim" is essential. This is not to say that black parents should not try to raise nonvictim children just because it may not be widely accepted. I do feel, however, we should be aware of the pressures on our children as they become less easily dominated, victimized, and exploited, in *all* ways.

In general, my overall assessment of the book is a positive one, and I would strongly recommend this book to any concerned parent. I have only one major criticism of the book. This book is written for a particular audience—those concerned parents who have a well-developed degree of verbal skills. In many instances degree of verbal skill is tied to class background or orientation, regardless of race. For parents with poorly developed verbal skills, many of the exercises will seem difficult. However, if a parent is motivated to read this book, then he or she would probably be motivated to improve the required skills. Therefore, I feel that in the exercise for Part One it would be helpful to include a few references to help with this problem.

In addition, I feel that the book needs to include an explicit discussion of the role of opportunity in child sexual abuse (especially child molestation). Both my husband and I feel that some of this opportunity can be eliminated if parents seriously concern themselves with their children's activities. This goes beyond knowing where and with whom the children spend their time. Parents need to know not only what activities their children are engaged in, but also they must be willing to and available to intervene in those activities when necessary. It is surprising to what extent many children are left unsupervised for long periods of time. Even young children are left in a "safe" place for long periods of time without their parents checking on them. The book does discuss many of these issues, but they should be drawn together and discussed in one area.

I found the first part of the book to be valuable for several reasons. First, it provided a general definition of child abuse which made the issue something specific. The definition was helpful in seeing sexual abuse as a crime with boundaries. Secondly, it provided concrete information about the characteristics (e.g., a strong self-concept, nonstereotyped sex roles, legitimacy, and territoriality) to help a child develop that would prevent him or her from being victimized.

I found the section on helping the child to develop a strong self-concept to be informative and well done. Of course, helping children develop a strong self-concept is not a new idea. Unfortunately, it is the kind of goal which can get lost in everyday parenting. All too often parents forget to maintain a balanced blend of both praise and criticism towards their children and themselves. Sometimes we are overwhelmed by our daily activities and react only with general remarks or we don't react at all. My husband and I both make a strong effort to be specific in both our praise and criticism.

The section on sex-role stereotyping gave us the opportunity to sit down and ask ourselves to what extent sex-role stereotyping is a part of our family life. Although we have had numerous conversations about sex-role stereotyping, I don't recall any in which we discussed how the elements of it that are present in our family life affect our son. The questions reminded us that we have to constantly be aware of the stereotyping we do as well as that done by others. The following story shows that children develop sex-role stereotypes at an early age.

> Recently my son had his sixth birthday. He had a party and only a few girls were invited. After choosing toy submarines and spinning tops for the boys, I asked my son what he thought we should get for the girls. He said, "I know just what they like —makeup and jewelry." I was shocked and pointed out to him that many girls don't like such things. We compromised by getting toy watches and jacks for the girls.

I was upset that my son had such stereotyped ideas, especially since we make a conscious effort to break those kinds of stereotypes. Later, as I was repeating this story to my husband, he asked me why I felt the girls needed different toys. This question was obvious, but I hadn't asked it.

The discussion of television's role in stereotyping is important, and black parents have an additional danger to watch out for. The recent "trendy" portrayals of black families on TV, such as "Good Times" or "The Jeffersons" are insulting and inaccurate. With the addition of "Diff'rent Strokes" black children are only portrayed as obnoxious, precocious, "street-smart" kids who know more than any adult. I believe this is not healthy for black children as it encourages them to believe they are inherently worldly and it makes the black family look like a joke rather than a place where adults are respected and children are cared for. There are few healthy models for black children on television.

While reading this section, I wondered how many black parents concern themselves with the problems of sex-role stereotyping. The little black girl is more likely victimized as a black person than as a female, and sometimes in fighting the many daily battles we must all fight, sex-role stereotyping might seem unimportant. At the same time, black adults and children, like anyone else, might genuinely believe in the male dominant/female subservient scheme talked about in this book. Still others might adopt it believing it "keeps life simple" and should not be at the top of the list of challenges we would take on. I believe we must all try to be aware of the limitations sex-role stereotyping puts on our children.

The discussion of helping children to develop a sense that their concerns are legitimate was important. It was a good reminder that being listened to and being able to ask questions are important for *both* children and adults. We always try to listen to our son but sometimes we are just too busy or tired to do a very good job of it. However, the discussion of listening in terms of how it contributes to a child's legitimacy will help us to redouble our energies in this area. Knowing that his concerns are legitimate will also help to reinforce our child's sense of territoriality, i.e., what others have the right to ask and expect of him.

We have always told our son that what he feels and thinks is one of the most important things in any situation (in which he has to make a choice), and that we want him to express his opinions, even if they don't agree with ours. We are usually very consistent about reinforcing this. Although there are times when other considerations are more important, we still want to know how he feels. This way we can help him to understand. However, two recent incidents have shown me (my husband didn't need to learn this lesson) that there is still work to be done in this area.

A female friend, who is a single parent, baby-sat for us one afternoon. When we returned to pick up our son she pointed out that he was very critical. "He certainly has his own opinion about things." My response was to explain to my son that everyone does things in a different way.

Our son disliked the same friend's son. And on several occasions he didn't want to visit their house and play with the boy. However, we went anyway and every time our son was rude and hostile to the boy. After each occasion I told my son that he should be more tolerant of other children.

In both of these stories I was guilty of infringing on my son's territoriality. In the first case I didn't respect his opinion because another adult felt uncomfortable with it, and so I tried to restrict his ability to express opinions. In the second case, I tried to involve my son in a friendship which he would never have chosen for himself. I had encouraged him to express his opinions but in those two instances I hadn't respected those opinions.

Both my husband and I felt that the exercises at the end of Part One were useful to parents, as either beginning or supplementary techniques, to help in building a child's self-concept. We liked the exercises because they are simple to do and their purpose is quite explicit. My husband liked the exercises because they are consistent with advice that he would give. Although his patients suffer from a variety of problems, most of them also have weak self-concepts and low self-esteem.

The second part of the book was the most difficult for me to read. I felt a certain reluctance to examine any detailed information about child sexual abuse. However, both of us agree with Ms. Sanford that in order to help children protect themselves, parents must understand the nature of the crime. Actually, reading this chapter was important for me because it diminished much of my anxiety.

The knowledge that the crime can be viewed as two components: (1) an external component based on the differences between the offender and the victim in terms of power, knowledge, and resources; and (2) an internal component which is the offender's responsibility. It is in the area of the external component that parents can have the most effect.

Knowing that child sexual abuse is rarely a spontaneous or random crime was reassuring to me. In particular, child molesters have a preference for the sex and the type of victim as well as for the desired circumstances of the crime. Child molesters have several criteria to meet before they even attempt the crime. They usually want to have a relationship with the child. This factor can be useful to parents because they can help their children avoid being involved in many potentially harmful situations. If children have a strong and positive self-concept (power), they know what child sexual abuse is (knowledge), and they have been told what to do if anyone approaches them (resources), then parents have done a great deal toward preventing their children's victimization.

The section on incest dealt with family dynamics and I am not sure how much of this is applicable to black families. Again, the situation is more dependent on the family's economic status, but I discerned two important differences. First, the mother's emerging independence—such as returning to school, taking a job—was sometimes, in the father's mind, the precipitating event of the incest. Many black women have not had the luxury of being timid, dependent homebodies, so that factor would be different, although it's important to remember that the precipitating event seems to be almost anything. Secondly, after discovering the incest, many women are in conflict because they feel an economic dependence on their husbands. Among the many black women who work to partially or totally support their families, this would not be of such great importance. Black families must still be concerned about the possibility of incest, but I feel there are, in some situations, differences in the dynamic.

The last part of the book was the most valuable to me because it provided specific ways in which to warn a child about sexual abuse. Left to themselves, many parents wouldn't attempt to discuss sexual abuse because they don't know how to initiate the discussion, and they are afraid of frightening the child.

The book provides a straightforward and reassuring way in which to go about providing this information. Immediately a context is established from which parents can view the discussion and establish when this discussion needs to take place (see questions on pp. 221–22, 227). Parents don't often categorize the information which they provide children. But a large percentage of it is survival information. We would consider ourselves remiss if we didn't warn our children about possible physical dangers in the environment. In the same context, child sexual abuse is also a danger in the environment. When presented in an ordinary and matter-of-fact way, this information need not be frightening to children.

One of the first tasks is to divest genitalia of their mystery and exoticness. Children should know the proper names and functions for genitalia because this makes them ordinary and understandable. Our son knows this and he sees nothing mysterious about them.

> When we had our initial discussion with our son, his first reaction was amazement. "Why would anyone want to do that?" He thought the idea that anyone would want to touch his penis was weird. His tone conveyed the impression that touching it was pointless.

Our next step will be to provide our son with specific examples. At this point the technique of the "What if . . . ?" game will be invaluable. Before reading this book, we would not have thought of all the various levels on which child sexual abuse could originate. Consequently, we would have failed to provide a complete warning. Granted our son will probably never need this information, but if he does, he will have it. In addition to the above game, we feel that parents should also use techniques that are more reality based. Parents can discuss: (1) articles and stories in the newspapers or on television with children, and/or (2) the parents' own experiences as children when they were in the same or similar situations. I feel that this will be helpful because in many ways, playing "What if . . . ?" games is perfectly natural to children. They do it all the time. And they know that in many cases the results of the games never happen. Finally the repetition of the games along with the reality-based discussion will help children to develop their judgmental abilities for a crisis situation.

Another issue discussed in this part was the secret. I know that this was a supplementary issue, but it provided me with an important insight. Our family loves surprises, both to give and receive them. And we have always used the words, secret and surprise, interchangeably. I have been aware for some time of the negative potential of secrets. Unfortunately, I have never come to grips with this particular problem. The discussion of secrets helped me to clearly see the negative aspects of secrets and to clarify the distinction between secrets and surprises. By knowing that surprises are to be shared and that they are only kept for specific periods of time, children will be less vulnerable to hiding things under the guise of secrets.

Finally, the exercise for Part Three will help to ensure that parents move beyond a theoretical discussion of how to tell their children about sexual abuse, by providing the opportunity to practice the crucial elements involved in giving that information.

Practicing body language and proper terminology for genitalia, along with discussing the case studies with another adult, will be helpful and reassuring to parents. But most importantly, by developing and practicing a series of "What if . . . ?" stories at various levels, the parents will gain valuable insight into what they are helping children to avoid.

In conclusion, I would say this book is relevant for black parents interested in the prevention of child sexual abuse. It is an issue that cuts across racial or economic lines. It is a fear common to most parents and I believe this book will help prepare both parents and children for the prevention of this crime.

## Asian Parents

BY ELAINE KANZAKI WONG

Elaine Kanzaki Wong is a Sansei (third-generation Japanese American) married to a first-generation Chinese American and is the mother of two children: York, Jr., age 8, and Tara, age 4. She is an active member of the Asian community in her hometown of Tacoma, Washington, and recently spent a year living in American Samoa.

Asian parents, like all parents, try to equip their children with survival skills. For many of us who are third- or fourth-generation Asian Americans, a book of this type, which emphasizes building assertiveness and healthy "self-sufficiency," can be very useful and informative. We and our children are products of American society, so we identify with the situations and circumstances outlined. My children, for example, have been warned about the candy-and-strangers routine, have seen violent renditions of kidnapings à la TV detective stories, but also have a clear idea of what is unacceptable adult behavior.

For me, and for parents like myself who are raising their children in the mainstream of American culture, development of positive self-images for our children is especially valuable.

Asians are *perceived* as different. We *are* different from white Americans; my kids are different in appearance and ethnic consciousness from the Anglo kids down the street, Jason Jones or Kim Smith. As a parent it is my job to help them feel good about being different; to enhance who they are, so they don't feel inferior to or become isolated from their neighborhood friends; so they can handle being confronted by racial and ethnic prejudice as well as the next step of being assertive enough to be among the nonvictims. These two go hand in hand, for Asian-American children must learn early in life that they will be teased or bullied until they stand up to the bully. Once armed with that self-confidence, perhaps they can cope better with future crises, maybe even the advances of an offender.

It is certainly true that parents today are raising children differently than they themselves were raised and even more radically from the way their parents or grandparents were raised, and it is understood that the country and the times have changed, and along the way parenting techniques changed too. For Asians in America this is further complicated, because we have to bridge not only a generation gap, but a cultural gap as well. This is to say that young Asian parents might be anywhere on a continuum from, on the one extreme, a first-generation recent immigrant with children born in Asia, all the way to the other end of the spectrum, of fourth-generation Asian Americans raising their children who only vaguely realize that their great-great-grandparents came from Asia. In between are all the variations in shades of yellow.

Recent immigrants will probably continue for several years, if not for an entire generation, to parent in the traditional ways of the country of their origin, based on a society unlike America. Many are quick to learn external stateside ways (modes of dress and use of processed food, to name a couple), and, if their children are born in the United States, will be forced to change more rapidly, to keep pace with growing Americanization, but basically those parents' orientation will be toward an Asian country. By strong contrast, the fourth-generation parent has probably never visited the land of his or her ancestors and has learned subliminally the culture, teaching, and parenting of Asia. Their orientation, like everyone else here, is middle-class, white America, with all its media hype, both good and bad.

It is my intention to point out some of the similarities and dissimilarities between these two populations of Asian parents and to show how this book might relate to both.

Let us start out with the notion of self-concept. In addition to those ideas mentioned above, we need to look at self-concept for children of immigrant parents. Healthy self-concept for children is often based on healthy adult outlooks, and parents struggling to learn a foreign tongue, a foreign culture, and at the same time keep in step with the growth of their children in fast-paced America sometimes lose their sense of authority or become objects of ridicule to their children.

Take the case of an Asian wife of an American serviceman now living in the United States. She might have been an independent, self-sufficient woman in her own country when she met and married her husband, but once transported away from family, friends, familiar language, and shared culture, her dependency on her husband grows. In our mobile society chances are slim that she would be transplanted into a close, nurturing, extended family on her husband's side, like the one she left behind, and therefore she is truly a stranger in a strange land, with everything to learn, including such oft-forgotten, simple things as credit-card shopping, check cashing, driving, public-transportation routes, school-parent-teacher meetings/conferences, etc. These are everyday occurrences for most of us, to be sure, but each is a mammoth obstacle for her. This dependency, if taken to an extreme, can lead to subservience, as she must lean on her husband not only for economic support for her very survival, but also he becomes the only source of psychological support too. This is a natural setting, as we saw in the section entitled "The Special Friend," for the incestuous father whose mate is losing control of her role as wife and mother.

It is to be remembered that this woman is in a period of transition, and the fact that she had the courage and confidence to venture to a new country, casting off her established support systems, indicates to me that she is a *strong* woman with *survival skills* intact and will possibly in time emerge from the upheaval positively, and even pass on these same skills to her children.

Imagine the debt Asian-American women owe to women of this caliber who were among the group of women who are our grandmothers and great-grandmothers. Our own sense of present-day self-worth is gleaned from images of women who came to the States clad in kimonos or cheong-sans, worked side by side with their immigrant husbands in fields, factories, mom-and-pop stores, and gave of their strength and courage to their children and grandchildren.

Besides the "new immigrant/established fourth-generation Asian-American" split, there is the overall definition of what comprises Asians in America. We are a very diverse group indeed, with backgrounds based in countries like China, Japan, Korea, Cambodia,

Vietnam, and Laos, and South Pacific islands like the Philippines, Guam, Samoa, Fiji, and our own state of Hawaii. The cultures, languages, and traditions are all unique, and it is only in America that we are put together under the hyphenated title of "Asians-Pacific Islanders."

There are many dissimilarities, and it would be foolhardy for any one person to try to speak on behalf of all these peoples, but as an Asian-American woman, I do find that there are consistent similarities that often astound me, for geographically and culturally we *are* so diverse. We are, for example, all Asian; all of us are viewed by statisticians as "model minorities"; all of us are lumped together by white America as "ethnically nonwhite"; all of us are subject to *negative* stereotypes (aggressive, sneaky, inscrutable, smelly) and not-so-positive, *positive* stereotypes (unaggressive, studious, industrious, mystical, quiet, superclean). And all of us have to struggle daily with being outside of the majority population.

We *do* have traits and character in *common* despite the diversification, especially as it relates to our parenting. All of our cultures are based on strong patriarchal societies. All of us would agree that there has been, and continues to be, strong emphasis to obey our elders; that the family unit is paramount to our very existence; and that all Asians in America have an ethnic consciousness to some degree.

Let's consider these commonalities one at a time. First, historically the father was the primary decisionmaker in Asian countries, and in some countries, like Japan, women had little control of their own destinies. Of course, much of this has changed in modern-day Japan, but current news articles indicate that widowed and divorced women raising children have a very difficult time, depending on grandparents and other relatives for support, because the state does not provide even minimal subsistence support.

Recently a Sansei (third-generation Japanese American) woman friend of mine who traveled to Japan to study and search out her deeply buried roots, realized quickly that her identity in Japanese society was measured against her uncle's position, and that he felt it necessary to extend his male protective status to her, though she lived alone in a dinky flat, was economically responsible for her own well-being, and was quite capable of fending for herself, having done so for several previous years. If this be the case in modern-day Asia for a full-grown, self-sufficient woman, what of the female children? Obviously boy children in most Asian countries, where property and lineage are male, are seen as both more desirable and potentially powerful. So when we read statistics like 97 per cent of the reported offenders are adult male and 66 per cent of the victims are female children, then indeed countries that are still entrenched in male dominance give rise to disenfranchised females, and feed into the helpless-female-victim syndrome. I'm convinced that there is as much child molestation in Asian countries as in Western countries, but fewer incidents are reported in Asia.

What remnants of this strong patriarchal upbringing remain in the memories of Asian Americans is hard to measure, but by and large, we still adhere to the idea that *father* is the head of the family.

Second among the similarities across the spectrum is the idea of respecting one's elders, which is so much a part of Asian parenting that I frankly can't remember my parents telling me to "respect your elders." I guess it was absorbed through osmosis or passed down from my older cousins. In any event, it was assumed that I knew enough not to be arrogant, cheeky, obnoxious, or even too talkative in the presence of older people—namely, parents, aunts, uncles, grandparents, and other adults close to my family.

Ethics and codes of behavior that work well in Asian countries with all the other checks and balances for a well-ordered society, sometimes go askew when transported to America. So it is with the case of unquestionable obedience to elders, for it does not take into account the alienation of America's elderly.

Think back, if you will, to the older man who befriended and later molested Robin in the section, "The Shared Secret." He was a man expected to compete with the young, while at the same time being stripped of his job and status in the community. His family was dispersed, and in general he was outside the mainstream of American life. The role of the elderly in Asian societies is very different: Children are in contact with secure elders with long-established seniority by virtue of their age, life experiences, skills, and wisdom, who do not feel displaced by youth or deprived by their country. In Asian societies the strict adherence to traditional values seldom leaves children vulnerable to attack, and instead can give them guidelines for highly acceptable elderly behavior and a glimpse into their own future. Not so in America.

We see our second- and third-generation teen-agers, in their insecure need for peer-group acceptance, rejecting those instilled values even to the point of feeling ashamed of their grandparents who speak "broken English." On the other hand, the positive side of this rejection of culture, perhaps, is that in the United States *trust* cannot be expected just because a person is older, and our children will stand in better stead if they learn to trust their own feelings above all.

The third example of similar experience among Asians is the all-pervasive family unit, whether it be a tight nuclear family, as is often the case with Japanese Americans (statistically they are below the average birthrate in the United States), or the Chinese (who have a national program geared to population control), to the amorphous, extended family (*aizas*) of the Samoans, which can include hundreds. It is what makes Asians have a sense of who they are, where they are, and what they will be. On the subject of incestuous relationships within the family unit, I feel that it may well be the strongest taboo for Asian people, but little has been written along these lines to document it to date. Asian cultures may have more or less stringent guidelines for determining what constitutes incest. Unlike the case of the father in "Two Scenarios" who almost commits incest because he sees no alternatives outside of the family for fulfillment, some Asian countries do not have a culture like ours based on puritanical ethics, but have more flexible, societally approved, sanctioned outlets for sexual expression that do not victimize children.

Last, the notion of ethnic consciousness that I spoke of earlier can best be summarized in the sentence I heard often as a child: "Be a good girl, for others will judge your whole race by your example." What a heavy burden to place on a small child—even granting that the time and the place for such admonitions were in the Midwest shortly after World War II, when racism toward Japanese Americans, recently relocated from concentration camps, was still running rampant. Yet compliance and politeness, mannerliness and respect for authority have been the descriptive words used over and over by white teachers in their relationships to their small Asian charges since the first Asian child entered a public school in the U.S.A.

Media messages and Hollywood-produced films that exploit Asian women and place in jeopardy Asian children by implying their inherent vulnerability provide opportunities for the child molester to take a cue from them to blame the victim.

The plots in the grade B movies of the 1940s and 1950s are repeatedly the same, often superficial story lines with heavy emphasis on sex, which somehow manage to convey the message that Asian girls/women are not valued and are defenseless in determining their future.

An example is the scenario of the young Asian girl who is given away by her parents to a rich, lecherous old man in order to assure the survival of the remaining members of her family; or the young girl who enters a lifetime of servitude to men when she is casually spotted by a professional geisha and later sold by her parents (for her own good, mind you) to the geisha house. Of course, there is always the young girl in a war-torn Asian country who becomes a teen-age hooker to sustain herself. But most damaging of all is the real-life scenario that irresponsible American journalism, in the guise of providing newsworthy news, gave full vent to recently as they provided all the gory details of the numerous rapings of adolescent girls among the "boat people."

Unhappily, these messages will remain as long as our society sees a profit to be gained from the use of racist and sexist exposure. And, also unhappily, it will continue to be a source of rationalization and stimulation for the offender, as he bridges the gap between Asian girl/child and Asian woman and blames the intended victim for his acts of molestation.

Asian children cannot avoid being victims of stereotypes, for they abound in American society, and our children are not exempt from watching the same racist portrayals on the "boob tube" that all children are watching. We all know the type of grade B movie that gets aired on "The Late, Late Show" that portrays Asian women, usually in a war movie, with a setting somewhere in Asia (the United States has been, after all, involved in wars in Asia and the South Pacific for almost forty years), as a mysterious, exotic, erotic, highly obtainable, and readily available piece of merchandise. The main male actor is usually the all-American boy who has left his virginal high-school sweetheart behind and is "horny as hell." *He* is seduced by *her* is the implication of this film, because he is *too innocent* to know any better. (Incidentally, he has just killed a whole platoon of the Asian enemy.) She is tiny, younger, dainty, maybe even a foot shorter than the so-called naïve raw-boned country boy from Nebraska, but we are expected to believe that *she* is the aggressor.

Advertising also blatantly uses Asian women as sex objects to sell cosmetics, clothing, and trips to the Orient or the South Pacific. Some men actually believe women run around bare-breasted in the South Pacific. Maybe they do if they're posing for *Playboy*, but missionary influence over the past 150 years has made island women much more modest in their dress than the average fashion-conscious U.S. working woman.

As an Asian-American woman who was raised with a heightened sense of ethnic consciousness, I realize that it has been inflicted on our children to keep them in line; not to make any waves that will cause the majority culture to point an accusatory finger at a particular group of people based on their ethnicity. And as an Asian-American parent I feel that it is necessary to *release* our children from this hamstrung position of being responsible for anyone other than themselves. Asian children can continue to understand their differences from the host culture, have a genuine sense of ethnic pride, hang onto those value systems that make us a proud and enduring people, and still be assertive and self-confident enough not to end up as one of the thousands of silent children presented in this book.

## Hispanic Parents

BY CARLOS LOREDO, PH.D.

> Carlos Loredo was born and raised in Cuba and has lived in a number of different Hispanic communities in the United States. He currently lives in a city of approximately 350,000, with an ethnic breakdown of roughly 60 per cent Anglo, 25 per cent Hispanic, and 15 per cent black. He is a clinical psychologist, and his professional experience has included work with minority children and families as well as with perpetrators of child sexual abuse. He is the father of a 3½-year-old son.

Although I am not speaking for all parents or all Hispanics, my background, social development, training, and professional experience allow me to make several generalizations. As a society we unwillingly promote the problems of child sexual abuse, for both the victims and the offenders.

### THE HISPANIC WOMAN

The Hispanic woman, as well as women throughout the world, have been programmed to be likely targets for sexual exploitation. The culture expects and demands that the women be quiet, passive, obedient, dependent, and subservient to "their man," as well as toward society in general. Women are also to be sexually uninterested and virgins until the day they wed. They are continually told that true meaning and fulfillment will only be attained once they have married, have numerous children, and raise their family. A woman is also instructed not to assert herself: Her rights and her individuality are only allowed expression within certain constraints. Assertion would be perceived and taken as aggression: Within the Hispanic culture, assertion (most often incorrectly expressed as aggression) is supposed to be the sole domain of the man.

Women in a sense are treated as chattels or property, as possessions. There are clearly defined expectations for women: To deviate from these codes for conduct is to be devalued by the Hispanic community and be treated as a "bad girl" or a "bad woman." These controls are at times so rigidly entrenched and enforced that the woman must ask permission of "her man" to go out or attend any functions.

### THE HISPANIC MAN

The Hispanic man, on the other hand, adheres to the *macho* ideology, an attitude and belief that men are to be outspoken, aggressive, dominating, competent, and all-knowing. Men are expected to be sexually experienced and constantly "on the make." For the Hispanic male, his sexual prowess (the Don Juan syndrome) is the central and overriding theme for most of his social interactions with women. It is the means by which he attempts to exercise control and domination of all women.

### THE HISPANIC CULTURE

As one would expect from the previous discussion, there is a tremendous amount of sex-role stereotyping within the Hispanic community. In general these culturally determined expectations can be summarized as follows: Women are to stay at home and be the passive "takers," and the men are to be out on the street and be the aggressive "doers."

The culture as a whole differs markedly in several ways from the prevailing Anglo culture. For the Anglo, personal excellence and improvement are the orders of the day. Anglos are also unwilling to simply "let things be." Hispanics, however, have very different cultural determinants. For the Hispanic, the critical elements are (1) social control: an attempt to make things work as they have for the past few hundred years—to "let things be" and to get along with other people; and (2) external validation: personal meaning is derived and obtained from the society, the community, the family, and the (primarily the Catholic) Church.

For the Anglo, the code of ethics and control comes primarily from within. For Hispanics, it comes from without. The Anglo views the world as something suitable for his impact. This notion is at variance with the Hispanic view of the world: The world is taken as a given, and one's function and role in this life is to assimilate into the society.

## THE HISPANIC FAMILY

Within the Hispanic family, certain rules of conduct exist. One is to avoid *verguenza* (shame or dishonor) at all costs. There is also the sense of the family taking care of its own problems. If there are suffering, trauma, or other difficulties within the family or affecting the family, one must endure and resolve the problem without assistance from others. The family does not ask or seek "outside" help. Since pride is so highly valued, asking for help might appear as if the family could not take care of or cope with its problems: For many, receiving "outside" help is equated with a burden to society. For the Hispanic family, outside intervention or assistance brings about dishonor and shame.

Coping strategies again revolve about the code of ethics. Personal injuries committed against a family member will be met by personal, familial revenge. Within the family, nonnormative behavior by a family member will be met with a sense of dishonor, loss of respect, and guilt. For the family, conformity to the culture and to tradition are of paramount importance.

## IMPLICATIONS

Cultural expectations are clearly defined for both boys and girls, and they are expected to conform to these codes. Although sexual curiosity and exploration are part of every young person's psychosocial development, sex is rarely discussed within the Hispanic family. Genitalia are perceived as filthy and dirty; development of secondary sexual characteristics are passed over or ignored; and the emotional, psychological, and physiological aspects of sexuality are typically not talked about. The basic message that is portrayed is that boys should go out and become sexually experienced and practice on the "bad girls," so guys can be prepared for marriage. Girls, on the other hand, should abstain from sexual interactions and interests, lest they be labeled as one of the "bad girls." Once they become married, however, women are to become sexually interested and be the perfect sexual partner for "their husband."

Few children receive sexual education within the family. Due to the cultural ethics, Hispanic women will not speak of sexual matters in front of strangers or outsiders. It is especially difficult for a Hispanic woman to speak about sexual victimization in front of strangers, family members, or friends. For the woman, such a revelation would bring about dishonor and loss of respect for both herself and the family. She would be seen as the "spoiled virgin"—not only by her community, but by her family as well. For these reasons, the sexually victimized Hispanic woman or girl may keep quiet rather than endure cultural disgrace.

The theme that emerges is that of woman as the perpetual victim and man as the persistent aggressor. In many ways the culture demands and expects these roles; the parents model such behaviors; and the children act these attitudes out.

The Hispanic community needs to recognize the magnitude of sexual-abuse victimization within their community. Sexual victimization of children by adults and juveniles is occurring within the Hispanic community, but various family and cultural pressures prevent or hinder identification and treatment of the problem. To confront the problem and address preventive measures that are necessary requires change.

### INTERVENTIONS

This author has recommended numerous helpful strategies to combat sexual victimization of children. The following suggestions may be particularly helpful for Hispanic parents:

1. *Sexuality:* The Catholic Church still has what I consider very repressive, outmoded, and factually incorrect ideas about sexuality. Most children and adolescents do masturbate—masturbation does not send one to hell, cause death, warts, or brain damage. Genitalia and sexual interactions are not "dirty." The point is that children must be correctly and *properly* informed about sexual matters. Typical sexual curiosity and exploration, by both boys and girls, need to be viewed as normal parts of any child's development, and not viewed as sinful, despicable behavior. Sex is not dirty—it is our attitudes about sexuality that are often distorted.

2. *Sexual stereotyping:* The culturally determined expectations
that were previously discussed do not produce the "inner voice" that
is so necessary for internal validation. This internal validating mech-
anism produces self-confident and assertive individuals, thereby re-
ducing the likelihood of their victimization. Sexual stereotyping limits the potentialities of all individuals, boys and girls and men and
women alike. It is important then to raise all of our children as
unique individuals, and to encourage them to be self-actualized,
strong, and assertive individuals.

3. *Self-concept:* It is important that children have a feeling of
self-worth. Feeling good about oneself is one of the necessary ingre-
dients for positive, constructive personal growth. Hispanic parents
could provide a very facilitative home atmosphere by promoting
the attitude that "liking yourself is not selfish"; that thinking good
things about how we feel, how we act, and what we believe is a
valuable attitude to have. Parents should also realize that induce-
ment or creation of guilt is not one of the better ways of promoting
feelings of self-worth and positive self-concept.

4. *Listening:* Children must feel that they have accessibility to
their parents. Children must know that they will be heard by their
parents, even when what the children have to say contradicts the
word of another adult. We must realize, as parents, that all adults
do not tell the truth. We must also recognize that although it is
important to be polite and respect others, some individuals are not
looking out for the best interest of the child: They may try to exploit the child's naïveté, obedience, and trust to commit a sexual
assault. There is also the issue that we as parents or adults always
know what is best for the child. Children who are led and directed
solely by their parents' wishes and demands are likely to heed, without question, the commands and requests of another adult. As parents, we cannot participate in much listening, or expect to be
approached by questions from our children if we persist with the
notion that *we* always know what is best for them. An open, non-
punitive channel of communication is an essential between parents
and their children.

5. *Children need to know:* Children need to know the implica-

tions and "meanings" of various situations. For example, children need to know that their body is their own and that other people do not have the right to touch them in various parts of their body. This information can be conveyed in a nonthreatening, comforting manner to the child by the parent. Children can also be told that whenever they feel uncomfortable or someone is making them feel uncomfortable, they should come home or call immediately. A well-informed, assertive child is not as likely to be victimized. Even if such a child were to be assaulted, the resulting aftershock would not be as great, because the child would have the personality traits, skills, and necessary support from his or her parents.

A sad but all too familiar vignette illustrates many of the points addressed in this section. The following is an excerpt from an interview with a ten-year-old victim of sexual assault, several weeks following the assault:

> O.K., I didn't take candy from a stranger, and I didn't ride in someone's car that I didn't know. But it was my teacher, and I believed what he told me. I knew that what he was telling me and asking me to do was wrong, but he was right: If I told you [parents], you would not believe me. He said he would do it only that time and leave me alone, so I went along with it.

### COMMENTS

This book provides much helpful information for parents and does so in an organized and constructive fashion. Various exercises and suggestions are clearly outlined and designed. This book provides a much-needed tool for all parents. But it is particularly useful for those parents who have been afraid or have not known how to approach the issue of child sexuality and child sexual assault.

I would like to expand on several issues alluded to by the author. The first of these is "man as the aggressor." It is definitely true that men have been given free rein to dominate and control throughout the centuries. My comments are in no way intended to minimize men's (or anyone's) responsibility for their behavior. To understand the problem of child sexual abuse and to be able to establish and develop preventive measures, we must understand the dynamics of the offender.

In my work with both juvenile and adult sex offenders, it is readily apparent that a great majority of them were sexually or physically abused as children. Their fear, embarrassment, and rage over their own victimization in many ways predisposed them to commit these inappropriate sexual offenses. These offenders were also child victims of many of the notions discussed in the book: uninformed sexuality, lack of "inner voice," sexual stereotyping, double standards, and sexual victimization. So it is important to view the offender, as well as the victim, as products of their environment.

It is also important to note that women and mothers do commit sexual offenses against children. Oftentimes these cases, when reported, are minimized or dismissed. In a case of sexual victimization of a juvenile by an adult woman, the presiding judge dismissed the case because it was a "good and normal experience for any guy to go through." Other therapists indicate that within a specified sample of convicted adult sexual offenders, at least 40 per cent of them had admitted to sexual victimization by their mothers (Prendergast, 1979). Because sexual victimization is such an important issue and difficult problem, it should not be viewed as solely a problem of "women as prey" and "men as the perpetrators." Currently, the reports of women (mothers) victimizing children sexually are few, but the reported numbers are steadily increasing.

This brings me to the last and final point: boys as victims of child sexual abuse. It was once thought that female child victims outnumbered male child victims nine to one. The statistics of *reported* cases in the past were correct, but the implication that boys were not as often sexually abused as girls is incorrect. We are finding that male child victims are equally as likely to be reported as victims of child sexual abuse (compared to girls). Given the double standard and sexual stereotyping, it is much more embarrassing and demeaning for a boy to report sexual victimization. He will often be labeled as a "fag" by his friends, and may be treated as something less than a man by his family. Boys as well as girls need to be seen as individuals, with unique qualities and difficulties. Both sexes need to be informed, aware, inner-determined, cared for, heard, and treated with all the dignity that should be accorded to all human beings.

Source:

Prendergast, W. "Rehabilitation of the Sex Offender," panel discussion presented at the National Organization of Victim Assistance, Inc. Philadelphia, Pa.: Oct. 29, 1979.

# Native American Parents

BY SARAH H. HUTCHINSON

Sarah H. Hutchinson is an instructor at the University of California at Davis, in the Department of Applied Behavioral Science's Native American Studies Program, and she teaches Native American courses on cultural values, research, and counseling. Before joining the university staff she taught school at the elementary, junior-high, high-school, and junior-college levels and was a psychiatric assistant and therapist for severely mentally ill children and adults. She has for a long time held a marriage, family, and child counselor's license.

Born to Cherokee Indian parents in Claremore, Oklahoma, in 1920, the second of eight siblings, she obtained United States citizenship by an Act of Congress on June 2, 1924.

Educated in Oklahoma public schools and universities, she obtained two college degrees in three years, five months.

Having no children of their own, she and her husband parented eighteen children and adopted her nephew, Roger.

A multitude of simultaneous messages swims through my mind as a result of reading this book. Most of them are best described as regret, sorrow, and trauma about the way little girls are treated in this great nation. The fact that one in four little girls in this country will experience incest, child molestation, or rape by the time she is eighteen causes me to believe that some loathsome wickedness permeates the social structure of this country, a condition that serves as an indictment on America!

My reactions are strong but they are right out of my Indian heritage, out of a matrilineal society where women are highly regarded, have positions of authority, have property rights, and where blood descent is traced through the mother. Indian women are expected to make decisions and to keep close watch on the course of affairs that affects the welfare of their children, their parents, and their relatives. Her thoughts and actions, guided by spiritual beliefs, tell her it is wrong to abuse children in any way. And sexual abuse of children is absolutely unforgivable!

Indian religion and spiritual beliefs guide and permeate the teaching and training of an Indian woman's children, and she teaches her children carefully. Starting before the children walk, she continues the training until they are adults. Her training and teaching methods consist almost wholly of advice and counsel.

She advises and counsels to commit certain acts or not to commit certain acts not because the acts are inherently right or wrong, but because certain acts are to the child's benefit and others are to the child's disadvantage. She does not use the abstract principles of right and wrong when she teaches her children. Her teaching goals are respect and sanction; positive public opinion is rewarded, and condemnation is dreaded. The child's pride and ambition are appealed to, and a reward of sweets or promises of privileges for good behavior are not offered.

The Indian mother is not alone in her thoughts and actions about children. Indian men are guided by the same spiritual beliefs and are companions to the idea that children are sacred.

Indian men and women bestow upon children the fullest expressions of affection and solicitude. Indian men and women who attend my classes at the University of California voluntarily refrain from participation in sexual intercourse after the birth of a child for an extended period of several months. This abstinence from intercourse is to ensure that the mother's lactation will not halt, because it is important not to jeopardize the healthy development of the child. These students believe that a child should be nursed as long as possible to ensure good health.

Indians today are encouraged by the World Health Organization's announcement of Friday, October 12, 1979, that "it is preparing strict global rules against any promotion of baby food designed to discourage the natural method of breast-feeding infants" (El Paso *Times*). WHO has invited its 135 member governments to set strict national rules to protect and encourage breast feeding. Traditional Indians believe breast feeding is in the best interest of the infant's health and that an infant's health is more important than a mother's convenience.

Indians do not separate themselves from children; Indians take their children to meetings, to activities, and sometimes to class. Sometimes they take their children to work with them. This is to say that Indians live public lives, and observation is not only easy but is also expected by everybody in the Indian world.

I have observed Indian children in their development of the "inner voice" and have heard two-year-old children say to themselves, "I better not do that." They make statements to themselves about their own behavior—means of putting them in a more favorable position. At age four, Indian children have for the most part developed the "inner voice," which guides their behavior as long as they are with Indians.

In all my experience as a teacher or counselor I have never heard from an Indian man or about an Indian man molesting his daughter, nor a mother her son.

Indian conversation frequently mentions incest, but incest has a unique meaning for Indians. Incest is a repulsive crime, a taboo, and not only between parents and their children. Incest extends to distant cousins (eighth cousins for my tribe) and to anyone in the clan. It even extends beyond blood relatives to politically created divisions.

Without exception, mating between Indian women and men who are in any way blood relatives is regarded as incest. Moral obligations for incest are extreme, and for Indians who commit incest with a blood relative or a member of some allied political group, punishment is severe. These persons are considered unfit to live on earth. And there are no generally applicable limits for the incest taboo or the rule that requires persons to marry outside a specific social or political group.

I adhere to the above-mentioned morals, ethics, and values, and for this reason reading this book was a traumatic experience. Little children are helpless! How can little girls defend themselves against fathers whose "inner voice" tells them it is permissible to molest, rape, or commit incest with their daughters? What can a mother possibly be thinking when she allows a man to get away with this horrific behavior?

I know of no one, including veterinarians, who has witnessed male dogs, cats, or pigs sexually abusing their female puppies, kittens, or piglets.

White Western man is supposed to enjoy a higher social status than women, Indians, and animals. But the chance that one in four little girls in America will be the victim of incest, child molestation, or rape by the time she reaches the age of eighteen is a powerful indication that he should not deserve the supposed higher status.

Rape, child molestation, incest, and alcoholism did not exist among American Indians before the advent of Western man's arrival in this country. My contention is that they did not exist because of the status of Indian women.

Indian women were created simultaneously with Indian men; each of them were endowed with unique qualities and sensibilities that made them dependent upon each other. The idea that they were created equal is an idea that is accepted by moral traditions that reach back into the vaults of history.

Historically Indian women goddesses enjoy equal if not more-than-equal status with male gods.

Indian women have enjoyed respect and equal status with Indian men, but they are not the only women who did. History is replete with captive alien women who shared this respect and status. Two cases in point are reported by Mary Rowlandson and General James Clinton. Mary Rowlandson, a clergyman's wife, was captured by the Narrangansett Indians for three months. In 1676 she told about being alone and in company with the Narrangansett Indians, sleeping, all sorts together, and not one of them offered unchastity or abuse, in word or in action.

General James Clinton, fighting the Iroquois Indians noticed, in 1779, that they never violated the chastity of their women prisoners.

It strikes me that Mary Rowlandson and General Clinton expected the Indians to abuse the women prisoners' chastity. This is my interpretation, of course, but I am not surprised at the protection and respect given the women prisoners. Respect and protection of Indian women and of white women are commonplace in the Indian culture.

Indian women and white women respond differently in threatening situations. I recall a classroom situation in which the women exhibited culturally motivated responses during our thirty-minute class-discussion period that followed a lecture in my Native American morals, ethics, and values class at the University of California.

The students wanted to discuss the East Area rapist incident of the night before.

The East Area rapist is a notorious character who had terrorized people in Sacramento's East Area by breaking into their homes in the predawn hours, awakening them by shining a powerful flashlight in their eyes, threatening and ordering the wife at gunpoint to bind the husband's feet with a rope and to bind his hands behind his back and place a stack of dishes on his chest. He threatened to kill the husband if he heard the dishes fall to the floor. Taking the woman to another room, he raped her with vacuum-sweeper-handle tubes and bottles.

The students were upset because the East Area rapist had moved his base of operations from Sacramento to Davis. And their attempt to discuss the subject was difficult, very slow, and at times almost impossible. My home is in the Sacramento East Area, and I was able to assist in their discussion. Just as the discussion was rolling along nicely, everyone was surprised at the handsome blond man with blue eyes who kept smiling with eyes dancing, as if he were enjoying the discussion very much. He raised his hand to talk and said he had an idea that would help women.

His idea was to write a grant proposal, get funds, open an office, and hire counselors to help women accept rape because accepting rape was their only problem as he saw it.

The Indian women in the class asked him what kind of nut he was and laughed. The white women gasped, drew themselves up, bent forward in their seats, and with eyes dancing with anger held their body posture, but they never said a word.

He continued with his idea. He had figured out a way, a foolproof way to rape women by jogging alongside the women in the early mornings on campus. Just jog up alongside of them and ease them off in the bushes. And he said he planned to draw a map of all the bushes on campus for anyone who was interested.

The white women settled back into their chairs defeated; the Indian women wanted to fight him but decided to leave the class instead. At this point he wanted to know what I thought of his idea.

I told him I would show him if he would join me in jogging the next morning, and I tried to get an agreement from him. He asked again what I thought, and again in a serious voice I tried to get him to agree to meet me. And he said he was sorry he brought the subject up.

The class period ended and another class was scheduled to begin, but the white women crowded around me at the desk and would not leave. Finally we inched out the door and down the stairs to the ground floor; in a clutch we stood outside the building. After a while I sat down on the steps and waited for them to say something. They did not speak for the longest time. They couldn't speak, and when I realized it I asked if they wanted to run with me the next morning. Like little girls they sat down on the ground in front of me and with smiling faces sat in silence.

For a while I thought they might think I was teasing them. And we spent a silent thirty-minute period just watching people enter and leave the building. I asked them to come into my office if they wanted to talk, to come at any time. And I left.

During the weeks that followed they came to talk and revealed that they were terrified beyond words at the student with crazy ideas. "Frozen in fear," one student said as she told about her feelings.

I learned that defending themselves is foreign to their thinking processes. I will never forget these women.

On another occasion, after reading a paper at the VI International Forum for Psychoanalysis, in West Berlin, and waiting for nine hours on an airplane at Heathrow Airport in London, England, because the Terminal Tower employees were on strike, we arrived in New York and had to reschedule our flight in order to reach our destination. The airline made overnight reservations and we stood outside the terminal to hail a taxi in order to get to the motel. When we got to the motel the night clerk told us he had no rooms and asked who sent us. We told him but he said he had nothing. I asked who was the manager and told him we would sleep on the floor in the lobby. He got the manager and I showed him the list of names and addresses and a letter that was being composed to send to the president of the airline and to an attorney. We were assigned to rooms, and my roommate was a beautiful blond thirty-eight-year-old schoolteacher from Kansas who had toured Europe for six weeks on a limited budget.

She was impressed with the luxury of the motel room.

When I asked her what she would do if someone tried to break into the room, she kept talking about the beautiful room. I asked again. But she didn't seem to understand.

I told her that if someone tried to break in, I would run quickly to the door and slam my briefcase on the door to startle the person on the outside of the door. She didn't say anything.

After sleeping for fifteen minutes there was a terrible clatter, as if the door would come off its hinges. I ran to the door and slammed the briefcase against it with all the strength I possessed. All was quiet in the hall.

Returning to the bed, I noticed her face as the rays from her bedside table lamp fell on her face. She was frozen in fear, rigid with fear, and unable to talk.

Observations like the above-mentioned ones cause me to think that white women are unable to take the responsibility to defend themselves. Defending themselves appears to be foreign to their thinking and behavior. Why should they be unable to take responsibility in their own defense? What experiences instill such overwhelming fear? Do these responses have cultural roots?

The Preface in David B. Lynn's book *Daughters and Parents: Past, Present, and Future* (1979), includes the following statement: "This book is directed toward redressing the neglect of females and looks specifically at daughter/parent relationships as a means of doing so. So that we may increase our understanding of parental influences on the development of women . . ."

In Lynn's book he has devoted a whole chapter to the American daughter's historical heritage and traces that heritage to ancient Greek, Hebrew, and Roman societies. This chapter serves to increase our understanding of parental influences on the development of women.

The Greeks not only valued daughters less than sons but also rarely raised more than one daughter. They put the baby girls out to the weather, a form of infanticide, when the father decided not to keep the child; the mother carried out the act. Daughters were sold by fathers, and daughters could not under any circumstances inherit family property after marriage.

Hebrew parents desired children, but the father sold daughters to strangers, married them as he saw fit, and had control over them after marriage. The Hebrew father could punish his children by death.

In Roman society the father had unlimited power: He could grant life or death to his wife, his children, and his slaves, and he practiced exposing female babies to the weather. Women were not recognized by early Roman law as legal persons, but some women held high places of esteem in private and social life. Toward the later years of the Republic the status of women changed, and some rose to political power.

Anglo-Saxon and Germanic tribes during the Middle Ages granted fathers the power of life or death over female babies by putting them out to the weather; however, they could not put them out to the weather if the baby had tasted food. Infanticide continued even after a law against it had been passed. Fathers could send their daughters to convents and keep them there against their will.

During the seventeenth century, preference was strong for boy babies. Daughters received harsh punishment even though they were grown. And girls were not allowed to play outside.

During the eighteenth century a development of parental love began to blossom, and parents became concerned about their children's education and future. Discipline was severe, and marriages were still arranged by parents. Daughters' chastity became of great concern, and they were warned to stay away from brothers, their own fathers, pages, and servants. Education for children became a reality because educators wanted to protect children from the corrupting influences of adults.

In 1792, Mary Wollstonecraft complained that education and treatment of women caused them to be weak and dependent.

All European countries in the nineteenth century still preferred boys, and physical punishment of girls continued.

In America daughters were inheritors of the powerful European, Roman, Hebrew, and Greek cultures, and the powerful patriarchal pattern described in the Old Testament. Discipline was very harsh, and breaking down children by beating was common.

In the southern colonies wealth was greater and easier to attain because of the prevailing attitudes and slavery. Fathers had greater power in the South but this power dissipated after the South's defeat in the Civil War.

Girls were allowed to attend the early schools. Before these early schools were established, children of wealthy families were sent to boarding schools in Europe.

During and after the Civil War, movements like industrialization, democratization, and the feminist movement stirred imaginations and forced changes for women in America. The women's movement found roots in the antislavery movement that preceded the Civil War; the women's movement blossomed after the war ended. In 1869 the National Suffrage Association was organized, and in 1920 women gained the right to vote.

New colleges for women were built, an admission that women were not too weak to stand the strain of mental labor.

Women made more progress between the Civil War and World War I than they made between the Revolution and the Civil War. Just as the women's movement found roots in the antislavery movement, the women's liberation movement found roots in the affirmative-action movement during the late 1960s and the early 1970s.

Clearly, culture is the carrier of systems of belief that are inherited and that condition thoughts and behavior. The above overview of the cultural roots of Indian mothers and daughters and of white mothers and daughters sheds light on individual and collective self-concepts. The two races differ drastically, are almost diametrical opposites.

It appears that the Indian girl is in the better position during the earlier years because the Indian mother's style of teaching is directed toward feeling good about oneself, knowing that the parent will listen, learning to master the environment, acting in the child's own best interest for the future, accumulation of conquered situations, action-oriented confidence, and willingness to take action.

Indians talk about kinship ties on every occasion when they meet. This talking about kinship is a technique used to keep alive the incest taboo, not between father and daughter but regarding marriage of blood relatives of any degree. Indians talk for hours and days about kinship, and individual relatives have a good opportunity to know who they are. It helps develop self-concept.

Teaching children about child sexual abuse among Indians is relatively easy because parents rarely separate themselves from their children. Adults never ask their children to leave the room if they wish to say something they don't want the child to hear. Adults get up together and leave together if they want to talk about something a child shouldn't hear. When this happens it is often to save face—that is, the one-to-one contact is used when one wishes to talk about another who is not present. Sex is discussed openly by everyone, and the Indians joke a lot about sex. But they never tell "filthy stories" for the sake of telling "filthy stories," and I've never heard Indian men tell dirty stories about women.

The teasing about sex is surface joking, or making reference to sex, and is used to keep the incest taboo alive.

Indian children talk easily, especially if a grandmother is around, not the paternal or maternal biological grandmother necessarily, but an older woman who is addressed as "Grandmother" by all Indian children. Figuratively, if a child says "Grandmother" in a group of people, all the older women will all but stand to attention. And it is not uncommon for an Indian child to walk up to an older woman and say, "Grandmother, will you watch me?" The child's mother may be only several feet away. The child simply wants to be watched over by a grandmother; children like the relationship. Tiny children when in the presence of their parent and an older woman will ask: "A grandmother?" If the parent answers in the affirmative, the tot is likely to throw out his hands and run to the grandmother.

Indian children frequently do what I call "reporting," but what is known in the white world as tattling.

Sex-role stereotyping for Indian children is important, because to be a female is to be respected. Females and males are expected to have natural differences. Each individual is expected to have a natural difference; none are expected to duplicate the behavior of others for status.

If a child is restless, hyperactive, cranky, or flighty, the old ones say the child is hunting his umbilical cord, meaning that the child is unhappy on earth, does not know his place on earth. And we make religious ceremonies so that the child may find happiness on earth.

Indian children, because of their heritage, develop a healthy "inner voice" and self-respect at an early age if their family and culture are intact. But if they have been raised in government schools or orphanages they will have all the problems white children have. It is in these cases that Indian teachers, therapists, and foster parents need to follow the exercises in *The Silent Children*.

Two portions of this book "jumped off the page," so to speak. Father-daughter incest is forbidden to such a great degree in Indian culture that it severely disturbs all Indians even to see this abuse discussed in print. The other disturbing portion concerned the direction to look the child directly in the eyes. In Indian culture, to look one directly in the eyes is an invasion of privacy that is considered an insult. In white culture the expression "look him square in the eye" is commonplace. For whites, not to look one in the eyes is thought to mean that one is lying.

The phrase "honest Indian" results from the Indians' reverence for truth, their search for truth. Simple truth. It results from our inability to understand why white men say one thing and do another, or the mere fact that they complicate and camouflage or disguise the truth. The thought that an Indian is lying because he doesn't look one in the eyes puts the Indian in a double bind.

From my experience as an Indian woman and my response or ability to respond to the needs of children and their protection from sexual abuse, I would encourage white women to think about Mary Wollstonecraft, who in 1792 complained that education and treatment of women caused them to be weak and dependent. That woman stood up for women 187 years ago. Consider the progress of women and the prevailing atmosphere of that time. What courage! A great woman! I would wish that mothers and daughters keep struggling for fair treatment, dignity, and pride.

Sexual abuse of children is unforgivable!

In my opinion, the overall usefulness of this book makes it one of the best books that has been written in the past ten years on the subject of child sexual abuse.

## Single Parents

BY MARINELL REDUS

> Marinell Redus is a forty-one-year-old single mother of three children, ages twenty-four, eighteen, and fifteen. She states her first child was born when she was seventeen and thanks to an aware and kind mother-in-law, Marinell began a lifelong interest in learing how to be a good parent and in how to pass on that information. She now lives in a small town north of San Francisco with her fifteen-year-old daughter and the man she has chosen to share her life with. She works for a YWCA child-care program for child abuse victims and families in crisis, and has a solid commitment to the feminist movement.

I recently had the opportunity to have some detailed conversations with my three grown or nearly grown children. I had just started to read this book so I was able to keep them and their experiences in mind as I continued to read it. I was also aware of them as my children and of me as their mother and of how we had all managed to become who we are. My children were very young when I became a single parent and for most of their growing up years I was the only adult in the home. Fortunately I had several very close women and men friends whom I often talked with at length about the problems that came up for me as a single parent. I read avidly all the books I could find concerning child rearing and I remember hours and hours of wondering, thinking, and trying to figure out how to do the right thing.

As a young mother, I knew that I wanted above all to keep the lines of communication open and well used, and to listen, really listen, to my children as consistently as I possibly could. This has often been extremely difficult and often impossible, but generally I have tried to hold to these guidelines. I noticed that the hardest ways for me to be as a mother were the ways in which I had chosen to be different from my own mother's ways. She did not listen very well to me and I can remember hearing her murmuring "uh-huh" and "yeah" when I knew she was a million miles away. I remember feeling isolated and lonely when that happened, yet when I tried to be different, those old learned models were most difficult to break down.

As my children grew and as I grew, I began to see through reading, talking to others and observation, that I wanted to give my children independence and a sense of responsibility to themselves. I tried to treat them as individuals always, and not as three little beings to form as I saw fit. As they grew, I was amazed at the enormous differences in them. The author of this book has given some really excellent ways of helping parents to give their children the tools not only to avoid sexual abuse, but also tools that will help them live strong, fulfilling lives. But I would like to emphasize how each suggestion always has to be considered in conjunction with *who* the child is. It is not difficult to fit the suggestion to the child, and we should be aware of this.

The teaching conversations I had with my older daughter were not always appropriate ones to have with my younger daughter. And my son was still a third personality. Sometimes this may have been due to their age differences, but most often it had to do with their uniqueness.

I worked hard at helping them to have a high sense of self worth and this was another difficult task. As parents and particularly as single mothers we often find ourselves constantly reprimanding or reminding our children of what they did not do or should have done. This can really get in the way of building self worth, but how can we manage to do both? I found that I had to really build a new habit for myself; I had to get in the habit of praising things I often took for granted. At one time a daughter of mine who was four, seemed to become more negative and harder to live with. She would wake up in the morning with a frown and the day continued in that way. I tried to look into what was going on in her life and to help her with her struggle, but I also started praising her on those mornings when she awakened with a smile and we would sing "Oh What A Beautiful Morning" together. When my son took his plate to the kitchen without being asked, I tried to remember to praise him. Often the problems of being a single parent made me forget to praise, but I tried to remember. A little child needs to be thanked for remembering to flush the toilet. There are a million little ways we can reinforce a child's self esteem, and high self esteem can help carry them through attempted sexual abuse.

I discovered quite early in my parenting that I made serious errors and mistakes, and that afterwards I felt guilty. I was taking all the responsibility of parenting and it was often more than I could manage. I stumbled onto a simple and invaluable way of helping my children to know that I am not always right, and that I make plenty of mistakes. I simply learned to apologize to them, and to explain honestly why I had behaved as I had. Sometimes this happened after I had punished them unjustly, or perhaps it was after I had treated them gruffly or very harshly because of my own state of mind. It might have been when I found myself not listening to them or realizing I had told them something that wasn't really true. An adult would have expected or even demanded an apology, or we think it is necessary to give them one. But we don't remember that our children need and deserve the same courtesy and thoughtfulness. Apologizing is recognizing your own humanness, and it can make an obvious difference in relationships with parents and children.

Our children can then see that we are not perfect, therefore they do not have to be perfect—or disappointed in themselves when they discover they are not. They can see that we value them and their feelings as much as we do other adults, and they learn to value themselves and their feelings. They learn that grownups are not always *right:* in fact sometimes grownups are jerks! I needed to be so perfect it seemed, since I was the only parent they were with, but once I started allowing myself to be vulnerable and began to show my weaknesses and mistakes, life was easier for me and the children. All these things will help children to be able to feel good about themselves and to hopefully avoid sexual abuse.

Another important point is to allow children to make their own judgments and to value them. If they don't like someone, they should be heard and appreciated. I remember very well when I was seven years old, my Mother started going out with a new man. I was used to her going out from time to time and I had never had bad feelings about the men in her life, but this particular one I simply hated. I wanted so badly to tell her how I really felt, but I knew I was supposed to like him and she was lonely. She never talked about it and

I think I felt responsible. She looked so pretty when she was getting ready to meet him and I could feel her happiness. So I didn't say I liked him, but I didn't say I hated him either. He brought me presents and I would not play with them, or I would break them. My Mother either refused to notice or she really wasn't aware of it and she married this man. Both of our lives became miserable. He was a violent alcoholic we soon discovered, and we both lived in a great deal of fear for three or four years. I always felt really creepy about him and I hated to be in the house alone with him—in fact I rarely was. I still believe he would have easily abused me sexually if I had been at all open to his friendliness. He did physically abuse my mother and on occasion I received the same treatment. If my children tell me they don't like someone, I try to listen and believe in their feelings.

There is an area of parenting that the author has mentioned but I believe it needs to be stressed more. Parents need to allow children to become angry at adults and to be able to say "no" to adults. This is of course a bit tricky, because any parent knows how easy it is for a two-year-old to say no and how hard it is for them to say yes. Also, a single parent may be all the child has and it may be harder for the child to say no to the only solid thing they know. I believe in the importance of listening to your child and learning to discern when you need to allow the child to say "no" to you, and even encourage disagreement. The anger they feel needs to be expressed in some way (my 15-year-old daughter says loudly, "Mom! You make me so mad!"). I remember when my children were small, I sometimes had to ask them in the middle of their tears, if they were very angry with me, and if they were, it was okay. They would often nod their heads and finally they learned to speak up with a "Yes!" After all, I had no trouble showing my anger to them—why should they not be allowed their feelings? And if they said "No, I don't want to go to the park today" or "No, I don't want to wear that today," I tried to give them those opportunities to be allowed to say "No" and to be respected.

The sections of this book that deal with sex stereotyping are very helpful. Sexual abuse of children *does* depend on the child being a victim and most sexual abuse is done to female children. The statistics given concerning children's TV programs can't be ignored. I wanted my children, male and female, to grow up believing in their own ability to take care of themselves. How can they do that if they see the people they are most trying to emulate, either relying on others to take care of and protect them or simply allowing themselves to be victims? When my husband and I were still living together, we both participated in our daily lives as two individuals. He allowed me to be as strong as I am and I rarely felt victimized. Of course we are products of sexism in our families, and we were often unaware of teaching our children sexist roles. As the wife and mother I felt responsible for everyone's feelings. I am sure this was passed on to my daughters. We began working years ago to try and correct our old patterns.

As a single parent I have tried to provide a strong role model and I tried not to be a victim. Sometimes I failed and all I wanted was my old security. This brings to mind another important issue in raising children to protect themselves; be honest. Particularly as a single parent, there have been times when I felt depressed, sad, lonely and stupid. I learned to share those feelings with my children (mindful of their ages and their ability not to be afraid of my unsureness), to some degree. As they grew older, I learned to share more completely what was happening to me and my feelings. I was afraid at first to be *so* vulnerable, but to my surprise they gave me such wonderful support and they were so relaxed to be able to *know* what was going on and to know that I trusted them, that I soon relaxed. My honesty about my own feelings with them began to promote their sharing with me. This process helped us to be able to have the conversations about sexual abuse that I mentioned earlier. Now that they are no longer children, we have become a group of friends as well as remaining a close family. They shared their experiences and feelings with me and I learned some things I did not know.

My first experience with sexual abuse involving one of my children happened when my son, the first child, was nearly four years old and his father and I were still together. I picked him up from nursery school every day and we rode the city bus home in the late afternoon. The bus was usually crowded, and one day we were standing up close to the front beside the front sideways seats. We were standing right in front of the people seated there. My son was in front of me and were both facing an older man in his late sixties.

He was looking at Ricky in a very fond way, and at first I saw it as an old person looking with pleasure at a young person. Then he began to mumble something to my son and took his hands and put them around Ricky's hand. Then I could see that something I did not like at all was happening right before me. The old man seemed not to know anyone else was there as he began to stroke Ricky's hand and then his chest. Ricky was pushed up close against the man's legs. It all happened very quickly and in no time I felt a very hot flush that I believe was anger and not knowing exactly what to do, I quickly maneuvered around so that Ricky was standing in front of me and my back was turned to the old man. I had the feeling of being vulnerable exposed to him myself and I could hardly wait to get off the bus. I felt such revulsion and anger. When we got off the bus, I asked Ricky if he had realized what had happened. He told me that he had felt kind of strange and uncomfortable when the old man touched him. We talked about the possibilities of sexual abuse then and what he should do. I felt guilty because I did not confront the man immediately. I felt some kind of personal lack of power. My husband didn't seem to fully appreciate any of the feelings I had. He was briefly angry at the old man and he talked with our son a bit about what to do in the future. Later in the first grade, Ricky was approached by another man near his school, who tried to offer him gifts if he would go with him. Ricky ran away to the school office and reported what had happened. The man was supposedly picked up by the police, but I was never contacted by them. My son says that he cannot remember any incidents after this one of being approached with any overtones of sexuality as a child. He does not remember the first incident, except to say he feels a slight ring of recognition when he hears about it.

When my younger daughter, Sylvia, was ten years old, she went to live with her father for a year. She had lived with me for a long time and she felt she wanted to go live with her father for a while. Her father and I have always been in good communication and the children have visited back and forth with no real problems. Sylvia told me that one night while she was in Colorado, she was staying over at a friend of her father's, because there were many guests and the friend had offered his house. Sylvia was the only child and was put to bed in the friend's (Leno) bed to be moved later. He came to bed much later and got in bed with her. He reached over and put his hands on her very young breasts. She said she pushed his hand away and said, "Don't do that, Leno." He put his hands back and told her that it was all right. He told her he often did that with young girls in his family. She told him it was not all right with her and pushed him away again. He made no further attempt.

My heart was in my throat as I listened, for the situation seemed physically and emotionally dangerous to me. I mean what was he doing in the bed with her in the first place? I did not know the man, but I had heard from many people about how wonderful he was. I had heard nothing but good things, and I suppose Sylvia's father had the same image of him as the other people had presented. Sylvia didn't mention it to her father (she felt "funny" about saying anything), and nothing else ever happened. I did not know about it for five years. When we talked about it, she said that the man had not seemed threatening to her and that she believed he viewed it as a very normal thing to do. He is from a very large family and is in his late sixties. Sylvia thought it was not at all normal. She said she felt really uncomfortable about it. I had read this book and thought about the training she received to protect herself. I believe she was saved by her high self-esteem, her ability to say "no" to adults, and the knowledge she had of sexual matters. She also realized what boundaries existed for her.

Sex education started at our house at a very early age and has always seemed to me to be generally relaxed and healthy. Sylvia told me that her sound knowledge of sex helped her. But I don't remember ever really stressing the importance of specific incidents of abuse and the immediate need to report them to me. I was more general in my advice, although I do remember talking very frankly about the possibilities of sexual abuse and how to avoid it. They knew about sex by then, for how can you warn a child to stay out of the street if they don't know what a street is? Now I can see that I should have made more of an issue of reporting the incidents. I wish for her own feelings that she had been able to tell her father right away.

As we talked, Sylvia reminded me of an incident that I had not thought of. After she came back to live with me, we were living in a house in the mountains outside of Santa Barbara. Our house was somewhat isolated, but just across the highway was a community of houses. She frequently went over there to visit friends, and through these friends she had been asked to babysit for a woman who had two small children. The woman shared the house with other people, one of whom was a young man about twenty-five years old. One time Sylvia came home after babysitting at this house and told me that she did not want to go back over there. I asked her what had happened and she told me that in the past when she had gone over there and Peter had been there, he always made comments to her about how beautiful she was and how he really particularly liked very young girls with long hair. He had been there that day and tried to get her to "get stoned" with him and told her more things about how much he liked really young girls. He said that they turned him on and that she should relax and get high with him. I knew this man very slightly, from a class at the local college, and he had invited me to come over on particular evenings when his drama group did Shakespeare readings. I had wanted to, but never made the effort. I had absolutely no reason to suspect him of ever doing what he did, but I knew I never wanted Sylvia to be around him again. At that point in my parenting I had reached a place where I felt confident and successful. I feel I gave Sylvia support and the opportunity to tell me about what happened. I never considered reporting him, although I did tell some of the parents in the area. I was not at all aware of the possibility of him being attracted to the young child who lived in the house with him and I don't know if that was likely. I don't believe I handled it properly as far as he was concerned. I would do it differently now; I would talk to the woman who was the mother of the children where he lived and I would have talked to him. Maybe I could have offered some way for him to help himself. I have realized the importance of not just forgetting an incident just because *my* child is all right.

Sylvia has always been a very trusting, warm person and I remember incidents in her childhood when I tried to help her keep that warmth and trust but still become aware of the possibilities of harm. I tried to help her understand *why* people may be the way they are and this has facilitated her ability to understand herself as well as other people.

I have another daughter who talked with Sylvia and me. She said she had never had any experience at all with sexual abuse as a child. She said she knew of the possibility for as long as she could remember and that she remembered me telling her about being cautious about people approaching her in an intimate way or if she had a funny feeling about someone. She said she was never afraid, but that she felt she knew what to look for and that she would have told me right away. She also felt she had been given a very good background in matters of sex education and felt she had "always" known about "babies and making love."

One of the things that I have not read in this book is any information for parents about their own sexual feelings towards their children. In the years I have spent raising my children and talking to other parents I have found this is a subject that hardly anyone wants to talk about. I believe that talking about it and learning about it is another step in aiding potential victims and molesters. I don't mean to say that all parents are potential molesters or that we will avoid molesting our children by recognizing our sexual feelings towards them. However, bringing any subject out of hiding and shedding light on it is bound to help everyone, particularly those who have problems in that area. Also parents who became more comfortable with their own feelings are more easily able to talk to their children about all areas of sexuality.

When my two daughters were very young, my husband woke up one morning in a horrible state. He was holding his head and just coming out of a dream. He moaned. "Oh, my God, what have I done?" I woke up quickly and asked him what happened and he told me in almost sobs that he had dreamed he had had intercourse with our oldest daughter. He felt sick inside and we talked a long time. We had both read enough to know that just because he had dreamed about it did not mean that he really wanted to molest her. There are normal sexual feelings involved in parenting. Children are very sensuous creatures, and although the feelings I experienced as a very physically affectionate mother were never specifically sexual, I have deeply appreciated their wonderful bodies, lovely skin, and generally breathtaking physical perfection. Having such a dream as my husband experienced is not hard to imagine, particularly when we know that dreams don't necessarily need to be taken literally. I dreamed that I had intercourse with my son when he was about thirteen and I felt strange about it when I woke up. I find nothing strange about having these feelings when I consider it because I know I am not going to act on any of them, or even fantasize about them. In recent years, as my children have become adults, we have talked about these feelings and dreams. Not too long ago, my son and his girl friend were visiting me when he suddenly remembered having a dream the night before of making love to me. He grabbed his head (interesting father-son reaction) and said, "Oh my God, I just remembered I dreamed I made love to you." I feigned hitting my head with my hand and we all laughed. I am pleased to know we can laugh about something like this, even though he had a moment of feeling awful when he remembered his dream. After all, there is a very strong taboo against incest.

One of the most important things to know about parents and children and sexuality is that parents must learn to be open with each other about these thoughts, however brief they may be. A single parent must have someone to share these thoughts with. I was very fortunate to have a very dear friend I have known since I was eighteen. We have remained like sisters over the years and she has raised a son by herself. We helped each other many times in sharing problems as single parents. I would like to emphasize that all the people in our family know that these are simply feelings and will never be acted on. We have no desire to act on them. But a father or stepfather in a house with a beautifully developing teenage girl needs to know that it is normal for him to occasionally see her as she is to other men. People can have all kinds of feelings and still know that they do not have to act on them. A stepfather who moves into the house with a woman who has teenage daughters has to frequently confront the attraction he may feel to those young women. Again, communication is extremely important. The two adults *need* to be able to share their feelings and get comfortable with them. However a single mother needs to have spoken with her children about what the child would do if someone the mother loves very much asks them to rub them in intimate places, or asks them to undress, etc.

The section in the book that speaks of being comfortable with conversations about sex is important. In the last few years it seems that people are finding it a little easier to talk openly about sex. I would like to see a time when people having a conversation about sex don't stop talking when children come into the room. I have often been in conversations with other mothers involving some sexual topic, and when the children come into the room, the conversation suddenly stops. Now, I realize that you really can't just say absolutely anything to a four-year-old that you might say to your good friend or your spouse, but stopping the conversation in midstream is not good either. Finishing a sentence or two and pausing to see what needs to be done is a better way. Also children need to know we aren't keeping sexual secrets and that they don't need to.

I can remember feelings that I had when I was having conversations with my children about sexual matters. Often the conversation would have happened because of some question they had or perhaps something I had read or talked about with a friend. I was aware of trying to be "easy" in my voice and manner, for there was a certain amount of uneasiness for me in talking very specifically about sex. At the same time I felt some kind of excitement, because I felt something good was happening. It was the same feeling I had when I talked to them about anything that I was particularly interested in. It was easy to smile and I tried to remember to "lighten up" when the conversation became too deadly serious. All three of my children were able to have the benefit of their Father's presence in the house when they were very young. He easily participated in their sex education, and I can remember him teaching them the correct names of their genitalia, along with some sweet nicknames. Later when their father was not there, I had male and female friends who helped out in this very important way.

For my parenting, it has been important to listen closely to my own inner voice and to listen closely to my child. Sometimes I have a very gut level feeling of something not being right for one of my children and I know it is important to follow that feeling and see if there is something bothering them. Often enough they are in need of someone who cares and can help out by supporting them or doing any number of things that need to be done. We parents need to listen really well. Sometimes a child says something just to see if you are listening, and if they know you are, they will be able to say what is really on their minds.

Many single mothers have an older child who steps in as a second parent figure. This can be a setup for incestuous behavior with the power and authority the older child has over the younger ones. The younger children may feel insecure and want to be loved. The older child needs to be allowed to develop at her/his own pace and rate and not be given a parental role.

I feel some discomfort and disagreement in the section of the book that deals with adolescent molesters and how they got to be that way. The author speaks several times about the use of pornography as a tool in the normal sexual learning and orientation process. She says at the end that she wouldn't recommend it, but nevertheless the message is clear that it apparently helps an adolescent boy to orient sexually to a female his age. For me, this is a little like taking something that causes cancer in order to get rid of another problem. I agree that pornography is used extensively, but I can only see this as causing other problems. The problems may not be related to molesting children, but they certainly pertain to how young men will view, stereotype, and relate to women. No thanks.

This book for parents offers sound methods for preparing children and ourselves for the prevention of child sexual abuse. Single parents particularly may be helped with suggestions and thoughts they may not have discussed with anyone. I have learned a great deal from reading it and would highly recommend it to every parent as a valuable aid in their parenting process. I would like to say again that we must listen to our own inner voice and learn to apply our learning in a way that fits our own feelings and hearts to those of our children. We parents need all the knowledge and help we can find.

## Parents of
## Developmentally Disabled Children

BY MAURA BRADY

Maura Brady is a fifteen-year-old high-school student who lives in
Vermont and is an avid writer. Both of her parents are active in
services for the developmentally disabled.

As children, if my sister and I asked our parents why Sheila had
been exempt from punishment for a certain misdemeanor, they said
to us, "Well, Sheila's special—" and that was that. There were no
arguments; we accepted it as part of family life. But the subject
rarely came up; most of the time the three of us played together
without giving it a thought.

Later, as we grew older, we learned exactly what made Sheila
"special." She was born with a condition called Down's syndrome,
which made her moderately retarded, although we weren't sure how
or why.

Now she is seventeen. We live in a small community in southern
Vermont. Since the town doesn't provide the kind of educational
facilities she needs, each day she is taken fifteen miles away to a
high school where she can learn to function almost independently.

The three of us don't play together anymore; we are occupied
with schoolwork, and Sheila has drifted into a world of her own.
She divides her time among television, her records, and writing
letters to her television boyfriends. She talks incessantly with her
imaginary acquaintances about television shows and her fictional
romances. This is virtually her whole social life, except for school
and an occasional school dance.

She is very aware of being the oldest of we three girls. This is
an extremely unusual situation because, since the chances of having
a developmentally disabled child increase with age, most Down's
syndrome children are born to older parents with other children.
Sheila has the idea that the oldest child should have the most re-

sponsibilities, and therefore it is hard for her to accept being given fewer responsibilities than her *"younger* sisters." When we were young, basically the same things were expected of us—picking up after ourselves, not talking back. But as we have grown older, the gap has widened between the extra tasks we have taken on and that Sheila was either not allowed to do or not capable of doing, such as answering the door or taking phone messages. She is put out when she realizes that we're doing something she is not.

Punishments in our family are usually meted out with equal severity. This is also true of the distribution of specific praise or criticism. But for moderately retarded children like Sheila, the stress should be placed on *balance* between the two. Many parents of retarded children I have known tend to lavish praise on their child for small things ("You really caught that ball good! How about a cookie?"), thereby giving the child a false sense of competency.

As for development of Sheila's "inner voice," it is difficult to tell how it has progressed. As she has retreated farther into her own imaginary world, she has become extremely shy with people outside of the family, and is therefore unwilling to perform for strangers. She is content to divide herself between her family and her imaginary friends; she doesn't feel required to make new friends. As far as I can see (it is hard for me to generalize, being only her sister), this is unusual for kids on her level of retardation. Others I have known are very gregarious and outgoing. They *do* feel obliged to perform for others, and thus are more of a target for potential molesters.

Sheila has a very good self-image. She knows nothing of the popularity rat race or high-school cliques; it has never occurred to her that someone might not like her. This is the case with most moderately retarded children, unless parents label them or tell them that no one will like them because they're different. But usually as the degree of retardation lessens, the child's awareness of his difference will rise; thus the mildly retarded child usually has a worse self-image.

The bad side of her socially innocent nature is that she automatically trusts almost anyone (even though she may be too shy to speak to them). She doesn't understand that "some people who have trouble making friends might ask you to do something you shouldn't." She doesn't really know that she should say "no," although she wouldn't appear eager to comply. Developmentally disabled children need, probably more than normal children, to be taught that it's O.K. to say "no" to someone.

Of all the sections in Part One, the most relevant to Sheila is the section on sex-role stereotyping. Sheila eagerly patterns herself after the female stereotype, and accepts attitudes toward women as well; she wants to use makeup and be passive when it comes to men.

Her attitude can probably be attributed to the amount of television she watches. Her fantasies reflect its influence; one of her favorites is to be kidnaped (held at gunpoint) and then be rescued from her fate by her idol, Shaun Cassidy. Being "sexy" is very important to her. Of course, she is told by her fantasy people that she is sexy, but she likes to hear it from others—especially men. Because of this she is susceptible to a potential molester; she would probably be glad to do anything "sexy" women do.

She also likes to be referred to as an "older woman," and will loudly correct anyone who calls her a "kid" or a "little girl." Even the rewards she responds to now tie in with her "older woman" image; where food used to be able to get her to do something, now offers of nail polish or lip gloss will do the same.

As an "older woman," Sheila is anxious to date, and was shocked when "the youngest" started going out last year. Later she asked many questions about how old you had to be to date—very obviously thinking that, since she was the oldest, she should have started first.

In general, I would say that most mildly to moderately retarded people are more susceptible to stereotype propaganda because of the amount of television they watch, compounded with a lack of real experiences to check their information against.

There has never been a serious problem concerning the amount of attention we pay to Sheila, because she is a very verbal person and has unusually good speech and vocabulary skills for a Down's syndrome child. Many Down's syndrome children become frustrated when trying to communicate, and are therefore vulnerable to the "someone who will listen" approach.

Unfortunately, many retarded children are kept from discovering what people can expect from them by overprotective parents. All the child knows is what Mom and Dad expect from him or her—that is, not much. This "you can't do that" attitude of parents often unnecessarily limits the child's growth. Reactions to such an overprotective attitude could differ. It could be that the child would be afraid of new people without Mommy and Daddy by his side, or it could happen that he would be so devoid of worldly-wise knowledge that he would immediately trust anyone, especially if the person offered companionship.

Sheila is given a relatively free rein to discover her limitations (or as free as possible, given the isolation and lack of suitable social functions in the state), but occasionally her fantasy world takes over and she imagines that she is capable of things she is not. When we visit the coast of Maine in the summer, she paddles in the Atlantic and later tells her gym teacher that yes, she can swim. She has dreams of going on to college to become a detective. However, when pressed for details about what a detective does and how to become one, she admits that she might be a waitress instead. She will play around in the shallow end of the pool, but won't go off the deep end. If she is forced to be realistic, she will admit her limitations.

We tried out one of the exercises in the book and asked Sheila what she liked best about herself. She gave some "funny" and irrelevant answers: "Oliver" (our puppy) and "Shaun Cassidy." She doesn't like to talk about herself to the family—she fulfills this need through her pretend people. We have tried to coax her into conversation with us, but she laughs it off or, if she is in a particularly bad mood, ignores us.

Other Down's kids who are normally less verbally active and have a smaller vocabulary than Sheila's might be unable to answer such questions, and the games would be ineffective. If used, they would have to be modified considerably. For example, in teaching a developmentally disabled child to say "no," repetition of a certain "What if . . . ?" situation would be useful—not changing the wording, but keeping it the same each time it is repeated, until a new example can be substituted.

Of all the molestation approaches described in the book, the ones Sheila would probably be most susceptible to are "the special friend" and "the shared secret." Because of her imaginary friends, she would probably be eager to have a *real* "special friend." Because keeping secrets appeals to her imagination (Sometimes I will hear her talking with her invisible friends and, when she hears me coming, she will say, "Shhh—here comes Maura. Remember: It's a secret!"), she would be even more vulnerable to the "secret" approach.

Probably the best protection for retarded children would be high visibility in the neighborhood; if the child is a familiar sight in the neighborhood, people will be able to tell something is wrong if the child's routine is off. When Sheila was about nine, she followed a stray dog for a couple of blocks and wound up at the local five-and-ten-cent store. We received a call from the sales clerk, who knew Sheila, and who told us that Sheila had a big pile of toys at the counter she was insisting on taking home with her. Of course, she is also known to those in the sex-offender category, but caring people are in the majority.

For city children, of course, this method of protection would not work. An alternative might be a companion for the child until she or he is older. Playing "What if . . . ?" situation games would also be more important, since the chances of molestation are greater in cities.

Unfortunately, many people look upon developmentally disabled children as "freaks," and breathe a sigh of relief that they aren't responsible for them. Anyone who lives in a community with a retarded child has a responsibility to do everything in his power to protect the child from tragedies such as child molestation. If only they would, it could, if only slightly, lighten the burden for the parents.

# Parents of
# Physically Handicapped Children

BY ROBERT H. DOMBRO AND ELLI GUERRERA

Robert H. Dombro is the executive director of the Vermont Achievement Center in Rutland, Vermont, and is the father of a twenty-one-year-old handicapped son who is a communications major at the University of Arizona. He works and lives in a rural area.

Elli Guerrera, M.S.N., is a registered nurse and is presently the coordinator of follow-up services at the Vermont Achievement Center. Previously her experiences have included educational clinical positions at Boston College and Yale-New Haven Medical Center in the areas of birth defects and surgical nursing. She also has been director of convalescent child care at the Caverly Child Health Center in Pittsford, Vermont, and at the Vermont Achievement Center.

A child with a physical disability who is growing and living in our society has all the usual influences to contend with during this maturing period as well as others related to the effects of his or her handicap.

For this chapter, even though the number, type, and degree of possible disabilities affecting people are infinite, this definition of a disability was chosen: a motor or sensory handicap present that is severe enough to have caused significant limitations regarding the expected developmental patterns and alterations in the usual lifestyle. Also, those afflicted were to be of at least average intelligence, to be sincere and reliable, and to have had a relationship with at least one of the authors.

A cerebral-palsied child fits the above description, and in his early years may become very dependent regarding the need to communicate, to feed himself, to socialize, and to take care of ordinary needs such as toileting. He also may build an unusual amount of trust for those people who care for him, since these persons are responsible for his functioning on a day-to-day basis. His relationship with his siblings and peers may be unnatural in that he is unable to participate in their daily activities of attending a community school, taking part in recreational activities at the local center, or camping in a wilderness area. The disabled child does not usually progress along the continuum of growth acquiring the developmental milestones leading to independence, self-confidence, self-esteem, and mature competence in the same easy manner as his able-bodied peers. These types of exclusions can have a lasting effect on a child and make him vulnerable to anyone who shows consideration and kindness. This vulnerability can very well lead a child to become a victim of a molester.

A child confined to a wheelchair is not in complete control of his environment. There may be little opportunity to play or socialize with his siblings or peers. This situation is bound to have an effect of helplessness on the child, and anyone who helps him overcome this feeling would be considered a valued and true friend, a friend who could very well take advantage of the child.

There is a possibility that resentment by both the family members and the child will develop as the child matures. The parents and siblings, realizing that they may have to be caretakers to the child for possibly a lifetime, are not happy with the prospects. The child, understanding his position in the family circle as being a burden and a hindrance, can harbor lasting negative feelings. This unhealthy situation places the child and family in untenable positions and may cause the child to look outside the family circle for enduring and meaningful relationships. Such attempts may lead to forms of sexual abuse which the child would find hard to refuse.

The handicapped child in today's family could be an intensifying factor for stress. The need to provide constant attention in regard to just his schooling and social life might be too much to bear for a family where both his parents are working in order to survive in the shaky economic situation that affects most of the population today.

Family members may be ambivalent regarding their treatment of the disabled child. They may have been well prepared in parenting principles, but because of the child possibly being of high-risk status, these skills could not be fully utilized. Such a situation causes frustration and even anger both on the parents' part and on the child's and may cause him to seek and rely on acquaintances outside the family circle.

Let us imagine that the primary interest of the family is to have the child mature and leave home so that its members and the child can be independent. What insecure feelings can arise in this situation? "Can we let him go? Will he ever be able to take care of himself? Will he be employed? Will his living quarters be satisfactory?" And what are the child's thoughts? "How am I going to make it without their help? Will I be able to get a job? Can I get my wheelchair into my apartment? What happens if I get stuck?" These uncertainties can make the child an easy target for a stranger who forms a relationship and wishes to take sexual advantage.

The physically disabled child with his problems of mobility may have difficulty being accepted in his neighborhood. He has many problems coping with his daily life, let alone adjusting with neighborhood agencies. Participation, for example, in a recreation center may cause undue strain with transportation, and overcoming architectual barriers. He may be entered in a school with nonhandicapped students and have school-personnel and student adverse reactions to his attempts. His acceptance in clubs, the Boy Scouts, YMCA, and 4-H may be fraught with instances in which he or others are unable to adjust. Such negative experiences may make him susceptible to the advances of a possible sexual abuser.

There are instances when the handicapped child is placed in a foster or surrogate home, where he has to adjust to another set of unique problems. There are new people, new routines, and circumstances whereby the child may re-enter a more dependent life. The inhabitants may certainly look at the child as "easy pickings," and those who wish to make sexual advances may certainly succeed, since the child has become submissive in these surroundings.

A disabled child suffers in regard to his image through public information and awareness. Various organizations who cater to the needs of the handicapped publicize the child as being somewhat helpless and in need of educational and therapeutic help. The child is portrayed on crutches or in a wheelchair utterly dependent on those who serve him. The impression that a deviant gets is that here is a helpless child at an extreme who would be easy prey as a sexual object.

TV exposes a child in this light through telethons, where he is shown as being unable to navigate for himself, having to be pushed or carried from place to place by a well-built adult. Again, this is a sign of weakness for anyone wishing to gain sexual favors.

On the one hand, it is good that we find more television programs featuring the problems of the handicapped. In the past two years, there has been a dramatic increase in the number of programs about autism, epilepsy, hearing impairments, and about developmentally disabled people. But, on the other hand, this does not go far enough. It seems that handicapped people are either the objects of the programs, or they are not there at all. Handicapped people go to work, participate in classes, shop for groceries, and travel down the streets, yet they are conspicuously absent from programs where specific handicaps are not being presented. This gives the child a skewed picture of himself or herself: either the star or not there at all. Along with correction of sex-role stereotyping, television and movies could be improved by including handicapped people as they really are—functioning in everyday life.

We formulate our image of the victim from the media also, and many of us see *her* as someone like the little girl with the bare buttocks in the suntan-lotion ad who is provocative and cuddly at the same time. If parents of a handicapped child feel that their child (especially a son) does not fit this image, then they might wrongfully conclude that their child is safe from the attentions of an offender.

Sex education seems to be a taboo for children with disabilities. In checking with several child-care institutions serving the handicapped, the subject is thought about among the educators but very seldom introduced as part of the curriculum. The child is taught many self-care skills, but there is an avoidance of any discussion regarding sex. This lack of information distorts the concept and can leave the child at the mercy of his peers or the staff providing services. There are frequently instances of attacks on children by other, more able residents or personnel working at institutions that are reported in the news media.

Certainly, some children with handicapping conditions have had adequate sex education but are reluctant many times to express themselves. They lack confidence and experience and are concerned with "fumbling" the experience or being rejected. They are interested, however; and may accept sexual advances. They need to belong and be accepted, but perceptions of them as sexual objects may for the most part be limited by others.

To avoid molestation, the physically impaired child needs to develop inner strength from birth and have confidence that he will be supported by his family, other relatives, and those who provide supportive services. He must be a decisionmaker as soon as possible and be given viable choices. Every effort should be made to have him become independent in his thinking and knowledgeable about life processes both within his family and with those who serve him. It is important for him to gain an identity of being worthwhile and equal to those who are not handicapped. Common sense should be the order of each day. Frank discussions and decisions regarding daily living should be made co-operatively. There must be a trust established between the child and those who care for him. Values must be clarified and discussed openly. Disagreements should be aired and solved with mutual satisfaction. Social opportunities at all stages of growth should be provided so that the child has well-rounded experiences with a variety of people. These experiences should be discussed by his family members with him in order to clarify the positive and the negative effects.

The handicapped child must have options as he develops and matures, and various interests should be introduced. He should be encouraged to develop skills outside his daily life routines so that he can enjoy his leisure time now and as an adult. This will strengthen his concept of self-worth and make him a stronger, integrated individual. When the proper time occurs, his family members should discuss sex and its ramifications so that the child will be aware of unnatural acts and reject those who pursue them.

The handicapped child suffers the danger of being self-centered because of his condition and those serving him. It is commonplace for his needs to be considered and fulfilled first, before those of his siblings or peers, and for him to utilize the family's available resources of time, energy, emotion, and economic assets. The consequence of such a long-standing arrangement is that the disabled child does not acquire adequate skills of mutual social interaction with or concern for others. It is imperative that the child be given an opportunity to explore his surroundings and to be educated in a well-rounded manner. To treat the handicapping condition as the primary goal without providing necessary educational, recreational, and social programming in an equal manner is a severe injustice and will leave the child dependent, vulnerable, and a prime victim of those interested in taking advantage of him sexually.

The combined experience of the authors of this chapter in working with the handicapped numbers some forty years. There has been extensive work in a variety of children's hospitals, and rehabilitation centers and community-based programs. During these years, there has been very little direct experience with a child who has been molested and the molester. Children referred to hospitals or rehabilitation centers come for rehabilitative, therapeutic, or educational services such as physical therapy, occupational therapy, speech therapy, and special education. In checking the records of the children, there has been knowledge that some type of sexual abuse of some of the children has taken place, but staff people have been reluctant to take appropriate action either because they were squeamish, they were unable to prove abuse, or they were preoccupied with serving the child for the primary reasons for his admittance.

In most of these instances the responsible parent or guardian was knowledgeable concerning the abusive practices. To pursue the two issues together—the practice of sexual abuse and the rehabilitation program for the primary disability—would not likely be possible, since the first issue would cause tension in the parent-therapist relationship, and a very positive relationship is required to work on the second issue.

The authors have experienced children being admitted to an institution for short periods of time because of suspected molestation but have taken no investigative action personally. These children have been referred to appropriate agencies, the local department of social welfare, etc., who have experience in dealing with the situation. When referrals have been made, there has been reluctance on the part of staff of these agencies to get involved. There are too much red tape, bureaucracy, and legal tangles. The authors were unable to identify a family or an individual who would or could contribute this chapter because present relationships were not based on this issue, but they did approach twelve disabled people known to them who were of average or above-average intelligence, and articulate; all of whom had lived in community settings for most of their growing-up years. Some, as children, had lived exclusively with their families, and some had lived part of the time with foster parents or in other temporary residential arrangements.

At the present time, all are living lifestyles in the community, at various levels of independence. Some are still with their families, some reside in a college dormitory, some are sharing residential quarters with a friend or spouse, and some are living alone.

The group was chosen because a trustful relationship already existed with at least one of the authors. These people are presently inhabitants of small rural cities or towns that accommodate individuals with special needs. There are departments of social welfare, visiting nurses, mental-health clinics, and psychiatric services.

Before approaching these twelve individuals, the authors interviewed personnel from the above agencies in order to determine whether they had experiences with children who were molested, and if there were personnel who specialized in dealing with the problem. These personnel had a long range of service but had almost no direct service for children with a disability who had also been molested. Information was skimpy; all personnel had some experience that was similar to the authors'; also, they did not pursue possible instances of molestation for the reasons we have already stated.

In order hopefully to acquire information relative to this topic, conferences were held by one of the authors with twelve people who represented the frame of reference described at the beginning of this section. Following is a brief summary of the information from ten of the individuals interviewed; their ages ranged from fifteen to forty-two.

1. Margie had diabetes by age three. This resulted in low vision by age eight, and total blindness by age eighteen. Margie, unlike her siblings, was cared for by a "sitter" during her parents' absences until age seventeen, long after the age when children require such accommodation. Margie, over a two-year period, was sexually

abused by her sitter, an older man who was a close friend of her parents.

2. Laura contracted polio at the age of four; she was ambulatory with the use of crutches and bilateral long leg braces by the age of six. She was taken advantage of sexually several times by a neighbor who was requested by Laura's parents to watch out for her casually during a two-hour gap each afternoon after her mother left for work and before her father returned home.

3. At age nine, Libby was injured in an automobile accident that rendered her a quadriplegic thereafter. Libby was approached sexually by a neighbor, the uncle of one of her playmates.

4. Barbara has had spastic cerebral palsy involving all four extremities since birth. She is mobile in a wheelchair. During her early years, Barbara stayed in a temporary boarding home to be closer to the location of her rehabilitation program. Occasionally the boarding-home parents left her in the care of a family friend, who had an eighteen-year-old son, who molested her on more than one occasion.

5. Since birth, Marty has had a mixed type of cerebral palsy that has prevented her limbs from developing much strength. She also uses a wheelchair for mobility. As a young child, Marty was frequently cared for by her older brother, who often took her along with his own peers to such events as ball games. The friends of her brother frequently became her sexual offenders.

6. John has had arthrogryposis since birth. The absence of a complete set of muscle structures prevented him from developing hand skills that would enable him to acquire independence in self-care skills. John, from the age of three, lived in a foster home. Members of his foster family were his sexual molesters.

7. Since birth, Martha has a combination spastic and athetoid form of cerebral palsy involving all extremities as well as free-flowing speech. Throughout Martha's preteen and adolescent years she was subjected to excessive and almost constant sexual verbal abuse from her siblings and their friends.

8. Tommy has had severe speech problems caused by inadequately developed communication structures allowing him the ability to express himself which was at best difficult to understand; sometimes it was impossible. Tommy's parents carried on a lifestyle with him as well as his two siblings that frequently included sexual "games."

9. Bart has had osteogenesis imperfecta since birth and stated that there has been sexual advances and abuse during his childhood; however, he was reluctant to elaborate.

10. Sammy has had a spastic form of cerebral palsy since birth. He admitted to having been molested as a child by adults but refused to discuss the details because "it was too close to his family," whom he cared for greatly.

Ten of the twelve individuals admitted to having been victims of child sexual abuse, and eight gave the details of their experiences and named their assailants. Two admitted having had such experiences but refused to give details. Two of the twelve individuals interviewed denied having had any childhood experiences involving sexual abuse. Because of the population chosen, it is felt by the authors that the information was understood, reliable, and was honestly given. At the time of the molestations, none of the ten involved individuals reported or discussed the happenings with their parents, which leads us to believe that sexual abuse of handicapped children is grossly underreported.

In this book, the offender has been described as someone who needs to be a rescuer, a guardian angel. This holds true with the experience of the people we interviewed. If they tried to break off the relationship with the offender, they were called ungrateful and insensitive. The offender felt he was being "especially wonderful" to befriend/molest the handicapped child, and the child's wanting this to end was seen as a slap in the face. The offenders seemed to feel they were really meeting the needs of the child, giving him important things in areas where the child was deprived.

The interviewees were asked if they thought their handicap was in some way responsible for their being victims. Here is a summary of their answers:

1. They believed that limitations caused by their handicaps contributed to their vulnerability. They felt trapped by their physical disability.

2. They were very aware of how much care they required from their family members and were concerned that they not be more of a burden on their parents; this influenced them to endure the advances of sitters and those temporarily entrusted with their care.

3. They felt that to expose the situation would endanger their relationships with family members by creating disharmony among their parents and the offending relative, family friend, neighbor, or other siblings. Where siblings were the offenders, the disabled person felt that their parents loved the able-bodied, more attractive brother or sister better.

4. They were sure that their parents loved them and wanted only good for them; however, all were uncertain how much testing this love could take. A continued warm relationship with the parents was so important that to expose the offender, with the possibility of serious consequences, was, they felt, not worth it.

5. They thought that they had much fewer options to assert themselves than their siblings or peers, especially in being able to enjoy the company of people they liked, or not having to endure the company of people they didn't like. This was especially prevalent when they were so dependent on others for personal care.

6. They were sure that their parents held different standards of behavior and accepted different options for them in terms of when to leave home, when to work, who to have for friends, etc., than their siblings.

It appears that those who are physically handicapped are prime victims for the molester due to their vulnerability, the rejection suffered, the dependence endured, and uncertainty about roles in the family. The ten people interviewed are admittedly a small sample, but their experiences and comments should be looked at and listened to carefully by all those who are involved with this insidious problem.

## Parent of a Past Victim

BY CAROLYN SAYLES

Carolyn Sayles is the mother of six children: one daughter, age sixteen, and five sons, ranging in age from fourteen to twenty-four years. They live in a large summer-resort town, and she is a staff member of Tidewater Rape Information Services, Inc. (TRIS).

I was married when I was very young; I remained married for over twenty years. The incestuous relationship went on between my daughter and her father for approximately ten years. Her earliest memories are of her father molesting her. She told me when she was thirteen years old.

As I was reading the manuscript of this book it became a time of reflecting back over my life and the lives of my children. Even though I was not aware of the sexual abuse of my daughter until she was thirteen, I still own some of the responsibility for what happened to her.

The first chapter particularly (feeling good about yourself is the most important thing in the world), is such an important issue for a parent or parents to teach their child. But how can you teach a child if your own self-esteem is so low? For so many years I was a nonperson. I didn't like myself, so how could I teach my children to like themselves? Low self-esteem of the mother and the father in an incestuous family seems to be one of the key factors.

The role models the parents give their children are very important. My husband, for instance, was insecure, unpredictable, tyrannical, and always tried to act like such a "he-man." He was a heavy drinker, as is often true of an incestuous father. When he was drinking there was always a threat of violence.

I, on the other hand, was very passive, dependent, and nonassertive. I was so young when I married. I went from my parents telling me what to do, to my husband telling me. I never questioned this. It was how I believed things should be. My wants and needs were never important; the needs of my husband were first, and then those of the children. I remember long periods of depression, of feeling so terrible about myself and not caring. Of course, my husband was emotionally abusing me this whole time. He really knew how to keep me down. He made me feel worthless as a woman. It still hurts sometimes when I think of how I really bought into all the things he kept telling me. In the frame of mind I was in, it is no wonder that I was so unaware of what was happening. I believed women weren't important anyway.

These were the negative role models we gave our children. It is easy to see why my daughter was victimized for so many years, feeling as she did, and yes, how I had taught her to feel by my role model. She felt she couldn't tell anyone, because who would believe her, anyway? "After all, men are always right, and women are never right about anything." Her father was such a dominant figure that she felt no one was there to help her or protect her. And, of course, during this whole time he was reinforcing all of her feelings that no one would believe her over him. There were many threats: no allowance, not being allowed to do something she wanted to, or not getting that special present she wanted so much for Christmas. He also controlled the family finances. My daughter has since shared with me the times when, for instance, she would ask for a piece of gum, and he would reply, "What will you give me in return?"

One of the things that is so ironical is that during this time I really believed I was a good mother: I was involved with the children, I took an active interest in their activities, etc. This is how I survived all those years. My needs were met through my children. I have often wondered how many other mothers believe they are good parents, but are neglecting the most important things their child should be learning, things such as these: Everyone is important. Each and every one of us is special, and no one is better than you are, even an adult. And no one, no matter who, has a right to touch you if you don't want to be touched. Unfortunately, children who become victims are first victimized by their parents—not always victims of sexual abuse, but victims of emotional abuse.

This is one of the most important ways in which this book can be utilized by parents—by reading it and following the educational process to teach their children about feeling good about themselves, and also about sexual abuse.

I would like to think that if I had read this book when my children were small, I might have taught them differently. Considering my state of mind then, I'm not sure how effective I could have been. It is possible to use the book to teach your child after sexual abuse has taken place, but it is a much longer process. It is a matter of re-education after the fact.

My own daughter has since learned this, but it came too late to save her from a childhood of hell, too late to bring back her lost childhood. She and I went through this learning process together. We have come a long way and have gotten closer through this. I can look at her now without the pain that was once present. At one time, whenever I looked at her I thought of all the hurt she endured because of her father and because of me too, because I didn't teach her the basic things, things that I'd never learned either.

For all those years my daughter endured the pain because she didn't think I could make it on my own. She was afraid that the family would break apart and that someone or everyone would blame her. She also felt that I would be so hurt and so would everyone else in the family if she told. She rationalized it this way: As long as she kept "the secret," no one was being hurt but her.

When she was very small she said she used to ask her father about other girls and their relationship with their fathers. He told her that all fathers did this to their little girls, but it was like he always told her, no one is supposed to know, that it is a secret that all fathers share with their daughters, and that is why none of her friends ever talk about it. So she should never talk about it either. As she became older the abuse became more frequent and the threats changed too. He told her that he could do whatever he wanted with her and that if she ever tried to stop him he could rape her whenever he wanted to. He also wouldn't let her go out with her friends very often. I thought it was because she was our only daughter and he was trying to protect her. Her own self-image became lower and lower. By this time she was already feeling guilty and trapped. The only resistance she had ever put up was crying occasionally and asking him not to bother her anymore. She was old enough now to know that this was taboo in our society.

She was no longer the young, trusting child who believed, "Daddy knows best."

I think that what I have been trying to tell other parents is how my daughter became a victim and what it was like for her. Until we open our eyes to the realities of intrafamily sexual abuse, it will keep growing at the present overwhelming rate. Our society needs to learn that yes, it is happening right here in our cities and towns, large and small, in the best neighborhoods and in the worst ones. Incest knows no social, economic, or racial boundaries. Until we are able to accept that incest is happening, how can we effectively learn to treat the problem? There are, however, a growing number of professionals who recognize the magnitude of the problem. But there are many more who still think of incest as an isolated incident. Intrafamily sexual abuse is a painful subject for us as parents to think about, especially those of us who had a healthy, loving relationship with our own fathers. Perhaps someday we will be open enough to accept the realities of incest and it will no longer be a secretive thing that no one ever talks about.

Never in my experience have I seen a mother whose children are victimized within the family feel confident and sure of herself. Therefore a woman who is submissive, has a low self-image as I had and so is a very poor role model, sets the stage for incest to occur. This is why we so often hear of the mother who was aware of the abuse and did nothing to stop it or help her child. She is so unsure of her own capabilities, so overwhelmed by her husband. She has submitted so much of herself, her wants and needs, her very being. She bows once again to his power over her.

I can look back now and am amazed that I was capable of immediate action against him. I found an inner strength I didn't know existed within me. Of course, I was hurt and angry. I was so angry, I can remember, after he was arrested and was out on bail, pacing the floor at night and planning how I was going to kill him. The hate was at times almost unbearable. Then slowly I came to realize that killing him would never bring back my daughter's lost childhood, could never erase the damage or the hurt. It was at this point that we were really able to start putting our lives back together, finally understanding that I couldn't change what had already happened, so my choices were to continue with crying over the past or letting go of it and trying to rebuild our lives. We did this slowly, brick by brick. My daughter, my youngest son, and I spent over a year in therapy. We were fortunate. The professionals we saw were able to handle the many problems we were experiencing. There are many professionals who still have a hard time dealing effectively with the dynamics of an incestuous family. This is why I would encourage a family with such problems to call for a referral someone who knows their area and the professionals there, one who is aware of the work being done and who understands the problems these families are experiencing. This is where your local rape crisis center can help. We are aware of what is being done in our area. We are there to help in making a referral to a professional who understands the many, many difficulties and problems these families are dealing with. We are also there for support and to help through the court process if that is the choice of the family.

Sometimes these families try to handle these many problems themselves. They are afraid of someone outside of the family knowing. These feelings just add to the families' already overwhelming problems and nurture the seed of low self-esteem that has already been planted.

More and more of these problems are being brought out into the open as more people understand and are willing to help these families.

As an afterthought I would like to add that the children and I have been successful in building our lives up to where they should have always been. My daughter is quite a remarkable young woman, bright, intelligent, and with sensitivity and caring that are rare in someone her age.

I can see this book being a help after a parent finds that their child has been a victim, but I feel that no family can work through these many problems without professional help.

We have gone through hell and were able to crawl back up with the help of many caring people. We have a bright future and a true zest for life. We are examples that it is never too late to learn the many things this book has to say.

# NOTES

## PART ONE    THE FAMILY ATMOSPHERE

1. National Abortion Rights Action League, *The Facts About Rape and Incest* (825 15th St. NW, Washington, D.C. 20005 [1978]).

2. Dorothy Corkille Briggs, *Your Child's Self-esteem* (Garden City, N.Y.: Doubleday & Company, 1970), p. xiv.

3. Harold Bessell, Ph.D., and Thomas Kelly, Jr., *The Parent Book: The Holistic Program for Raising the Emotionally Mature Child* (Sacramento, Calif.: Jalmar Press, 1977), p. 33.

4. Briggs, op. cit., p. 37.

5. Bessell and Kelly, op. cit., p. 143.

6. Briggs, op. cit., p. 3.

7. Bessell and Kelly, op. cit., p. 17.

8. Mildred Newman and Bernard Berkowitz, *How to Be Your Own Best Friend* (New York: Random House, 1974), p. 35.

9. Jeanne Kohl Jenkins and Pam McDonald, *Growing Up Equal: Activities and Resources for Parents and Teachers of Young Children* (Englewood Cliffs, N.J.: Prentice-Hall, 1979), p. 18.

10. Ibid., p. 25.

11. Caroline Isber and Muriel Cantor, *Report of the Task Force on Women and Public Broadcasting* (Corporation for Public Broadcasting, 1111 16th St. NW, Washington, D.C. 20036 [1975]).

12. Linda Busby, "Defining Sex-role Standards in Commercial Network Television Programs Directed Toward Children," *Journalism Quarterly*, 51 (4) (Winter 1974), pp. 690–96.

13. Jenkins and McDonald, op. cit., p. 25.

14. Ibid., p. 26.

15. Briggs, op. cit., p. 185.

16. Bessell and Kelly, op. cit., p. 95.

17. Briggs, op. cit., p. 90.

18. Ibid., p. 51.

19. Bessell and Kelly, op. cit., p. 106.

20. Sherry Angel, "Don't Be Afraid to Say 'No'!," *Redbook* (July 1978), p. 40.

21. Ibid., p. 42.

22. Ibid., p. 44–46.

## PART TWO    OVERVIEW OF THE CRIMES OF CHILD MOLESTATION AND INCEST

1. Leroy Schultz, "The Child Sex Victim: Social, Psychological and Legal Perspectives," *Child Welfare,* Vol. LII, No. 3 (Mar. 3, 1973), p. 148.

2. Ibid., p. 690.

3. Vincent DeFrancis, "Protecting the Child Victim of Sex Crimes Committed by Adults: Final Report" (American Humane Association, P.O. Box 1266, Denver, Colo. 80201 [1969]), p. 38.

4. Edward M. Brecher, "Treatment Programs for Sex Offenders: Prescriptive Package" LEAA (Washington, D.C.: U. S. Department of Justice, Jan. 1978), p. 5.

5. Interview with Gerry Holtzinger, therapy supervisor, Western Washington State Hospital Sex Offender Program (Steilicoom, Wash.: Apr. 5, 1978).

6. A. Nicholas Groth, "Patterns of Sexual Assault Against Children and Adolescents," *Sexual Assault of Children and Adolescents,* Ann W. Burgess, A. Nicholas Groth, Lynda L. Holmstrom, and Suzanne M. Sgroi (Lexington, Mass.: Lexington Books, 1978), p. 4.

7. Arthur Jaffee, Lucille Dynneson, and Robert ten Bensel, "Sexual Abuse of Children: An Epidemiological Study," *American Journal of Diseases of Children,* Vol. 129 (June 1975), p. 689.

8. Schultz, op. cit., p. 691.

9. DeFrancis, op. cit., p. 46.

10. Joseph J. Peters, "Children Who Are Victims of Sexual Assault and the Psychology of the Offenders," *American Journal of Psychotherapy*, Vol. XXX, No. 3 (July 1976), p. 415.

11. Ibid.

12. Groth, op. cit., p. 23.

13. Interview with Gene Abel, M.D., and Judith Becker, Ph.D., Columbia University College of Physicians and Surgeons (New York: Mar. 27, 1979).

14. Brecher, op. cit., p. 24.

15. Jaffee, Dynneson, and ten Bensel, op. cit., p. 690.

16. Charles H. McCaghy, "Child Molesters: A Study of Their Careers as Deviants," *Criminal Behavior Systems: A Typology*, ed. Marshall B. Clinard and Richard Quinney (New York: Holt, Rinehart & Winston, 1967), p. 83.

17. Ibid.

18. Ibid., p. 85.

19. Groth, op. cit., p. 23.

20. Mervyn Shoor, Mary Helen Speed, and Claudia Bartlett, "Syndrome of the Adolescent Child Molester," *American Journal of Psychiatry*, Vol. 1:22 (1966), p. 784.

21. Interview with Toni Clark, Ph.D., and Gary Wenet, Ph.D., Program for Juvenile Sex Offenders, University of Washington Adolescent Clinic (Seattle, Wash.: Jan. 2, 1979).

22. Toni Clark, Gary Wenet, Bob Hunner, and Steve Sulzbacher, "Final Report: Development of Diagnostic and Treatment Programs for the Juvenile Sexual Offender," University of Washington Adolescent Clinic (Seattle, Wash.: Nov. 30, 1976), p. 29.

23. Clark et al., op. cit., p. 19.

24. Ibid., p. 20.

25. Ibid., p. 23.

26. Ibid., p. 22.

27. Groth, op. cit., p. 9.

28. A. Nicholas Groth and H. Jean Birnbaum, "Adult Sexual Orientation and Attraction to Underage Persons," *Archives of Sexual Behavior,* Vol. 7, No. 3 (1978), p. 178.

29. Bart Delin, *The Sex Offender* (Boston, Mass.: Beacon Press, 1979), p. 16.

30. P. H. Gebhard, J. H. Gagnon, W. B. Pomeroy, and V. Christenson, *Sex Offenders* (New York: Harper & Row, 1965), p. 142.

31. A. Nicholas Groth, "Sexual Trauma in the Life Histories of Rapists and Child Molesters," unpublished paper (Connecticut Correctional Institution, Box 100, Somers, Conn. 06071 [1979]), p. 7.

32. Interview with A. Nicholas Groth, Ph.D., director, Sex Offender Program, Connecticut Correctional Institution (Somers, Conn.: July 20, 1979).

33. A. Nicholas Groth, "Guidelines for Assessment and Management of the Offender," *Sexual Assault of Children and Adolescents,* op. cit., p. 26.

34. Groth, "Patterns of Sexual Assault Against Children and Adolescents," op. cit., p. 6.

35. Groth, "Adult Sexual Orientation and Attraction to Underage Persons," loc. cit.

36. A. Nicholas Groth, Ann W. Burgess, H. Jean Birnbaum, and Thomas S. Gary, "A Study of the Child Molester: Myths and Realities," *LAE Journal of the American Criminal Justice Association,* Vol. 41, No. 1 (Winter/Spring 1978), p. 20.

37. Interview with A. Nicholas Groth, loc. cit.

38. Groth, "Adult Sexual Orientation and Attraction to Underage Persons," loc. cit.

39. Interview with A. Nicholas Groth, loc. cit.

40. Alan P. Bell and Calvin S. Hall, *The Personality of a Child Molester: An Analysis of Dreams* (Chicago, Ill.: Aldine-Atherton, 1971), p. 38.

41. Ibid., p. 39.

42. Ibid., p. 36.

43. Jaffee, op. cit., p. 691.

44. Groth, "Patterns of Sexual Assault Against Children and Adolescents," op. cit., p. 12.

45. Ibid., p. 14.

46. Ibid., p. 13.

47. Ibid., p. 15.

48. Gebhard et al., op. cit., p. 12.

49. Steven N. Silver, "Outpatient Treatment for Sexual Offenders," *Social Work* (Mar. 1976), p. 136.

50. Gebhard et al., op. cit., p. 155.

51. Interview with A. Nicholas Groth, loc. cit.

52. DeFrancis, loc. cit.

53. David E. Newton, "Homosexual Behavior and Child Molestation: A Review of the Evidence," *Adolescence*, Vol. XIII, No. 49 (Spring 1978), p. 39.

54. Interview with A. Nicholas Groth, loc. cit.

55. Newton, op. cit., p. 36.

56. Gebhard et al., op. cit., p. 293.

57. Ibid., p. 282.

58. Ibid., p. 287.

59. Newton, op. cit., p. 38.

60. Ibid., p. 39.

61. Florence Rush, "Child Pornography," *The First Feminist Anti-Pornography Papers,* ed. Laura Lederer (New York: William Morrow & Company, 1980), p. 12.

62. Interview with Michael Murphy, special assistant to the executive director, Covenant House (New York: Mar. 28, 1979).

63. Testimony of Father Bruce Ritter before the U. S. Senate Select Committee on Crime (Nov. 14, 1977).

64. Robin Lloyd, *For Money or Love: Boy Prostitution in America* (New York: Ballantine Books, 1976), p. 32.

65. Testimony of Father Bruce Ritter, loc. cit.

66. Henry Giaretto, "Humanistic Treatment of Father-Daughter Incest," *Child Abuse and Neglect: The Family and the Community*, ed. R. E. Helfer, M.D., and C. H. Kemp, M.D. (Cambridge, Mass.: Ballinger Publishing Company, 1976), p. 4.

67. Rush, op. cit., p. 8.

68. Ibid.

69. Margaret Loeb, "The Good Shepherd of 42nd Street," New York *Sunday News Magazine* (Apr. 30, 1978), p. 1.

70. Lloyd, op. cit., p. 74.

71. Interview with Miriam Kerster, director, Juvenile Services Unit, Legal Aid Society (Brooklyn, N.Y.: Mar. 24, 1979).

72. Interview with Michael Murphy, loc. cit.

73. Ibid.

74. "No Place for a Child" (Covenant House, 260 West 44th St., New York, N.Y. 10036 [1979]), p. 4.

75. Suzanne M. Sgroi, "Child Sexual Assault: Some Guidelines for Intervention and Assessment," *Sexual Assault of Children and Adolescents*, op. cit., p. 135.

76. Peters, op. cit., p. 414.

77. Suzanne M. Sgroi, "Comprehensive Examination for Child Sexual Assault: Diagnostic, Therapeutic and Child Protection Issues," *Sexual Assault of Children and Adolescents*, op. cit., p. 149.

78. Schultz, op. cit., p. 91.

79. Giaretto, loc. cit.

80. S. K. Weinberg, *Incest Behavior* (New York: Citadel Press, 1977).

81. Sandra Butler, *Conspiracy of Silence: The Trauma of Incest* (San Francisco, Calif.: New Glide Publications, 1978), p. 15.

82. Giaretto, op cit., p. 9.

83. Judith Herman and Lisa Hirschman, "Father-Daughter Incest," *Signs: Journal of Women in Culture and Society,* Vol. 2, No. 4 (Spring 1977), p. 736.

84. Henry Giaretto, Anna Giaretto, and Suzanne M. Sgroi, "Co-ordinated Community Treatment of Incest," *Sexual Assault of Children and Adolescents,* op. cit., p. 233.

85. Susan Forward and Craig Buck, *Betrayal of Innocence: Incest and Its Devastation* (Los Angeles, Calif.: J. P. Tarcher, 1978), p. 20.

86. Herman and Hirschman, op. cit., p. 755.

87. Forward and Buck, op. cit., p. 74.

88. Ibid., p. 73–143.

89. Herman and Hirschman, op. cit., p. 736.

90. Forward and Buck, op. cit., p. 85.

## PART THREE  DISCUSSING CHILD SEXUAL ABUSE WITH THE CHILD

1. The material in this section is copyright © 1977 by Linda Sanford under the title, "Parent-oriented Prevention of Child Molestation and Incest Program." The author would like to acknowledge the assistance of Claudia Black, M.S.W., in developing the content.

## PART FOUR  CONCLUSION

1. Trudy Peterson, caseworker with Covenant House, New York City, "60 Minutes" (New York: Columbia Broadcasting System, 1979).

2. Florence Rush, "Child Pornography," *The First Feminist Anti-Pornography Papers,* ed. Laura Lederer (New York: William Morrow and Company, 1980).

3. Judith Coburn, "Trafficking in Innocence," *New Times* (Jan. 8, 1979), p. 71.

6/~
3

## Catalog

If you are interested in a list of fine Paperback
books, covering a wide range of subjects
and interests, send your name and address,
requesting your free catalog, to:

McGraw-Hill Paperbacks
1221 Avenue of Americas
New York, N.Y. 10020